Houghton
Mifflin
Harcourt

GO MATH!

Volume 2

Made in the United States
Text printed on 100%
recycled paper

Houghton
Mifflin
Harcourt

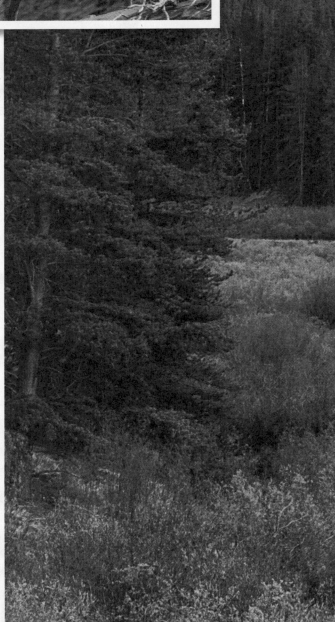

2017 Edition

Printed in the U.S.A.

ISBN 978-0-544-71055-9

9 10   0877   24 23 22 21 20 19 18

4500743148   D E F G

Dear Students and Families,

Welcome to **Go Math!**, Grade 1! In this exciting mathematics program, there are hands-on activities to do and real-world problems to solve. Best of all, you will write your ideas and answers right in your book. In **Go Math!**, writing and drawing on the pages helps you think deeply about what you are learning, and you will really understand math!

By the way, all of the pages in your **Go Math!** book are made using recycled paper. We wanted you to know that you can Go Green with **Go Math!**

Sincerely,

The Authors

Made in the United States
Text printed on 100% recycled paper

GO MATH!

Authors

Juli K. Dixon, Ph.D.
Professor, Mathematics Education
University of Central Florida
Orlando, Florida

Edward B. Burger, Ph.D.
President, Southwestern University
Georgetown, Texas

Steven J. Leinwand
Principal Research Analyst
American Institutes for
  Research (AIR)
Washington, D.C.

Contributor

Rena Petrello
Professor, Mathematics
Moorpark College
Moorpark, CA

Matthew R. Larson, Ph.D.
K-12 Curriculum Specialist for
  Mathematics
Lincoln Public Schools
Lincoln, Nebraska

Martha E. Sandoval-Martinez
Math Instructor
El Camino College
Torrance, California

English Language Learners Consultant

Elizabeth Jiménez
CEO, GEMAS Consulting
Professional Expert on English
  Learner Education
Bilingual Education and
  Dual Language
Pomona, California

VOLUME I
Operations and Algebraic Thinking

Big Idea Develop a conceptual understanding of concepts and strategies for addition and subtraction.

 Animals in Our World. I

Big Idea

GO DIGITAL

Go online! Your math lessons are interactive. Use *i*Tools, Animated Math Models, the Multimedia *e*Glossary, and more.

Chapter 1 Overview

In this chapter, you will explore and discover answers to the following **Essential Questions**:

• How can you model adding within 10?
• How do you show adding to a group?
• How do you model putting together?
• How do you show adding in any order?

Chapter 2 Overview

In this chapter, you will explore and discover answers to the following **Essential Questions**:

• How can you subtract numbers from 10 or less?
• How do you model taking apart?
• How do you show taking from a group?
• How do you subtract to compare?

Personal Math Trainer
Online Assessment and Intervention

© Houghton Mifflin Harcourt Publishing Company

vi

Addition and Subtraction Relationships 251

Chapter 5 Overview

In this chapter, you will explore and discover answers to the following **Essential Questions**:

• How can relating addition and subtraction help you to learn and understand facts within 20?

• How do addition and subtraction undo each other?

• What is the relationship between related facts?

• How can you find unknown numbers in related facts?

GO DIGITAL

Go online! Your math lessons are interactive. Use iTools, Animated Math Models, the Multimedia *eGlossary*, and more.

Chapter 6 Overview

In this chapter, you will explore and discover answers to the following **Essential Questions**:

• How do you use place value to model, read, and write numbers to 120?

• What ways can you use tens and ones to model numbers to 120?

• How do numbers change as you count by tens to 120?

Personal Math Trainer
Online Assessment and Intervention

VOLUME 2
Number and Operations in Base Ten

Big Idea Develop a conceptual understanding of place value.

Chapter 7 Overview

In this chapter, you will explore and discover answers to the following **Essential Questions**:

- How do you use place value to compare numbers?
- What ways can you use tens and ones to compare two-digit numbers?
- How can you find 10 more and 10 less than a number?

Practice and Homework

Lesson Check and Spiral Review in every lesson

Chapter 8 Overview

In this chapter, you will explore and discover answers to the following **Essential Questions**:

- How can you add and subtract two-digit numbers?
- What ways can you use tens and ones to add and subtract two-digit numbers?
- How can making a ten help you add a two-digit number and a one-digit number?

Big Idea

Chapter 9 Overview

In this chapter, you will explore and discover answers to the following **Essential Questions**:

- How can you measure a length and tell time?
- How can you describe using paper clips to measure the length of an object?
- How can you use the hour and minute hands of a clock to tell time to the hour and to the half hour?

Personal Math Trainer
Online Assessment and Intervention

Measurement and Data

Big Idea Measure using non-standard units and develop a conceptual understanding of time. Represent data in picture graphs, bar graphs, and tally charts.

 All Kinds of Weather 501

Represent Data 571

Chapter 10 Overview

In this chapter, you will explore and discover answers to the following **Essential Questions**:

• How can graphs and charts help you organize, represent, and interpret data?

• How can you look at a graph or chart to tell the most or least popular item without counting?

• How are tally charts, picture graphs, and bar graphs alike? How are they different?

• How can you compare information recorded in a graph?

Practice and Homework

Lesson Check and Spiral Review in every lesson

© Houghton Mifflin Harcourt Publishing Company

Big Idea

GO DIGITAL

Go online! Your math lessons are interactive. Use *iTools*, Animated Math Models, the Multimedia *e*Glossary, and more.

Chapter 11 Overview

In this chapter, you will explore and discover answers to the following **Essential Questions**:

• How can you identify and describe three-dimensional shapes?

• How can you combine three-dimensional shapes to make new shapes?

• How can you use a combined shape to make a new shape?

• What two-dimensional shapes are on three-dimensional shapes?

Chapter 12 Overview

In this chapter, you will explore and discover answers to the following **Essential Questions**:

• How do you sort and describe two-dimensional shapes?

• How can you describe two-dimensional shapes?

• How can you identify equal and unequal parts in two-dimensional shapes?

xii

Geometry

Big Idea Identify, describe, and combine both two- and three-dimensional shapes. Develop a conceptual understanding of equal and unequal parts.

 Vocabulary Reader On the Move 621

© Houghton Mifflin Harcourt Publishing Company

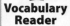
Around the Neighborhood

written by John Hudson

UNITED STATES POST OFFICE

We Deliver

COLLECTION TIMES

OUT OF TOWN

BIG IDEA Develop a conceptual understanding of place value.

The mail carrier brings letters to Mr. and Mrs. Jones. How many letters does she bring?

_____ ◯ _____ ◯ _____

Social Studies

How do mail carriers help us?

The mail carrier brings packages to the fire station. Then she brings more packages. How many packages does she bring?

_____ ◯ _____ ◯ _____

Social Studies

How do firefighters help us?

It is time for lunch. The mail carrier eats in the park. How many boys and girls are playing?

_____ ◯ _____ ◯ _____

Social Studies

How do parents help us?

The mail carrier brings 12 packages to the police station. "This person has moved," says the police officer. "You need to take these back." How many packages does the officer keep?

_____ ◯ _____ ◯ _____

Social Studies

How do police officers help us?

The mail carrier stops at City Hall.
She brings 8 letters for the mayor.
She brings 4 letters for the city clerk.
How many letters does she bring?

_____ ⊕ _____ ③ _____

How do city workers help us?

Write About the Story

One day, Mr. and Mrs. Jones each got the same number of letters. They got 12 letters in all. Draw the two groups of letters.

Vocabulary Review

add   difference

doubles   subtract

sum

Mr. Jones   **Mrs. Jones**

Letters for Mr. Jones   **Letters for Mrs. Jones**

Write the number sentence. _____ ⊖ 2 ⊖ ~~⊗~~

WRITE ▸ Math   Describe your number sentence. Use a vocabulary word.

6

_____

- -

_____

- -

_____

How Many Letters?

1. How many letters do ⬤ and ⬤ have in all?

   _____ ◯ _____ ◯ _____

2. How many more letters does ⬤ have than ⬤ ?

   _____ ◯ _____ ◯ _____

3. Circle the two that have 11 letters in all.

MATH BOARD Make up an addition story about the mail carrier bringing letters to you and a classmate. Write the number sentence.

Count and Model Numbers

Curious About Math with
Curious George

Dan and May like apples. They buy 15 apples in all. If Dan buys 10 apples, how many apples does May buy?

Name _____

Explore Numbers 6 to 9

Count how many. Circle the number.

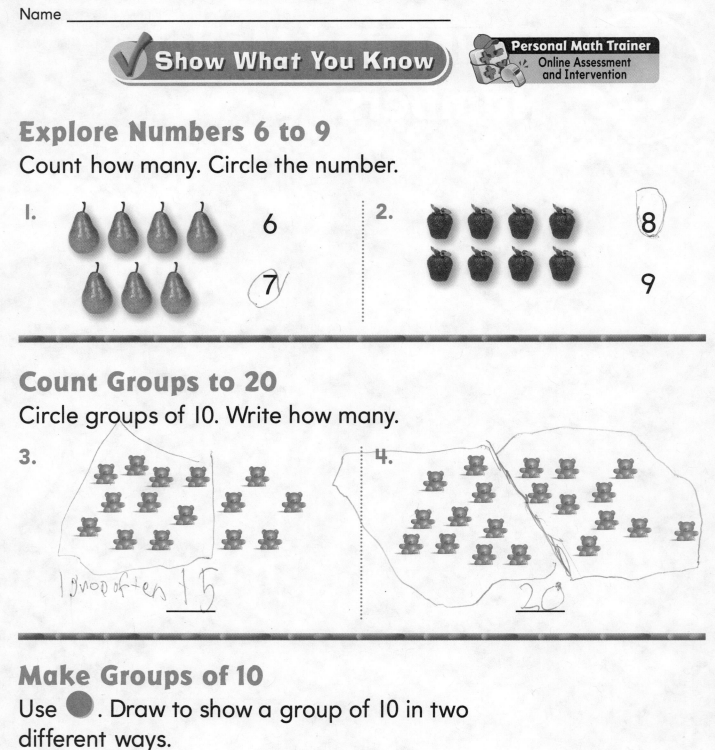

1. 6

    ⑦

2. ⑧

    9

Count Groups to 20

Circle groups of 10. Write how many.

3. 1 groop of ten 15

4. 20

Make Groups of 10

Use ⬤. Draw to show a group of 10 in two different ways.

5.

6.

This page checks understanding of important skills needed for success in Chapter 6.

Vocabulary Builder

Visualize It

Draw pictures in the box to show the number.

two

nine

five

Understand Vocabulary

Write a review word to name the number.

1.

_____

2.

_____

3.

_____

Game Show the Numbers

Materials • 👤 and 👤 • 🎯(spinner 1-6)
• 20 🔴 • ⬜ ten frame

Play with a partner.

① Put your 👤 on START.

② Spin the 🎯. Move your 👤 that many spaces.

③ Read the number. Use 🔴 to show the number on a ten frame.

④ Have your partner count the 🔴 to check your answer. If you are not correct, lose a turn.

⑤ The first player to get to END wins.

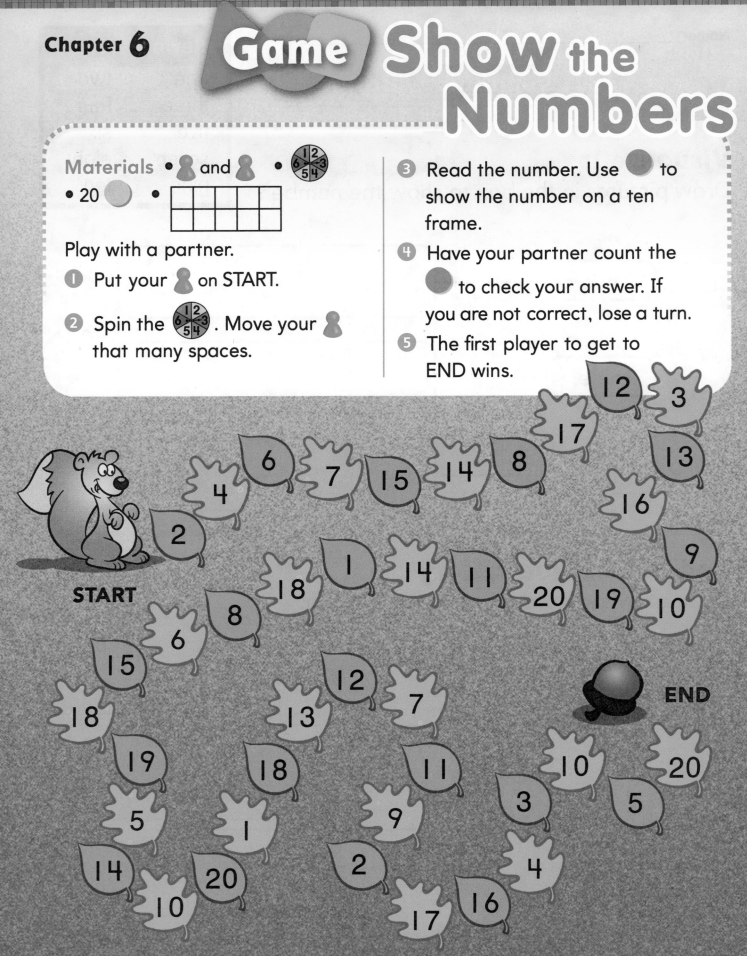

START

END

© Houghton Mifflin Harcourt Publishing Company

Chapter 6 Vocabulary

addend

sumando

2

difference

diferencia

13

digit

dígito

14

hundred

centena

29

ones

unidades

39

subtract

restar

52

sum

suma o total

54

ten

decena

57

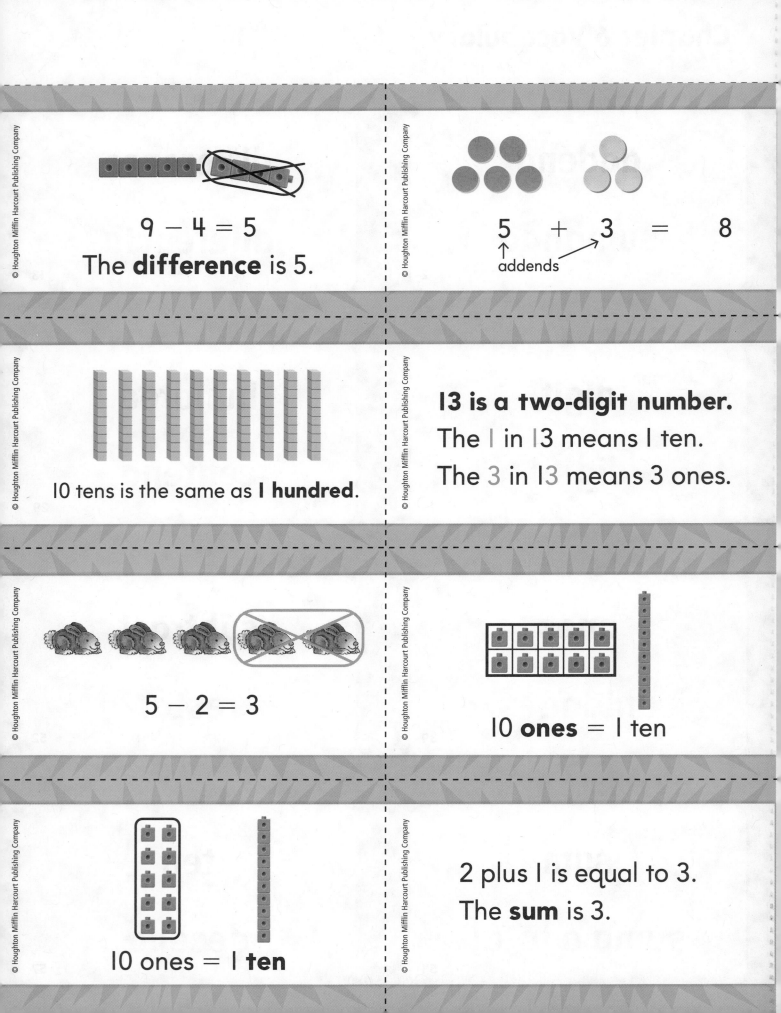

$9 - 4 = 5$

The **difference** is 5.

$5 \quad + \quad 3 \quad = \quad 8$

addends

10 tens is the same as **1 hundred**.

13 is a two-digit number.

The 1 in 13 means 1 ten.

The 3 in 13 means 3 ones.

$5 - 2 = 3$

10 **ones** = 1 ten

10 ones = 1 **ten**

2 plus 1 is equal to 3.

The **sum** is 3.

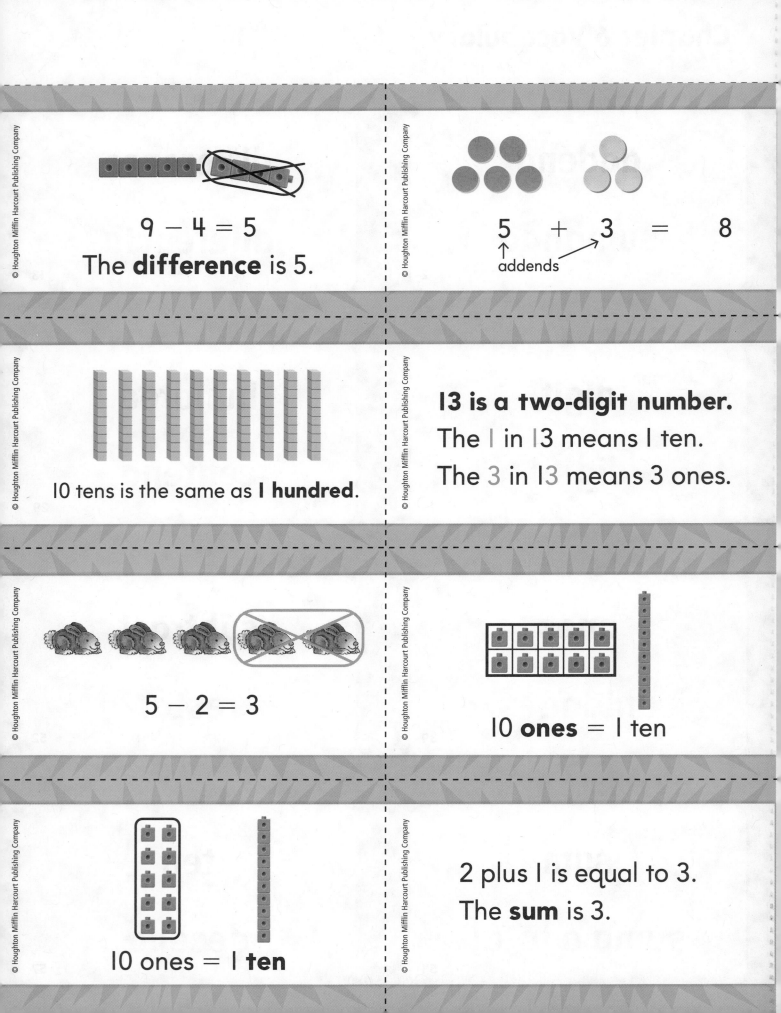

Going to Town

For 2 players

Word Box
- addend
- difference
- digit
- hundred
- ones
- subtract
- sum
- ten

Materials

- 1
- 1
- 1
- clue cards

How to Play

1. Put your on START.

2. Toss the to take a turn. Move that many spaces.

3. If you land on one of these spaces:

   Red Space Take a Clue Card. Answer the question. If you are correct, move ahead 1. Return the Clue Card to the bottom of the pile.

   Blue Space Read the word. Tell what it means, or give an example. If you are correct, move ahead 1.

   Green Space Follow the directions in the space.

4. The first player to reach FINISH wins.

Game

DIRECTIONS 2 players. Take turns to play. • To take a turn, toss the 🎲. Move that many spaces • Follow the directions for the space where you land. • First player to reach FINISH wins.

MATERIALS • I 📷 per player • I 🎲 • I set of clue cards

START

CLUE CARD

addend

Play in the park. Move ahead 1.

CLUE CARD

CLUE CARD

sum

Eat at the diner. Lose 1 turn.

digit

FINISH

Shop at the market. Take another turn.

CLUE CARD

difference

Wait at the post office. Go back **1**.

subtract

CLUE CARD

Go to the library. Trade places with another player.

The Write Way

Reflect

Choose one idea. Draw and write about it.

- Tell how you can use a counting chart to solve problems.

- Explain two ways that you can show a number as tens and ones.

Name _____

Count by Ones to 120

Essential Question How can knowing a counting pattern help you count to 120?

Learning Objective You will learn a counting pattern to help you count to 120.

Listen and Draw Real World

Write the missing numbers.

21	22	23	24	25	26	27	28	29	30
31	32	33	34	35	36	37	38	39	40
41	42	43	44	45	46	47	48	49	50
51	52	53	54	55	56	57	58	59	60
61	62	63	64	65	66	67	68	69	70
71	72	73	74	75	76	77	78	79	80
81	82	83	84	85	86	87	88	89	90
91	92	93	94	95	96	97	98	99	100

Math Talk

Math Processes and Practices ⑦

Look for Structure Explain how you know which numbers are missing.

FOR THE TEACHER • Read the following problem. Debbie saw this page in a puzzle book. Two rows of numbers are missing. Use what you know about counting to write the missing numbers.

Chapter 6

three hundred thirty-one **331**

Count forward.
Write the numbers.

1	2	3	4	5	6	7	8	9	10
11	12	13	14	15	16	17	18	19	20
21	22	23	24	25	26	27	28	29	30
31	32	33	34	35	36	37	38	39	40
41	42	43	44	45	46	47	48	49	50
51	52	53	54	55	56	57	58	59	60
61	62	63	64	65	66	67	68	69	70
71	72	73	74	75	76	77	78	79	80
81	82	83	84	85	86	87	88	89	90
91	92	93	94	95	96	97	98	99	100
101	102	103	104	105	106	107	108	109	110
111	112	113	114	115	116	117	118	119	120

10, __11__, ____, ____, ____

100, __101__, ____, ____, ____

110, __111__, ____, ____, ____

Share and Show MATH BOARD

Use a Counting Chart. Count forward.
Write the numbers.

Look for a pattern to help you write the numbers.

1. 114, ____, ____, ____, ____, ____, ____

2. 51, ____, ____, ____, ____, ____, ____

3. 94, ____, ____, ____, ____, ____, ____

4. 78, ____, ____, ____, ____, ____, ____

5. 35, ____, ____, ____, ____, ____, ____

6. 104, ____, ____, ____, ____, ____

Name _____

Math Processes and Practices **7** **Look for a Pattern**

Use a Counting Chart. Count forward.
Write the numbers.

7. 19, ____, ____, ____, ____, ____, ____, ____

8. 98, ____, ____, ____, ____, ____, ____, ____

9. 60, ____, ____, ____, ____, ____, ____, ____

10. 27, ____, ____, ____, ____, ____, ____, ____

11. 107, ____, ____, ____, ____, ____, ____, ____

12. **THINK SMARTER** Use a Counting Chart to write
the numbers counting forward.

____, ____, ____, ____, ____, 120

13. **THINK SMARTER** There is an unknown number in
the sequence counting forward. The number
is greater than 51. The number is less than 53.
What is the unknown number? ____

Problem Solving • Applications WRITE Math

Use a Counting Chart. Draw and
write numbers to solve.

14. GO DEEPER The bag has 99 buttons.
Draw more buttons so there
are 105 buttons in all. Write the
numbers as you count.

15. THINK SMARTER The bag has
56 buttons. How many more
buttons do you need to add to
the bag to have 64 buttons?

_____ buttons

16. THINK SMARTER Tito counts 105 cubes. Then he counts
forward some more cubes. Write the numbers.

105, _____, _____, _____, _____, _____, _____

TAKE HOME ACTIVITY • Take a walk with your child. Count aloud
together as you take 120 steps.

Name _____

Count by Ones to 120

Learning Objective You will learn a counting pattern to help you count to 120.

Use a Counting Chart. Count forward. Write the numbers.

1. 40, ____, ____, ____, ____, ____, ____, ____, ____

2. 55, ____, ____, ____, ____, ____, ____, ____, ____

3. 37, ____, ____, ____, ____, ____, ____, ____, ____

4. 98, ____, ____, ____, ____, ____, ____, ____, ____

Problem Solving Real World

Use a Counting Chart. Draw and write numbers to solve.

5. The bag has 111 marbles. Draw more marbles so there are 117 marbles in all. Write the numbers as you count.

6. WRITE Math Choose a number between 90 and 110. Write the number. Then count forward to write the next 5 numbers.

_____

_____

_____

Lesson Check

1. Count forward. Write the missing number.

110, 111, 112, _____, 114

· ·

Spiral Review

2. Solve. Write the number.
There are 6 bees. 2 bees fly
away. How many bees
are there now?

_____ bees

3. Solve. Draw a model to explain.
There are 8 children. 6 children
are boys. The rest are girls.
How many children are girls?

_____ girls

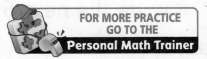

FOR MORE PRACTICE
GO TO THE
Personal Math Trainer

Name _____

Count by Tens to 120

Essential Question How do numbers change as you count by tens to 120?

Learning Objective You will count by tens from any number up to 120.

Listen and Draw

Start on 10. Count forward by tens.
Color each number as you say it.

1	2	3	4	5	6	7	8	9	10
11	12	13	14	15	16	17	18	19	20
21	22	23	24	25	26	27	28	29	30
31	32	33	34	35	36	37	38	39	40
41	42	43	44	45	46	47	48	49	50
51	52	53	54	55	56	57	58	59	60
61	62	63	64	65	66	67	68	69	70
71	72	73	74	75	76	77	78	79	80
81	82	83	84	85	86	87	88	89	90
91	92	93	94	95	96	97	98	99	100

Math Talk

Math Processes and Practices ⑧

Generalize Which numbers in the hundred chart did you color? Explain.

FOR THE TEACHER • Ask children: How do you count by tens? Starting at 10 on the hundred chart, have children count forward by tens, coloring each additional ten as they count.

Model and Draw

Start on 3. Count by tens.

1	2	3	4	5	6	7	8	9	10
11	12	13	14	15	16	17	18	19	20
21	22	23	24	25	26	27	28	29	30
31	32	33	34	35	36	37	38	39	40
41	42	43	44	45	46	47	48	49	50
51	52	53	54	55	56	57	58	59	60
61	62	63	64	65	66	67	68	69	70
71	72	73	74	75	76	77	78	79	80
81	82	83	84	85	86	87	88	89	90
91	92	93	94	95	96	97	98	99	100
101	102	103	104	105	106	107	108	109	110
111	112	113	114	115	116	117	118	119	120

THINK
When you count by tens, each number is ten more.

3, 13, 23, 33, _____, _____, _____, _____, _____, _____, _____, _____

Share and Show   MATH BOARD

Use a Counting Chart to count by tens.
Write the numbers.

1. Start on 17.

   17, _____, _____, _____, _____, _____, _____, _____, _____

2. Start on 1.

   1, _____, _____, _____, _____, _____, _____, _____, _____

3. Start on 39.

   39, _____, _____, _____, _____, _____, _____, _____

338 three hundred thirty-eight

© Houghton Mifflin Harcourt Publishing Company

Name _____

Math Processes and Practices ⑤ Use Patterns Use a Counting
Chart. Count by tens. Write the numbers.

4. 40, ____, ____, ____, ____, ____, ____, ____

5. 15, ____, ____, ____, ____, ____, ____, ____

6. 28, ____, ____, ____, ____, ____, ____, ____

7. 6, ____, ____, ____, ____, ____, ____, ____

8. 14, ____, ____, ____, ____, ____, ____, ____

9. 32, ____, ____, ____, ____, ____, ____, ____

10. **THINK SMARTER** If you start on
43 and count by tens, what
number is after 73 and
before 93? _____

11. You say me when you start
on 21 and count by tens. I am
after 91. I am before 111.
What number am I? _____

Problem Solving • Applications   WRITE Math

GO DEEPER Use what you know about a Counting Chart to write the missing numbers.

12.

6	
16	

	28	29

13.

	54	55
	64	
72		

14.

		15
32		

15.

97	98		

16. **THINK SMARTER** Use a Counting Chart. Count by tens. Match each number on the left to a number that is 10 more.

57 •   • 103

73 •   • 67

77 •   • 87

93 •   • 83

TAKE HOME ACTIVITY • Write these numbers: 2, 12, 22, 32, 42. Ask your child to tell you the next 5 numbers.

340 three hundred forty

Count by Tens to 120

Learning Objective You will count by tens from any number up to 120.

Use a Counting Chart.
Count by tens.
Write the numbers.

1. 1, ____, ____, ____, ____, ____, ____, ____, ____, ____

2. 14, ____, ____, ____, ____, ____, ____, ____, ____, ____

3. 7, ____, ____, ____, ____, ____, ____, ____, ____, ____

4. 29, ____, ____, ____, ____, ____, ____, ____, ____, ____

5. 5, ____, ____, ____, ____, ____, ____, ____, ____, ____

6. 12, ____, ____, ____, ____, ____, ____, ____, ____, ____

7. 26, ____, ____, ____, ____, ____, ____, ____, ____, ____

Problem Solving Real World

Solve.

8. I am after 70.
   I am before 90.
   You say me when you count by tens.
   What number am I? ____

9. WRITE Math Use numbers to explain the pattern you see when you count forward by tens.
   _____
   _____
   _____

Lesson Check

I. Count by tens.
Write the missing numbers.

44, 54, 64, _____, _____, 94

Spiral Review

2. Use the model. Write to show
how you make a ten. Then add.

___ + ___ + ___

___ + ___ = ___

So, ___ + ___ = ___

---

3. Write a number sentence
to complete the related facts.

$9 + 6 = 15$ $15 - 6 = 9$

$6 + 9 = 15$

---

342 three hundred forty-two

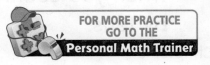

FOR MORE PRACTICE
GO TO THE
Personal Math Trainer

Name _____

Understand Ten and Ones

Essential Question How can you use different ways to write a number as ten and ones?

Learning Objective You will use models to find different ways to write a number as ten and ones.

 Listen and Draw Real World | Hands On

Use 🔲 to model the problem.
Draw the 🔲 to show your work.

Math Talk Math Processes and Practices ⑤

Use Tools How does your picture show the books Tim has?

FOR THE TEACHER • Read the problem. Tim has 10 books. He gets 2 more books. How many books does Tim have now?

Model and Draw

13 is a two-**digit** number.
The 1 in 13 means 1 **ten**.
The 3 in 13 means 3 **ones**.

THINK
10 ones and 3 ones
is the same as
1 ten 3 ones.

__1__ ten __3__ ones

__10__ + __3__

__13__

Share and Show MATH BOARD

Use the model. Write the number
three different ways.

1.

____ ten ____ ones

____ + ____

____

2.

____ ten ____ ones

____ + ____

____

Name _____

Math Processes and Practices **6** **Make Connections**

Use the model. Write the number
three different ways.

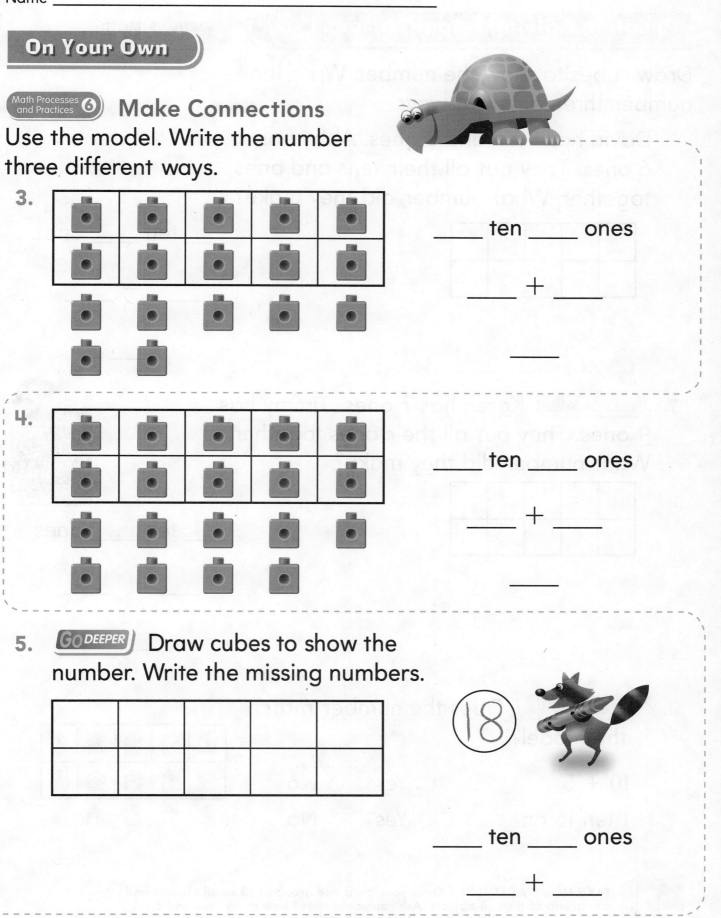

3.

_____ ten _____ ones

_____ + _____

_____

4.

_____ ten _____ ones

_____ + _____

_____

5. **GO DEEPER** Draw cubes to show the
number. Write the missing numbers.

⟨18⟩

_____ ten _____ ones

_____ + _____

Problem Solving • Applications (Real World) WRITE Math

Draw cubes to show the number. Write the number three different ways.

6. David has 1 ten and 3 ones. Abby has 6 ones. They put all their tens and ones together. What number did they make?

_____ ten _____ ones

_____ + _____

_____

7. THINK SMARTER Karen has 7 ones. Jimmy has 9 ones. They put all their ones together. What number did they make?

_____ ten _____ ones

_____ + _____

_____

8. THINK SMARTER Does the number match the model?

10 + 5   ○ Yes   ○ No

1 ten 15 ones   ○ Yes   ○ No

TAKE HOME ACTIVITY • Show your child one group of 10 small objects and one group of 8 small objects. Ask your child to tell how many tens and ones there are and say the number. Repeat with other numbers from 11 to 19.

Name _____

Understand Ten and Ones

Learning Objective You will use models to find different ways to write a number as ten and ones.

Use the model. Write the number three different ways.

I.

_____ ten _____ ones

_____ + _____

_____

Problem Solving Real World

Draw cubes to show the number. Write the number different ways.

Rob has 7 ones. Nick has 5 ones. They put all their ones together. What number did they make?

2.

_____ ten _____ ones

_____ + _____

_____

3. WRITE ▶ Math   Show twelve in four different ways. Use words, pictures, and numbers.

_____

_____

_____

Chapter 6

Lesson Check

1. Use the model. Write the number three different ways.

_____ ten _____ ones

_____ + _____ = _____

_____

....

Spiral Review

2. Use the model. Write the addition sentence. What number sentence does this model show?

_____ + _____ = _____

....

3. Write two subtraction facts related to $7 + 5 = 12$.

_____ − _____ = _____

_____ − _____ = _____

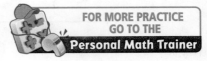

FOR MORE PRACTICE
GO TO THE
Personal Math Trainer

Name _____

Make Ten and Ones

Essential Question How can you show a number as ten and ones?

Learning Objective You will use objects, pictures, and numbers to show a ten and some ones.

Use ▪ to model the problem.
Draw ▪ to show your work.

Draw to show the group of ten another way.

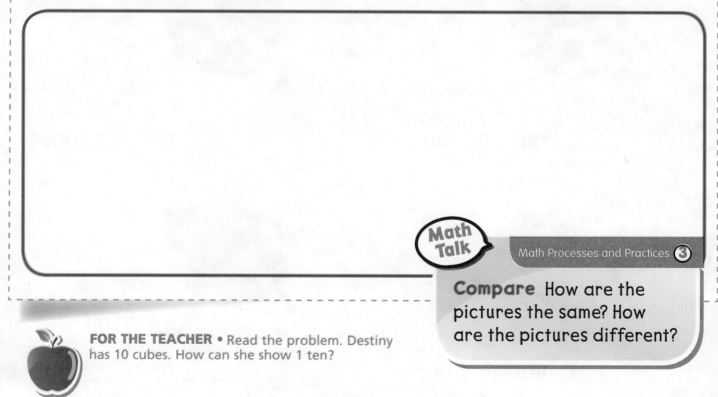

Math Talk

Math Processes and Practices ③

Compare How are the pictures the same? How are the pictures different?

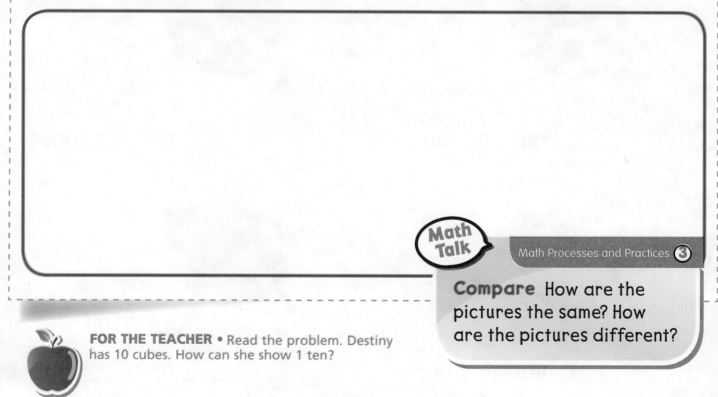

🍎 **FOR THE TEACHER •** Read the problem. Destiny has 10 cubes. How can she show 1 ten?

Chapter 6

Model and Draw

You can group 10 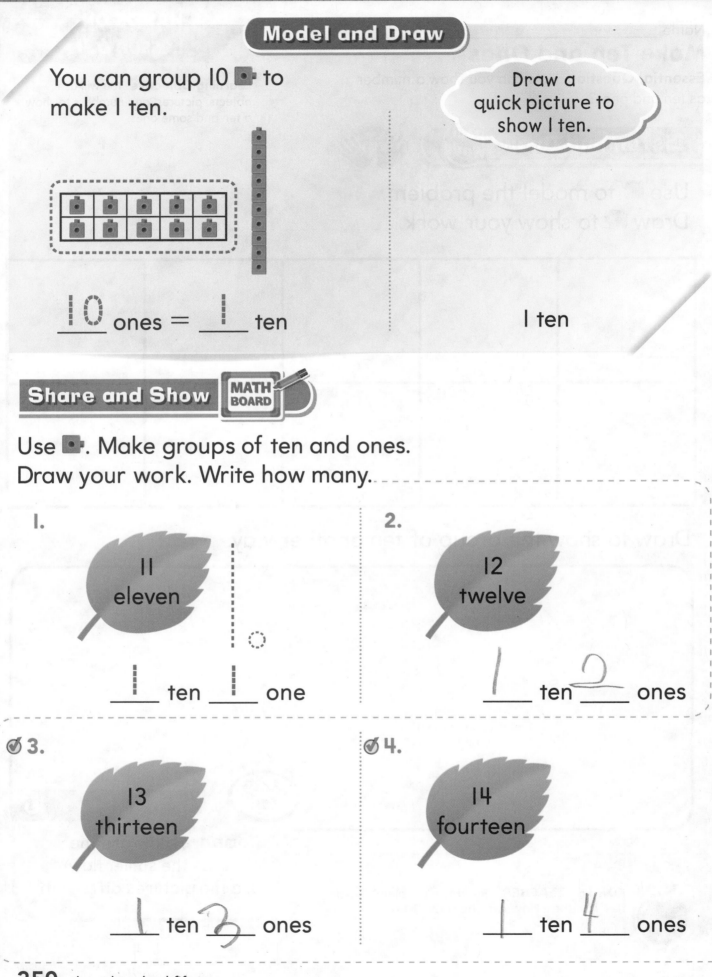 to make 1 ten.

Draw a quick picture to show 1 ten.

__10__ ones = __1__ ten

1 ten

Share and Show — MATH BOARD

Use 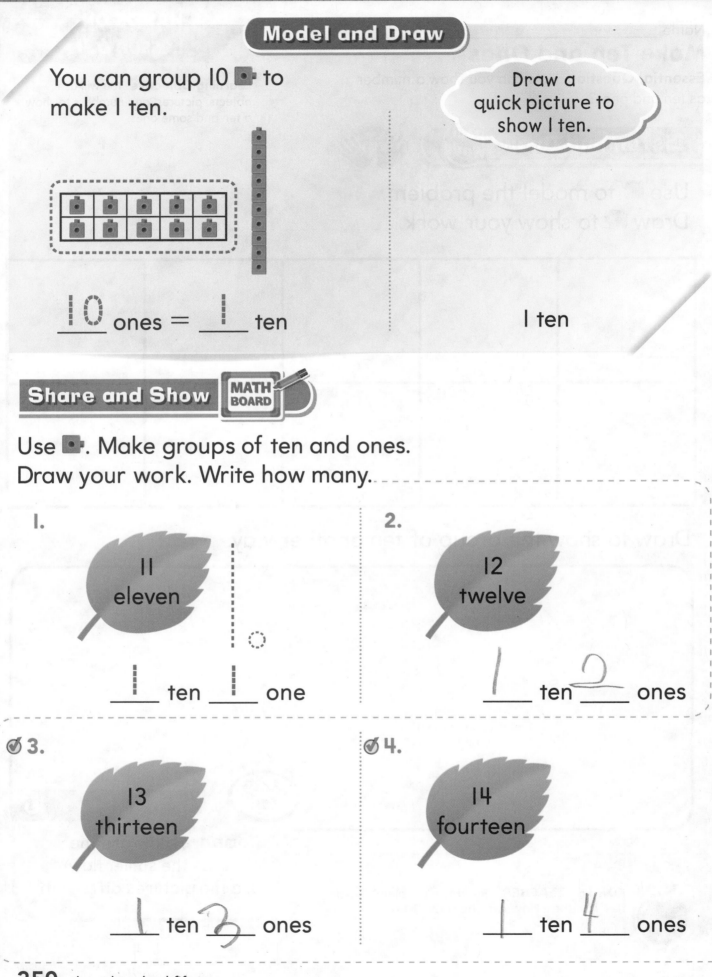. Make groups of ten and ones.
Draw your work. Write how many.

1.

11
eleven

__|__ ten __|__ one

2.

12
twelve

__1__ ten __2__ ones

✓ 3.

13
thirteen

__1__ ten __3__ ones

✓ 4.

14
fourteen

__1__ ten __4__ ones

Name _____

Math Processes and Practices **6**   **Compare** Use . Make groups of ten and ones. Draw your work. Write how many.

5.
15 fifteen

____1____ ten ____5____ ones

6.
16 sixteen

____1____ ten ___6___ ____ ones

7.
17 seventeen

____1____ ten ____7____ ones

8.
18 eighteen

____1____ ten ____8____ ones

9.
19 nineteen

____1____ ten ____9____ ones

Problem Solving • Applications (Real World)   WRITE Math

Solve.

10. **THINK SMARTER** Emily wants to write ten and ones to show 20. What does Emily write?

20
twenty

_____ ten _____ ones

11. **GO DEEPER** Gina thinks of a number that has 7 ones and I ten. What is the number? Draw to show your work.   _____

12. Ben drew this picture to show a number. What is the number?

_____

13. **THINK SMARTER** Circle the numbers that make the sentence true.

There are
| 1 |
| 4 |
| 10 |
tens and
| 1 |
| 4 |
| 10 |
ones in 14.

_____ ten _____ ones

🏠 **TAKE HOME ACTIVITY** • Give your child numbers from 11 to 19. Have your child work with small objects to show a group of ten and a group of ones for each number.

Make Ten and Ones

Learning Objective You will use objects, pictures, and numbers to show a ten and some ones.

Use ⬜. **Make groups of ten and ones. Draw your work. Write how many.**

1.

   14
   fourteen

   _____ ten _____ ones

2.

   12
   twelve

   _____ ten _____ ones

3.

   15
   fifteen

   _____ ten _____ ones

4.

   18
   eighteen

   _____ ten _____ ones

Problem Solving (Real World)

Solve.

5. Tina thinks of a number that has 3 ones and 1 ten. What is the number?   _____

6. **WRITE Math** Choose a number from 11 to 19. Write the number and number word. Use words and pictures to show how many tens and ones.

Lesson Check

1. How many tens and ones make 17?
Write the numbers.

17
seventeen

____ ten ____ ones

· ·

Spiral Review

2. Use the model. Write the
addition sentence. What
number sentence does
this model show?

___ + ___ = ___

· ·

3. Choose a way to solve.
Draw or write to explain.
Ben has 17 books. He gives
some away. He has 8 left.
How many books does
he give away?

____ books

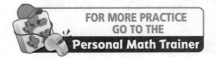

FOR MORE PRACTICE
GO TO THE
Personal Math Trainer

Name _____

Tens

Essential Question How can you model and name groups of ten?

Learning Objective You will model and name groups of ten.

Use ▪▪ to solve the riddle.
Draw and write to show your work.

Math
Talk
Math Processes and Practices 7

Look for Structure
What did you do to solve the first riddle?

FOR THE TEACHER • Read the following riddles. I am thinking of a number that is the same as 1 ten and 4 ones. What is my number? I am thinking of a number that is the same as 1 ten and 0 ones. What is my number?

Chapter 6

Model and Draw

You can group ones to make tens.

Draw a quick picture to show the tens.

20 ones = __2__ tens __0__ ones

__2__ tens = __20__
twenty

Use ▪. Make groups of ten.
Write the tens and ones.

Draw the tens. Count by tens.

☑ 1.

30 ones = ____ tens ____ ones

____ tens = ____
thirty

☑ 2.

40 ones = ____ tens ____ ones

____ tens = ____
forty

Name _____

Draw the tens.
Count by tens.

Math Processes and Practices 8 **Use Repeated Reasoning**

Use ▪. Make groups of ten. Write the tens and ones.

3. 50 ones

____ tens ____ ones

____ tens = ____
fifty

4. 60 ones

____ tens ____ ones

____ tens = ____
sixty

5. 70 ones

____ tens ____ ones

____ tens = ____
seventy

6. 80 ones

____ tens ____ ones

____ tens = ____
eighty

7. 90 ones

____ tens ____ ones

____ tens = ____
ninety

8. THINK SMARTER 100 ones

Math on the Spot

____ tens ____ ones

____ tens = ____
hundred

Name _____

✓ Mid-Chapter Checkpoint

Personal Math Trainer
Online Assessment and Intervention

Concepts and Skills

Use a Counting Chart.
Count forward. Write
the numbers.

1. 63, 64, ____, ____, ____

2. 108, 109, ____, ____, ____

Use a Counting Chart.
Count by tens. Write
the numbers.

3. 42, 52, ____, ____, ____

4. 79, 89, ____, ____, ____

5. Use the model. Write the number
three different ways.

____ ten ____ ones

____ + ____

____

Use . Make groups of ten and ones.
Draw your work. Write how many.

6.

15
fifteen

____ ten ____ ones

7. **THINK SMARTER** Choose all the ways that
name the model.

○ 60

○ 60 tens

○ 6 tens 0 ones

Tens

Learning Objective You will model and name groups of ten.

Use 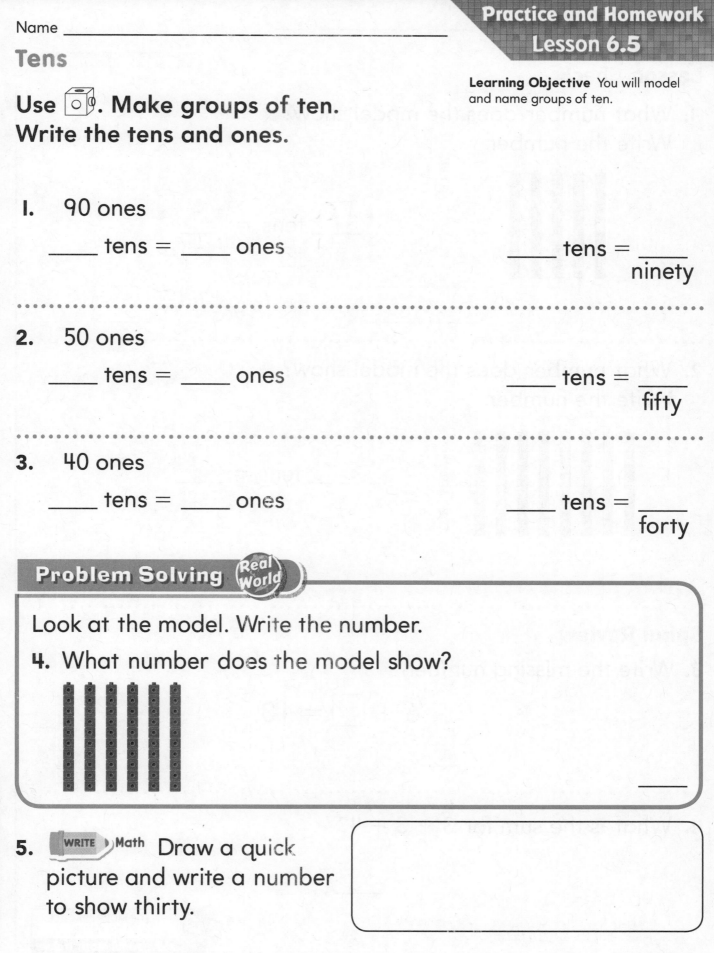. Make groups of ten.
Write the tens and ones.

1.   90 ones

   ____ tens = ____ ones

                                                                ____ tens = ____
                                                                          ninety

....

2.   50 ones

   ____ tens = ____ ones

                                                                ____ tens = ____
                                                                          fifty

....

3.   40 ones

   ____ tens = ____ ones

                                                                ____ tens = ____
                                                                          forty

Problem Solving Real World

Look at the model. Write the number.

4. What number does the model show?

   ____

5. WRITE Math   Draw a quick
   picture and write a number
   to show thirty.

Lesson Check

1. What number does the model show?
   Write the number.

_5_ tens = _50_

2. What number does the model show?
   Write the number.

____ tens = ____

Spiral Review

3. Write the missing number.

$$6 + \boxed{} = 13$$

4. What is the sum for $3 + 3 + 4$?

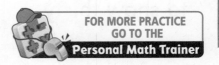

FOR MORE PRACTICE
GO TO THE
Personal Math Trainer

Tens and Ones to 50

Essential Question How can you group cubes to show a number as tens and ones?

Learning Objective You will group objects to show a number as tens and ones.

Listen and Draw

Use ▪ to model the number.
Draw ▪ to show your work.

Tens	Ones

Math Talk

Math Processes and Practices 4

Model How did you figure out how many tens and ones are in 23?

FOR THE TEACHER • Ask children to use 23 cubes and show them as tens and ones.

Model and Draw

The 2 in 24 means 2 tens.

The 2 in 42 means 2 ones.

__2__ tens __4__ ones = __24__

__4__ tens __2__ ones = __42__

Share and Show

Use your MathBoard and to show the tens and ones. Write the numbers.

1. __3__ tens __4__ ones = __34__

2. __2__ tens __0__ ones = __20__

✓ 3. __4__ tens __3__ ones = __43__

✓ 4. __1__ ten __4__ ones = __14__

Name _____

Math Processes and Practices 6 **Make Connections**

Write the numbers.

5. __3__ tens __3__ ones = __33__

6. __4__ tens __6__ ones = __46__

7. __4__ tens __0__ ones = __40__

8. __0__ tens __4__ ones = __4__

9. GO DEEPER Mary drew tens and ones to show 32.
She made a mistake.
Draw a correct quick picture to show 32.
Write the numbers.

Tens	Ones

Tens	Ones

____ tens ____ ones = ____

Problem Solving • Applications

WRITE) Math

Solve. Write the numbers.

10. I have 46 cubes. How many
tens and ones can I make?   ____ tens ____ ones

11. I have 32 cubes. How many
tens and ones can I make?   ____ tens ____ ones

12. I have 28 cubes. How many
tens and ones can I make?   ____ tens ____ ones

13. THINK SMARTER I am a number less
than 50. I have 8 ones and some
tens. What numbers could I be?

_____

Personal Math Trainer

14. THINK SMARTER + There are 35 ■. Jun says that there
are 3 ones and 5 tens. Rob says that there are
3 tens and 5 ones. Who is correct? Circle the name.

Jun   Rob

How can you draw to show 35?

TAKE HOME ACTIVITY • Write a two-digit number from 20 to 50,
such as 26. Ask your child to tell which digit names the tens and
which digit names the ones. Repeat with different numbers.

Name Z A (4

Tens and Ones to 50

Learning Objective You will group objects to show a number as tens and ones.

Write the numbers.

1.

__3__ tens __6__ ones = __36__

2.

__0__ tens __8__ ones = ____

Problem Solving Real World

Solve. Write the numbers.

3. I have 43 cubes. How many tens and ones can I make?

____ tens ____ ones

---

4. [WRITE] Math Write a number from 20 to 50 that has both tens and ones. Use pictures and words to show the tens and ones.

Chapter 6

Lesson Check

1. What number does the model show?
   Write the numbers.

   ___2___ tens ___0___ ones = ___20___

2. What number does the model show?
   Write the numbers.

   ___4___ tens ___2___ ones = ___42___

Spiral Review

3. Write the sum.

$$\begin{array}{r} 6 \\ +\ 3 \\ \hline \end{array}$$ 9

4. Show taking from. Circle the
   part you take from the group.
   Then cross it out.
   Write the difference.

   $6 - 4 = $ ___1___

FOR MORE PRACTICE
GO TO THE
Personal Math Trainer

Name _Zach_

Tens and Ones to 100

Essential Question How can you show numbers to 100 as tens and ones?

Learning Objective You will group objects to show numbers to 100 as tens and ones.

Listen and Draw

Use ▭▭▭▭▭ ▪ to model the number.
Draw a quick picture to show your work.

25

50

52

Math Talk

Math Processes and Practices ②

Reasoning How did you figure out how many tens and ones are in 52?

FOR THE TEACHER • Ask children to use base-ten blocks to show how many tens and ones there are in 25, 50, and 52.

Chapter 6

three hundred sixty-seven **367**

The number just after 99 is 100.
10 tens is the same as 1 **hundred**.

Draw quick pictures to show 99 and 100.

__9__ tens __9__ ones = __99__ | __10__ tens __0__ ones = __100__

Share and Show MATH BOARD

Use your MathBoard and ▭▭▭▭▭▭▭▭ ▪ to
show the tens and ones. Write the numbers.

1. ____ tens ____ ones = ____

2. __5__ tens ____ ones = ____

3. ____ tens ____ ones = ____

4. ____ tens ____ ones = ____

Name _____

Math Processes and Practices ② **Reason Quantitatively** Write the numbers.

5. ___9___ tens ___6___ ones = ___96___

6. ___6___ tens ___9___ ones = ___69___

7. ___8___ tens ___4___ ones = ___84___

8. ___7___ tens ___2___ ones = ___72___

9. ___10___ tens ___0___ ones = ___100___

10. GO DEEPER What number is the same as 7 tens and 20 ones?

_____

11. GO DEEPER What number is the same as 5 tens and 13 ones?

_____

Problem Solving • Applications (Real World) WRITE ▸ Math

Draw a quick picture to show the number.
Write how many tens and ones there are.

12. Edna has 82 stamps.

_____ tens _____ ones

13. Amy has 79 beads.

_____ tens _____ ones

14. **THINK SMARTER** Moe has a
group of 70 red feathers
and 30 brown feathers.

_____ tens _____ ones

15. **THINK SMARTER** Read the problem. Write
a number to solve.

I am greater than 14.
I am less than 20.
I have 6 ones.

16

TAKE HOME ACTIVITY • Give your child numbers from 50 to 100.
Ask your child to draw a picture to show the tens and the ones in
each number and then write the number.

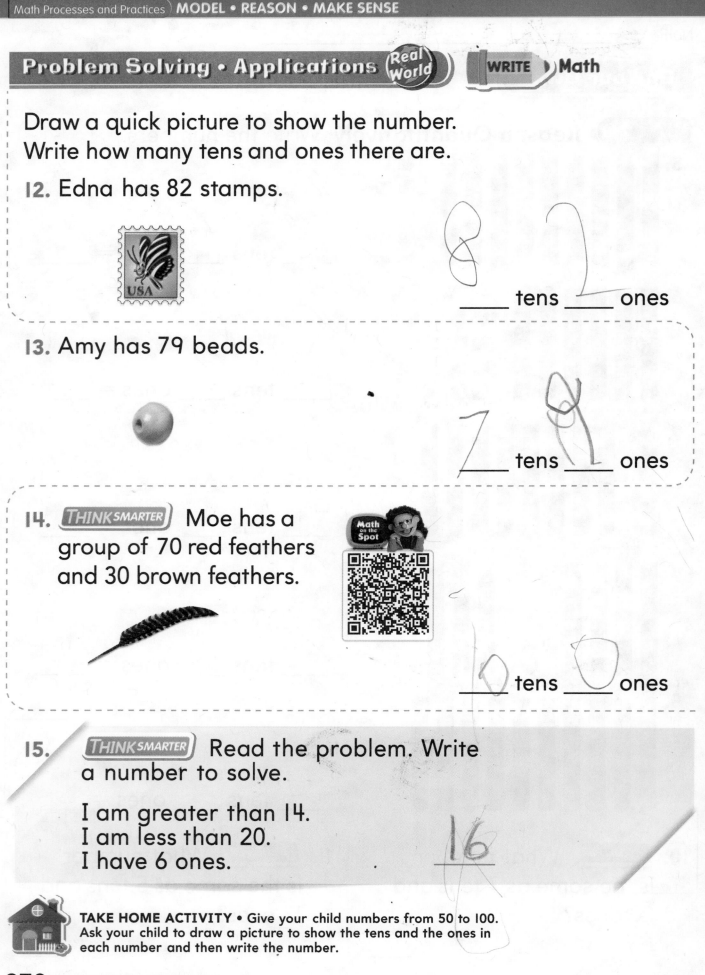

Name _____ ACH _____

Tens and Ones to 100

Learning Objective You will group objects to show numbers to 100 as tens and ones.

Write the numbers.

1. _____ tens _____ ones = _____

2. _____ tens _____ ones = _____

3. __7__ tens __5__ ones = __75__

Problem Solving Real World

Draw a quick picture to show the number.
Write how many tens and ones there are.

4. Inez has 57 shells.

__5__ tens _____ ones

5. ✏️ **WRITE** Math Use words and pictures to show 59 and 95.

Lesson Check

1. What number has 10 tens 0 ones?

100

2. What number does
the model show?
Write the numbers.

_7_ tens _4_ ones = _74_

Spiral Review

3. Barry knows that $6 + 5 = 11$.
What other addition fact does
he know? Write the new fact.

_5_ + _5_ = _10_

4. Count on to solve $2 + 6$.
Write the sum.

$$2 + 6 = \underline{8}$$

FOR MORE PRACTICE
GO TO THE
Personal Math Trainer

Name _____

Problem Solving • Show Numbers in Different Ways

Essential Question How can making a model help you show a number in different ways?

Learning Objective You will use the strategy *make a model* to help you show a number in different ways.

Gary and Jill both want 23 stickers for a class project. There are 3 sheets of 10 stickers and 30 single stickers on the table. How could Gary and Jill each take 23 stickers?

Unlock the Problem *Real World*

What do I need to find?

_____

__**two**__ different ways to make a number

What information do I need to use?

The number is ___23___.

Show how to solve the problem.

Gary	
Tens	Ones

23

Jill	
Tens	Ones

23

HOME CONNECTION • Showing the number with base-ten blocks helps your child explore different ways to combine tens and ones.

© Houghton Mifflin Harcourt Publishing Company

- What do I need to find?
- What information do I need to use?

Use ▭▭▭▭▭ ▪ to show the number two different ways. Draw both ways.

1. 46

Tens	Ones

46

Tens	Ones

46

2. 71

Tens	Ones

71

Tens	Ones

3. 65

Tens	Ones

65

Tens	Ones

Math Talk

Math Processes and Practices 6

Look at Exercise 3. **Explain** why both ways show 65.

© Houghton Mifflin Harcourt Publishing Company

Name _____

Use ▭▭▭▭ ▪ to show the number two different ways. Draw both ways.

4. 59

Tens	Ones

◯ =

Tens	Ones

5. 34

Tens	Ones

◯

Tens	Ones

6. **THINK SMARTER** Show 31 three ways.

Tens	Ones

◯

Tens	Ones

◯

Tens	Ones

On Your Own **Math**

Write a number sentence to solve. Draw to explain.

7. (Math Processes and Practices ④) **Write an Equation**

Felix invites 15 friends to his party. Some friends are girls. 8 friends are boys. How many friends are girls?

___ ◯ ___ ◯ ___ girls

GO DEEPER Solve. Write the numbers.

8. I am a number less than 35.
I have 3 tens and some ones.
What numbers can I be? _____

Personal Math Trainer

9. **THINK SMARTER ＋** Choose all the ways that show the same number.

🏠 **TAKE HOME ACTIVITY** • Have your child draw quick pictures to show the number 56 two ways.

**Problem Solving • Show Numbers
in Different Ways**

Learning Objective You will use the
strategy *make a model* to help you show
a number in different ways.

Use ⬚⬚⬚⬚⬚⬚ ▢ to show the number
two different ways. Draw both ways.

1.   62 | Tens | Ones | | Tens | Ones |

2.   38 | Tens | Ones | | Tens | Ones |

3. WRITE Math Draw to show 55 three different ways.

Lesson Check

1. What number does each model show? Write the numbers.

_____ − _____ = _____

2. What number does the model show? Write the number.

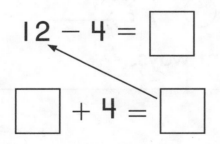

_____

Spiral Review

3. Subtract to solve. Then add to check your answer.

$$12 - 4 = \boxed{}$$

$$\boxed{} + 4 = \boxed{}$$

4. Write two ways to make 15.

15 = _____ + _____   15 = _____ + _____

FOR MORE PRACTICE
GO TO THE
Personal Math Trainer

Name _____

Model, Read, and Write Numbers from 100 to 110

Essential Question How can you model, read, and write numbers from 100 to 110?

Learning Objective You will model, read, and write numbers from 100 to 110.

Listen and Draw

Use .
Circle a number to answer the question.

1	2	3	4	5	6	7	8	9	10
11	12	13	14	15	16	17	18	19	20
21	22	23	24	25	26	27	28	29	30
31	32	33	34	35	36	37	38	39	40
41	42	43	44	45	46	47	48	49	50
51	52	53	54	55	56	57	58	59	60
61	62	63	64	65	66	67	68	69	70
71	72	73	74	75	76	77	78	79	80
81	82	83	84	85	86	87	88	89	90
91	92	93	94	95	96	97	98	99	100

Math Talk
Math Processes and Practices 7

Look for Structure
Why is 100 to the right of 99 on the hundred chart? Why is 100 below 90?

FOR THE TEACHER • Have children locate each number on the hundred chart. What number is the same as 30 ones? What number is the same as 10 tens? What number is the same as 8 tens 7 ones? What number has 1 more one than 52? What number has 1 more ten than 65?

Chapter 6

Model and Draw

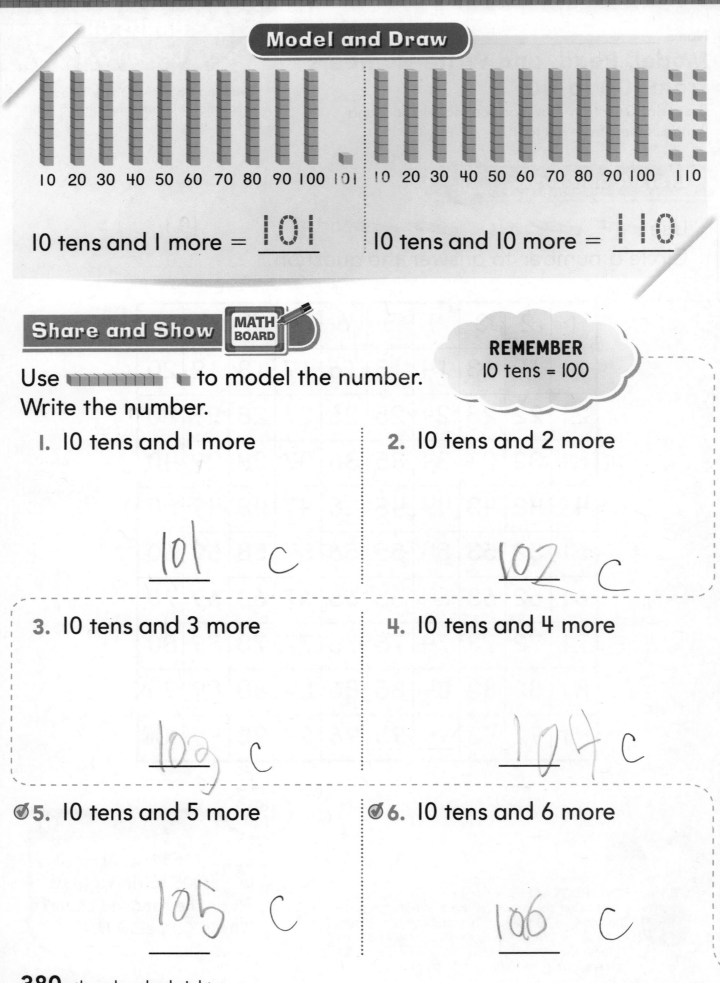

10 20 30 40 50 60 70 80 90 100 101

10 20 30 40 50 60 70 80 90 100 110

10 tens and 1 more = **101**

10 tens and 10 more = **110**

Share and Show MATH BOARD

REMEMBER
10 tens = 100

Use ▭▭▭ ▪ to model the number.
Write the number.

1. 10 tens and 1 more

101 c

2. 10 tens and 2 more

102 c

3. 10 tens and 3 more

103 c

4. 10 tens and 4 more

104 c

☑5. 10 tens and 5 more

105 c

☑6. 10 tens and 6 more

106 c

Name _____

Math Processes and Practices 4   **Model Mathematics**

Use ▭▭▭▭▭ ▪ to model the number.
Write the number.

7. 10 tens and
7 more

107 c

8. 10 tens and
8 more

108 c

9. 10 tens and
9 more

109 c

10. 10 tens and 10 more

110 c

11. THINK SMARTER   11 tens

111 c

Math on the Spot

Write the number.

12.

108 c

13.

101 c

14.

104 c

15.

105 c

Problem Solving • Applications   Real World   WRITE Math

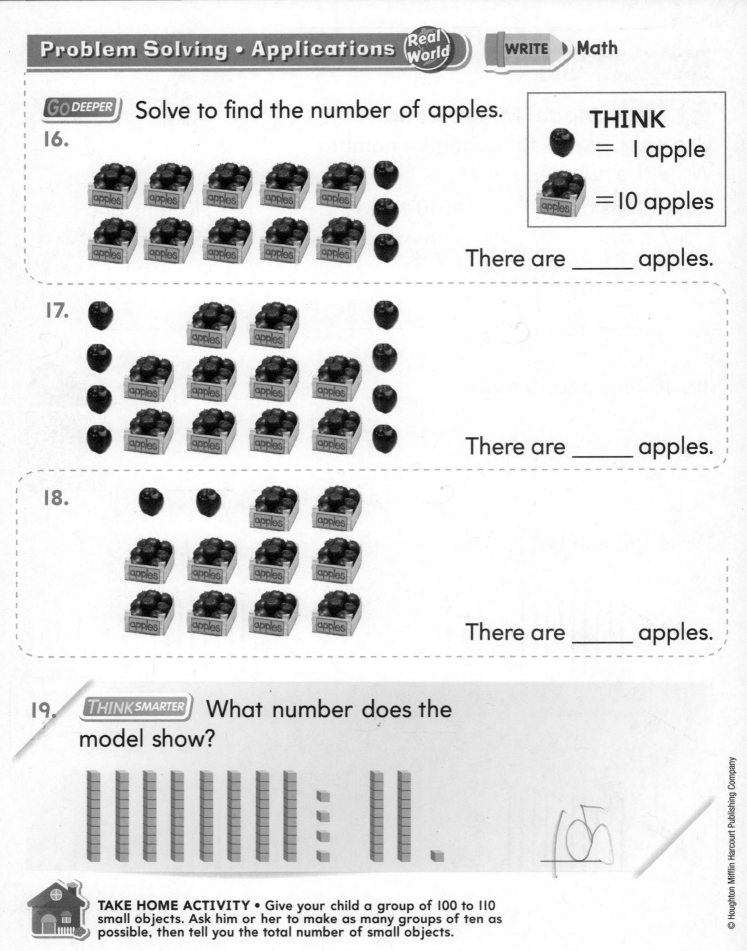

GO DEEPER Solve to find the number of apples.

16.

THINK

= 1 apple

= 10 apples

There are _____ apples.

17.

There are _____ apples.

18.

There are _____ apples.

19. **THINK SMARTER** What number does the model show?

TAKE HOME ACTIVITY • Give your child a group of 100 to 110 small objects. Ask him or her to make as many groups of ten as possible, then tell you the total number of small objects.

Name _____ ZACH _____

Model, Read, and Write Numbers from 100 to 110

Learning Objective You will model, read, and write numbers from 100 to 110.

Use to show the number.
Write the number.

1. 10 tens and 6 more

_106_

2. 10 tens and 1 more

_101_

3. 10 tens and 10 more

_110_

Problem Solving Real World

4. Solve to find the number of pens.

THINK

✎ = 1 pen

▭ = 10 pens

There are __104__ pens.

5. WRITE Math Choose a number from 101 to 110. Write it. Draw a picture to show it as 10 tens and more.

Lesson Check

1. What number does the model show?
Write the number.

|||||||||| o
           o
           o
           o

_____

....

Spiral Review

2. Show taking from. Circle the
part you take from the group.
Then cross it out.
Write the difference.

$4 - 3 =$ _____

....

3. Use the model to solve. Ken has
8 toy trains. Ron has 3 toy trains.
How many fewer toy trains does
Ron have than Ken?

8

3	

_____

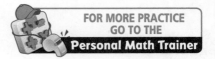
FOR MORE PRACTICE
GO TO THE
Personal Math Trainer

Name _____

Model, Read, and Write Numbers from 110 to 120

Essential Question How can you model, read, and write numbers from 110 to 120?

Listen and Draw *Real World*

How many shells are there?

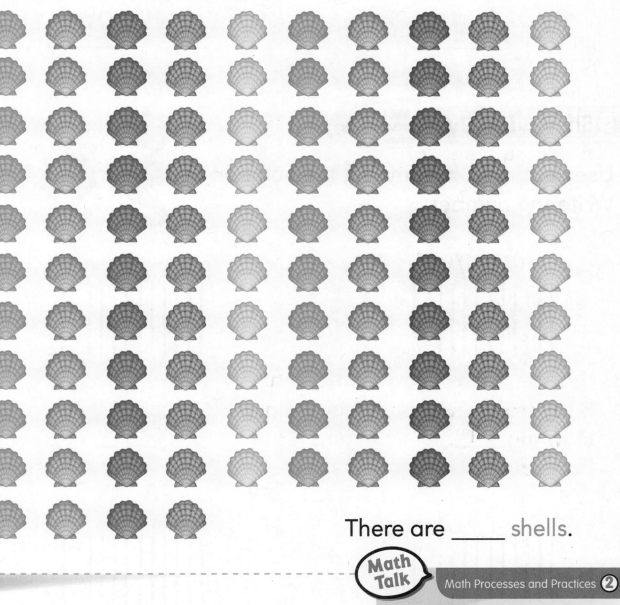

There are _____ shells.

Math Talk

Math Processes and Practices ②

Reasoning How did you decide how many shells there are? Explain.

FOR THE TEACHER • The picture shows the shells that Heidi has collected. How many shells does Heidi have?

Model and Draw

11 tens is 110.

120 tens is 120.

110

120

Share and Show   MATH BOARD

Use ▭▭▭▭▭ ▪ to model the number.
Write the number.

1.

111

2.

112

3.

119

4.

114

Name _____

On Your Own

Math Processes and Practices **4** **Model Mathematics**

Use to model the number.
Write the number.

5.

115

6.

116

7.

117

8.

118

9.

119

10.

120

Math on the Spot

THINK SMARTER Write the number.

11.

114

12.

111

13.

113

Problem Solving • Applications WRITE Math

GO DEEPER Choose a way to solve.
Draw or write to explain.

14. Joe collects toy cars. He can make
11 groups of 10 toy cars.
How many toy cars
does Joe have?

_____ toy cars

15. Cindy collects buttons. She can
make 11 groups of 10 buttons
and one more group of 7 buttons.
How many buttons
does Cindy have?

_____ buttons

16. Lee collects marbles. He can make
11 groups of 10 marbles
and has 2 marbles left
over. How many marbles
does Lee have?

_____ marbles

17. THINK SMARTER Finish the drawing to show 119.

Write to explain.

TAKE HOME ACTIVITY • Give your child a group of 100 to
120 small objects. Ask him or her to make as many groups of ten
as possible and then tell you the total number of small objects.

Name _____

Model, Read, and Write Numbers from 110 to 120

Learning Objective You will model, read, and write numbers from 110 to 120.

Use to model the number.
Write the number.

1.

‖‖‖‖‖‖‖‖‖ |

____

2.

‖‖‖‖‖‖‖‖‖ ∶ ⁰⁰ ⁰⁰ ⁰⁰ ⁰⁰ ⁰⁰

____

3.

⁰ ⁰ ⁰ ⁰ ‖‖‖‖‖‖‖‖‖‖

____

Problem Solving Real World

Choose a way to solve. Draw or write to explain.

4. Dave collects rocks. He makes 12 groups of 10 rocks and has none left over. How many rocks does Dave have?

____ rocks

5. **WRITE** Math Choose a number from 111 to 120. Write the number. Draw a picture to show it as tens and ones.

© Houghton Mifflin Harcourt Publishing Company

Lesson Check

1. What number does the model show?
Write the number.

_____

....

Spiral Review

2. Show how to make a ten to solve 13 − 7.
Write the number sentence.

| Step 1 | Step 2 |

___ − ___

___ − ___ = ___

So, 13 − 7 = ___.

....

3. What is the difference?
Write the number.

$$\begin{array}{r} 9 \\ -\ 4 \\ \hline \end{array}$$

FOR MORE PRACTICE
GO TO THE
Personal Math Trainer

✓ Chapter 6 Review/Test

Personal Math Trainer
Online Assessment
and Intervention

1. Felix counts 46 cubes. Then he counts forward some more cubes. Write the numbers.

46, _____, _____, _____, _____, _____, _____, _____

---

2. Count by tens. Match each number on the left to a number that is 10 more.

35 •   • 69

49 •   • 59

59 •   • 75

65 •   • 45

57 •   • 67

3. Does the number match the model?
Choose Yes or No.

10 + 10	○ Yes	○ No
1 ten 4 ones	○ Yes	○ No
1 ten 5 ones	○ Yes	○ No
10 + 5	○ Yes	○ No

4. Circle the numbers that make the sentence true.

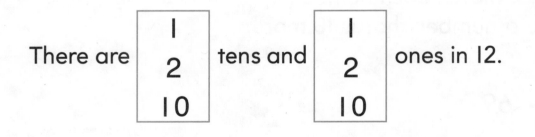

There are
| 1 |
| 2 |
| 10 |
tens and
| 1 |
| 2 |
| 10 |
ones in 12.

5. Choose all the ways that name the model.

○ 3 ones

○ 3 tens

○ 3 tens 0 ones

○ 30

6. There are 42 ◼. Lisa says that there are
4 tens and 2 ones. Elena says there are 2 tens
and 4 ones. Who is correct? Circle the name.

Lisa   Elena

How can you draw to show 42?

[ ]

---

7. Read the problem. Write a number to solve.

I am greater than 27.
I am less than 30.
I have 9 ones.

[ ]

8. THINK SMARTER + Choose all the ways that
show the same number.

Personal Math Trainer

○

○

○

○

9. What number does the model show?

_____

10. GO DEEPER Finish the drawing to show 118.

Write to explain.

11. Count the 🌰. Write the numbers.

How many tens? _____ tens

How many 🌰? _____

_____

12. Draw a quick picture to show 54 in two ways. Then write the number of tens and ones in each picture.

_____ tens _____ ones _____ tens _____ ones

Chapter 7

Compare Numbers

Curious About Math with
Curious George

How many colors do you see in the kite? Name the number that is one more.

Name _____

Model More

Draw lines to match.
Circle the set that has more.

1.

2.

More, Fewer

3. Circle the row that has more.

4. Circle the row that has fewer.

Draw Equal Groups

5. Draw a ball for each glove.

This page checks understanding of important skills needed for success in Chapter 7.

Name _____

Vocabulary Builder

Visualize It

Draw pictures in the box to show
more, **fewer**, or the **same** number.

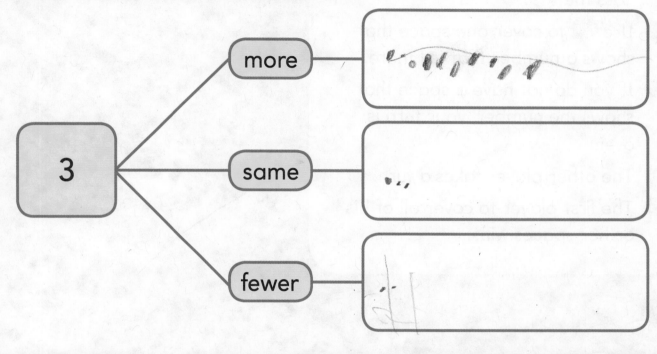

```
        ┌──── more ────┐
3 ──────┼──── same ────┤
        └──── fewer ───┘
```

Understand Vocabulary

Complete the sentences with review words.

1. I see 2 white cats and 4 yellow cats. I see _more_
   yellow cats than white cats.

2. Dave has 9 grapes. Ann has 6 grapes. Ann has _less_
   grapes than Dave.

3. 5 ducks and 5 swans are at the pond. There are
   the _same_ number of ducks and swans.

GO DIGITAL • **Interactive Student Edition**
• **Multimedia eGlossary**

Game Rainy Day Bingo

Materials • 🎲 • 9 🔵 • 9 🔵

Play with a partner.

① Toss the 🎲.

② Use 🔵 to cover one space that shows a number that is 1 more.

③ If you do not have a space that shows the number, your turn is over.

④ The other player takes a turn.

⑤ The first player to cover all of his or her spaces wins.

Player 1

4	5	2
3	6	4
2	5	7

Player 2

6	2	3
4	7	6
5	3	7

Chapter 7 Vocabulary

add

sumar

1

difference

diferencia

13

fewer

menos

19

is greater than (>)

es mayor que (>)

31

is less than (<)

es menor que (<)

32

more

más

38

subtract

restar

52

sum

suma o total

54

$9 - 4 = 5$

The **difference** is 5.

$3 + 2 = 5$

$32 > 24$

32 **is greater than** 24.

3 **fewer**

$5 - 3 = 2$

There are **more** .

$26 < 37$

26 **is less than** 37.

2 plus 1 is equal to 3.

The **sum** is 3.

$5 - 2 = 3$

Guess the Word

Word Box

add

difference

fewer

is greater than (>)

is less than (<)

more

subtract

sum

Materials
timer

How to Play
Play with a partner.

1. Choose a math word from the Word Box. Do not tell your partner.

2. Set the timer.

3. Give a one-word clue.

4. Your partner tries to guess the secret word.

5. Repeat with a new one-word clue until your partner guesses correctly or time runs out.

6. Take turns.

7. The first player to correctly guess 5 words wins.

The Write Way

Reflect

Choose one idea. Draw and write about it.

- Write two questions you have about comparing numbers.

- Explain how to compare 43 and 35.

Name _____

Algebra • Greater Than

Essential Question How can you compare two numbers to find which is greater?

Learning Objective You will model and compare two-digit numbers to find which is greater by using the > symbol.

Listen and Draw

Use ▭▭ ▪ or an *i*Tool to solve.
Draw quick pictures to show your work.

Tens	Ones

FOR THE TEACHER • Read the problem. Which number is greater, 65 or 56? Have children use base-ten blocks and draw quick pictures to solve.

Math Talk Math Processes and Practices 5

How did you **use tools** to decide which number is greater?

Model and Draw

To compare 25 and 17, first compare the tens.

2 tens are more than I ten.

__25__ **is greater than** __17__.

__25__ > __17__

If the tens are the same, compare the ones.

7 ones are more than 5 ones.

__17__ is greater than __15__.

__17__ > __15__

Share and Show MATH BOARD

Use your MathBoard and ▭▭▭ ▪ to show each number.

	Circle the greater number.	Did tens or ones help you decide?	Write the numbers.
I.	62 (65)	tens (ones)	__65__ is greater than __62__. __65__ > __62__
2.	84 48	tens ones	____ is greater than ____. ____ > ____
3.	72 70	tens ones	____ is greater than ____. ____ > ____

© Houghton Mifflin Harcourt Publishing Company

Name _____

Math Processes and Practices 5 Use a Concrete Model

Use ▭▭▭▭ ▪ if you need to.

Circle the greater number.	Did tens or ones help you decide?	Write the numbers.
4. 57 75	tens ones	_____ is greater than _____. _____ > _____
5. 94 98	tens ones	_____ is greater than _____. _____ > _____

Write or draw to solve.

6. **THINK SMARTER** Pam and Jake play a game for points. Pam's points are 1 ten 6 ones. Jake's points are 1 one 6 tens. Who has the greater number of points?

_____

7. **GO DEEPER** John has 51 cards. Paul has 32 cards. George has a number of cards greater than either Paul or John. How many cards might George have?

_____ cards

Problem Solving • Applications

WRITE ▶ Math

8. **THINK SMARTER** Color the balloons that show numbers greater than 56.

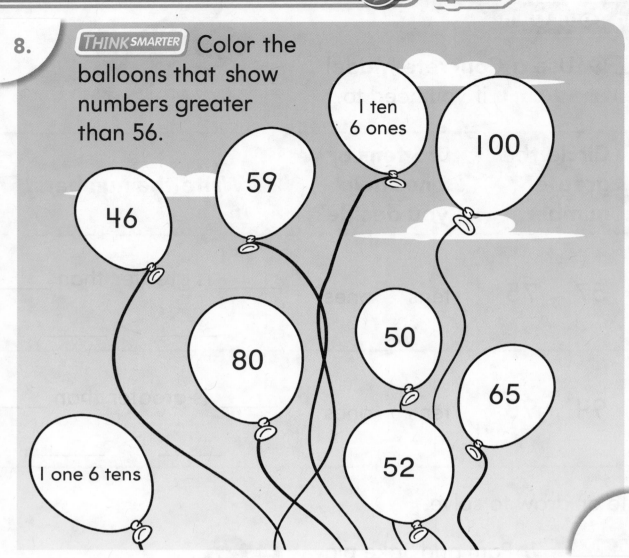

59

46

1 ten 6 ones

100

80

50

65

52

1 one 6 tens

9. **THINK SMARTER** Compare. Is the math sentence true? Choose Yes or No.

37 is greater than 43.　　○ Yes　　○ No

41 is greater than 39.　　○ Yes　　○ No

48 > 52　　○ Yes　　○ No

86 > 68　　○ Yes　　○ No

TAKE HOME ACTIVITY • Write 38, 63, 68, and 83 on slips of paper. Show your child two numbers, and ask which number is greater. Repeat with different pairs of numbers.

Algebra • Greater Than

Learning Objective You will model and compare two-digit numbers to find which is greater by using the > symbol.

Use if you need to.

Circle the greater number.	Did tens or ones help you decide?	Write the numbers.
1. 22 42	tens ones	____ is greater than ____. ____ > ____
2. 46 64	tens ones	____ is greater than ____. ____ > ____
3. 88 86	tens ones	____ is greater than ____. ____ > ____

Problem Solving (Real World)

4. Color the blocks that show numbers greater than 47.

5. WRITE Math Write a number that is greater than 29. Draw quick pictures to explain.

Lesson Check

1. Circle the number that is greater than 65.
Write the numbers.

37   49   56   66

___ is greater than ___.

___ > ___

2. Circle the number that is greater than 29.
Write the numbers.

19   20   28   92

___ is greater than ___.

___ > ___

Spiral Review

3. What is 5 + 7? Write the sum.

$$5 + 7 = \rule{1cm}{0.4pt}$$

4. Count forward. Write the number that is missing.

110, 111, ____, 113, 114

© Houghton Mifflin Harcourt Publishing Company

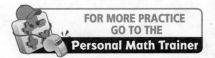

FOR MORE PRACTICE
GO TO THE
Personal Math Trainer

Name _____

Algebra • Less Than

Essential Question How can you compare two numbers to find which is less?

Learning Objective You will model and compare two-digit numbers to find which is less by using the < symbol.

Listen and Draw

Use ▰▰▰▰▰ ▪ to solve. Draw quick pictures to show your work.

Tens	Ones

Math Talk

Math Processes and Practices ③

Compare How does your drawing show which number is less? Explain.

FOR THE TEACHER • Read the problem. Which number is less, 22 or 28? Have children use base-ten blocks to solve.

Compare numbers to find which is less.

How do you know which number is less?

___43___ **is less than** ___49___.

___43___ < ___49___

Share and Show MATH BOARD

Use your MathBoard and to show each number.

	Circle the number that is less.	Did tens or ones help you decide?	Write the numbers.
1.	39 (36)	tens (ones)	_36_ is less than _39_. _36_ < _39_
2.	80 94	tens ones	____ is less than ____. ____ < ____
3.	57 54	tens ones	____ is less than ____. ____ < ____

Name _____

On Your Own

Math Processes and Practices 5
GO DEEPER

Use a Concrete Model
Use ▭▭▭▭▭ ▪ if you need to.

	Circle the number that is less.	Did tens or ones help you decide?	Write the numbers.
4.	(47) 48	tens ones	_47_ is less than _48_. _47_ < _48_
5.	82 (28)	tens ones	_28_ is less than _82_. _28_ < _82_
6.	96 (90)	tens ones	_90_ is less than _96_. _90_ < _96_
7.	(23) 32	tens ones	_23_ is less than _32_. _23_ < _32_

Write a number to solve.

8. **THINK SMARTER** Ella has 22 beads. Lauren has fewer beads than Ella. How many beads might Lauren have?

_____ beads

Chapter 7 • Lesson 2

four hundred seven **407**

© Houghton Mifflin Harcourt Publishing Company

Problem Solving • Applications 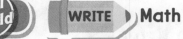 WRITE Math

Write a number to solve.

9. **THINK SMARTER** Nan makes the number 46. Marty makes a number that is less than 46. What could be a number Marty makes?

_____

10. **THINK SMARTER** Jack makes the number 92. Kit makes a number that has fewer ones than 92. What could be a number Kit makes?

_____

11. **THINK SMARTER** Write a number that is less than 67.

How do you know your number is less than 67?

_____

_____

 TAKE HOME ACTIVITY • Write 47, 54, 57, and 74 on slips of paper. Show your child two numbers, and ask which number is less. Repeat with different pairs of numbers.

Name _____

Algebra • Less Than

Learning Objective You will model and compare two-digit numbers to find which is less by using the < symbol.

Use ⬚⬚⬚⬚⬚ ▢ if you need to.

Circle the number that is less.	Did tens or ones help you decide?	Write the numbers.
1. 34 36	tens ones	___ is less than ___. ___ < ___
2. 75 57	tens ones	___ is less than ___. ___ < ___
3. 80 89	tens ones	___ is less than ___. ___ < ___

Problem Solving Real World

Write a number to solve.

4. Lori makes the number 74. Gabe makes a number that is less than 74. What could be a number Gabe makes? ___

5. **WRITE Math** Write a number that is less than 41. Draw quick pictures to explain.

Lesson Check

I. Circle the number that is less than 52.
Write the numbers.

25   52   64   88

_____ is less than _____.

_____ < _____

2. Circle the number that is less than 76.
Write the numbers.

100   81   77   59

_____ is less than _____.

_____ < _____

Spiral Review

3. What number does the model show? Write the number.

_____ tens _____ ones = _____

4. Count by tens.
Write the missing numbers.

8, 18, 28, _____, _____, 58

FOR MORE PRACTICE
GO TO THE
Personal Math Trainer

Name _____

Algebra • Use Symbols to Compare

Essential Question How can you use symbols to show how numbers compare?

Learning Objective You will use the symbols >, =, and < to show how to compare numbers.

Listen and Draw

Use ▭▭▭▭▭. Draw quick pictures to show your work. Write the numbers to compare.

_____ < 36   _____ = 36   _____ > 36

FOR THE TEACHER • Have children use base-ten blocks to show a number less than 36, a number equal to 36, and a number greater than 36.

Math Talk Math Processes and Practices ④

Represent Compare 47 and 32 in two ways. What two symbols do you use?

© Houghton Mifflin Harcourt Publishing Company

Chapter 7

Model and Draw

21 ⬤< 24
21 is less than 24.

24 ⬤= 24
24 is equal to 24.

30 ⬤> 24
30 is greater than 24.

Share and Show MATH BOARD

Use [image]. Draw to show each number.
Write <, >, or =. Complete the sentence.

1.

28 ◯ 35

28 _____ 35.

2.

16 ◯ 16

16 _____ 16.

⬤ 3.

46 ◯ 31

46 _____ 31.

⬤ 4.

51 ◯ 52

51 _____ 52.

Name _____

On Your Own

REMEMBER
< is less than
> is greater than
= is equal to

Math Processes and Practices ④ **Use Symbols**

GO DEEPER Write <, >, or =.
Draw a quick picture if you need to.

5.

45 〉 42

6.

38 〈 50

tehs

7.

90 〈 93

8.

87 〉 87

9.

64 〉 59

tens

10. **THINK SMARTER** Gill and Rob win tokens in a game. Gill has 86 tokens. Rob has 61 tokens. 70 tokens are needed for a prize. Who has enough tokens for a prize? Write the number.

Math on the Spot

86
9j7-1

THINK SMARTER Write numbers to solve.

11.
96 = 96

12.
53 > 20

13.
83 < 100

14.
40 < 200

15.
71 > 40

16.
29 = 28

🏠 **TAKE HOME ACTIVITY** • Have your child show you how to write <, >, and = to compare two numbers. Ask him or her to use words to explain each comparison.

✓ Mid-Chapter Checkpoint

Personal Math Trainer
Online Assessment
and Intervention

Concepts and Skills

Circle the greater number. Write the numbers.

1.   **38**   **83**   ___ is greater than ___.

___ > ___

Circle the number that is less. Write the numbers.

2.   **61**   **29**   ___ is less than ___.

___ < ___

3.   Matt scores 34 points and wins the game. Lee scores points and does not win. The number of Lee's points is less than the number of Matt's points. Is Lee's score 49 or 29?   ____

4.   **THINK SMARTER**   Circle the symbol that makes the math sentence true.

44 | > | 43
     | < |
     | = |

© Houghton Mifflin Harcourt Publishing Company

Algebra • Use Symbols to Compare

Learning Objective You will use the symbols >, =, and < to show how to compare numbers.

Write <, >, or =.
Draw a quick picture if you need to.

1.

38 ⬭ 31

2.

26 ⬭ 42

3. 88 ⬭ 78

4. 77 ⬭ 77

5. 91 ⬭ 89

6. 80 ⬭ 82

7. 33 ⬭ 44

8. 51 ⬭ 60

Problem Solving (Real World)

Write <, >, or = to solve. Circle your answer.

9. Tracey has 26 shells. Heba has 29 shells. Who has a greater number of shells?

Tracey   Heba

29 ⬭ 26

10. WRITE Math Choose some numbers to compare to 55. Use <, >, and =.

PP 4 55 5 1

Lesson Check

1. Compare each pair of numbers. Write <, >, or =.

22 ⃝ 28 ┊ 28 ⃝ 28 ┊ 22 ⃝ 22 ┊ 28 ⃝ 22

2. Compare each pair of numbers. Write <, >, or =.

78 ⃝ 87 ┊ 78 ⃝ 78 ┊ 87 ⃝ 78 ┊ 87 ⃝ 87

Spiral Review

3. What number does the model show? Write the number.

___7___ tens ___8___ ones = ___78___

4. Use the model. Write the number three different ways.

___1___ ten ___8___ ones

___18___ + ___0___

___18___

FOR MORE PRACTICE
GO TO THE
Personal Math Trainer

Name _____

Problem Solving • Compare Numbers

Essential Question How can making a model help you compare numbers?

Learning Objective You will use the strategy *make a model* to help you compare numbers.

Cassidy has the number cards shown below. She gives away the cards with numbers less than 49 or greater than 53. Which number cards does Cassidy have now?

Unlock the Problem

What do I need to find?

the __number cards__ that Cassidy has now

What information do I need to use?

number cards < 49

or > 53

Show how to solve the problem.

Cassidy has number cards __51, 52__.

© Houghton Mifflin Harcourt Publishing Company

 HOME CONNECTION • Your child made a model of the problem. The numbers crossed out are less than 49 or greater than 53. The remaining numbers are the solution to the problem.

Chapter 7

four hundred seventeen **417**

Make a model to solve.

1. Tony has these number cards. He gives away the cards with numbers less than 16 or greater than 19. Cross those out. Which number cards does Tony have now?

~~15~~   17   18   ~~20~~   ~~22~~

Tony has number cards ___17 18___ .
N = 2

2. Carol has these number cards. She keeps the cards with numbers greater than 98 or less than 95. Circle the number cards Carol keeps.

90   91   ~~96~~   ~~97~~   99

Carol keeps number cards __90, 91, 99__ .
N = 3

Math Talk

Model Explain how you can find the number cards Tony has now.

Share and Show MATH BOARD

Math Processes and Practices 4 **Use Models** Make a model to solve.

3. Felipe has these number cards. He gives away cards with numbers less than 60 or greater than 65. Which number cards does Felipe have now?

| 58 | 61 | 63 | 64 | 68 |

Felipe has number cards N=3(6 1 6 2 6)_.

4. **THINK SMARTER** Molly underlines the number cards greater than 76 and circles the number cards less than 84. Which number cards are both greater than 76 and less than 84?

| 72 | 75 | 78 | 82 | 85 |

Number cards _78 82_ are both greater than 76 and less than 84.

N=2

On Your Own   WRITE Math

Choose a way to solve.
Draw or write to explain.

5. GO DEEPER Some cows were in the field. 6 more cows walked there. Then there were 13 cows. How many cows were in the field before?

_____ cows

6. THINK SMARTER Ed has 6 marbles. How many marbles can he put in a red cup and how many can he put in a blue cup?

___ + ___ = 6

7. THINK SMARTER + Lani has these number cards. Write each number in the box to show **less than** 24 or **greater than** 24.

| 22 | 27 | 23 | 21 | 25 |

less than 24	greater than 24

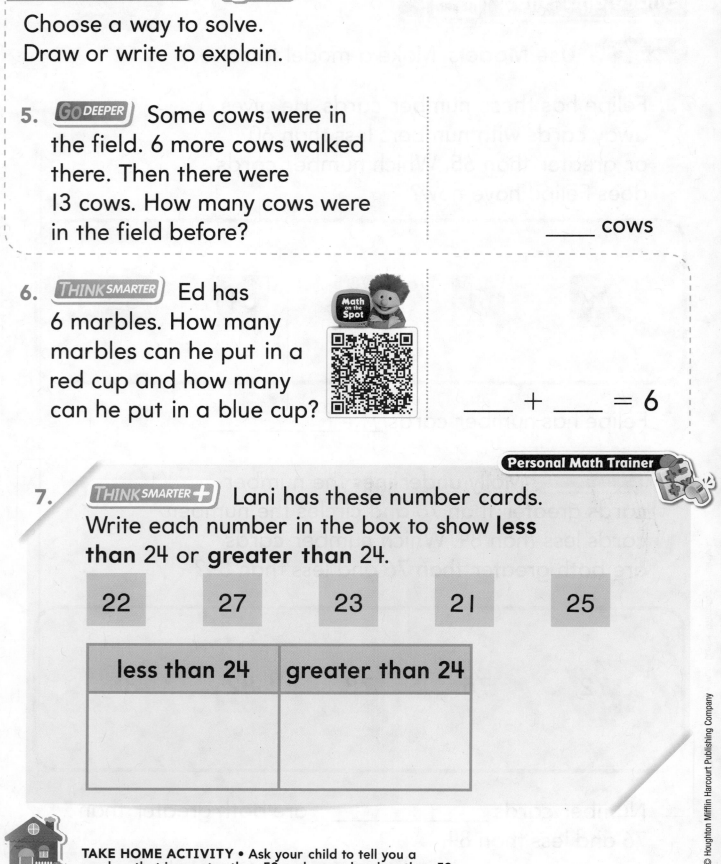

TAKE HOME ACTIVITY • Ask your child to tell you a number that is greater than 59 and a number less than 59.

Problem Solving • Compare Numbers

Learning Objective You will use the strategy *make a model* to help you compare numbers.

Make a model to solve.

1. Ava has these number cards. She gives away cards with numbers less than 34 or greater than 38. Cross those out. Which number cards does Ava have now?

   | ~~32~~ | ~~33~~ | 35 | 37 | ~~39~~ |

   Ava has number cards _35 37_ .

2. Ron has these number cards. He keeps the cards with numbers greater than 60 or less than 56. Circle the number cards Ron keeps.

   Ron keeps number cards _____ .

3. [WRITE Math] Write your own problem. Choose a secret number. Write clues about the number using the words *is greater than* and *is less than*.

   _____

   _____

Lesson Check

1. Juan crosses out the numbers that are less than 45 or greater than 50. Circle the numbers that are left.

43   44   46   49   52

....

Spiral Review

2. Count back 3.
Write the difference.

$$9 - 3 = \underline{6}$$

....

3. Write the numbers to complete the related facts.

$$4 + 7 = 11 \qquad 11 - 4 = 7$$
$$7 + 4 = 11 \qquad 11 - 7 = 4$$

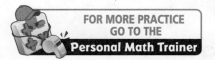

FOR MORE PRACTICE
GO TO THE
Personal Math Trainer

Name _____

10 Less, 10 More

Essential Question How can you identify numbers that are 10 less or 10 more than a number?

Learning Objective You will mentally find numbers that are 10 less or 10 more than a number.

 Listen and Draw

Use ▬▬▬▬▬ ▬ to solve. Draw quick pictures to show your work.

10 MARKERS

Pat

_____

Tony

_____

Jan

_____

Math Talk   Math Processes and Practices ⑥

What number has one less 10 than 12? **Explain.**

 FOR THE TEACHER • Read the following problem. Tony has 2 boxes of markers and 2 more markers. Pat has 10 fewer markers than Tony. Jan has 10 more markers than Tony. How many markers does each child have?

Chapter 7

four hundred twenty-three **423**

Model and Draw

Think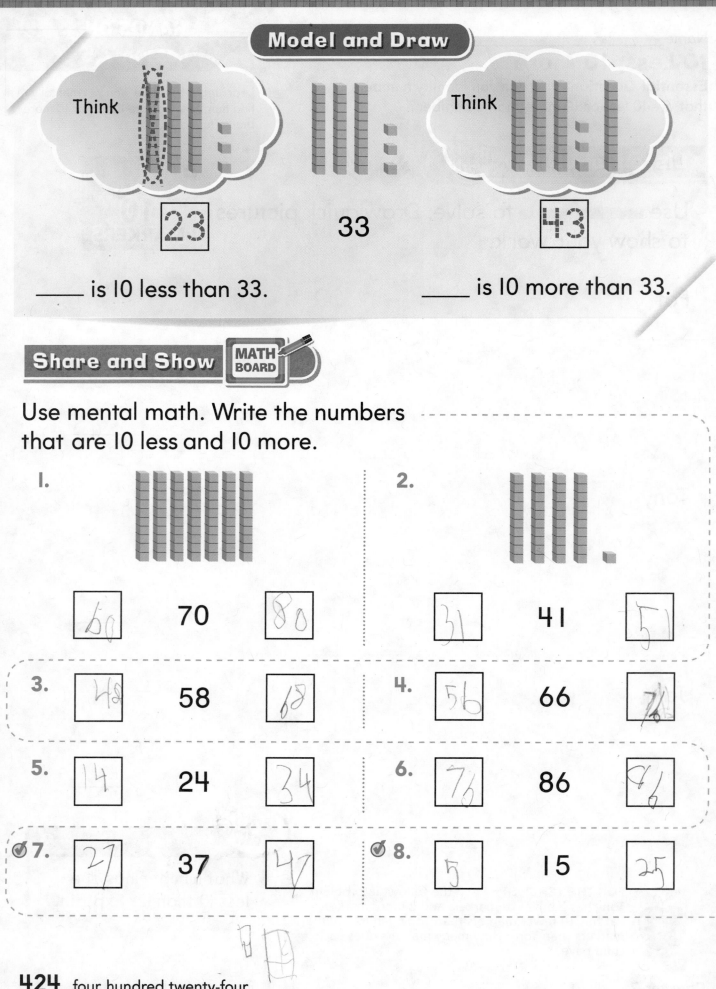

23

33

43

_____ is 10 less than 33.

_____ is 10 more than 33.

Share and Show MATH BOARD

Use mental math. Write the numbers that are 10 less and 10 more.

1. | 60 | 70 | 80 |

2. | 31 | 41 | 5⌐ |

3. | 48 | 58 | 68 |

4. | 56 | 66 | 76 |

5. | 14 | 24 | 34 |

6. | 76 | 86 | 96 |

⊘ 7. | 27 | 37 | 47 |

⊘ 8. | 5 | 15 | 25 |

Name ZACH

Math Processes and Practices ③ **Apply** Use mental math.
Complete the chart. Explain your method.

	10 Less		10 More
9.	2~~4~~	39	4~~0~~
10.	6~~1~~5	75	2~~6~~5
11.	~~5~~64	64	7~~2~~4
12.	8~~0~~	90	100
13.	3~~3~~	43	5~~3~~
14.	11	2~~1~~	3~~1~~
15.	6	~~16~~	26

16. **THINK SMARTER** Solve.
I have 89 rocks. I want to collect
10 more. How many rocks
will I have then?

_____ rocks

Problem Solving • Applications (Real World)   [WRITE] Math

Choose a way to solve. Draw or write to show your work.

17. The plant has 4 fewer ladybugs on it than the tree. The tree has 7 ladybugs on it. How many ladybugs are on the plant?

$7 - 4 = 7 - 4 =$

3 ladybugs

18. Amy has 7 ribbons. Charlotte has 9 ribbons. How many more ribbons does Charlotte have than Amy?

$8 - 7$

2 more ribbons

19. [GO DEEPER] Margo has 28 stamps. Chet has 10 more stamps than Margo. Luis has 10 more stamps than Chet. How many stamps does Luis have?

$28 + 10 + 10 = 48$

48 stamps

Personal Math Trainer

20. [THINK SMARTER +] Draw a quick picture to show a number that is 10 less than the model.

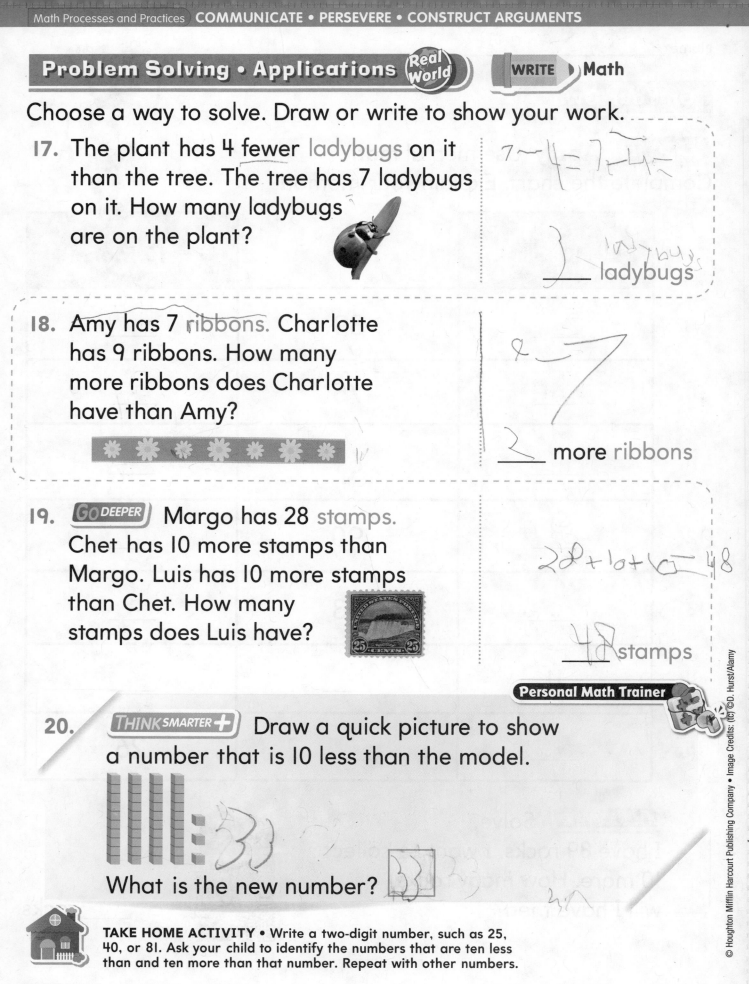

What is the new number? 33

TAKE HOME ACTIVITY • Write a two-digit number, such as 25, 40, or 81. Ask your child to identify the numbers that are ten less than and ten more than that number. Repeat with other numbers.

Name _____

10 Less, 10 More

Learning Objective You will mentally find numbers that are 10 less or 10 more than a number.

Use mental math.
Complete the chart.

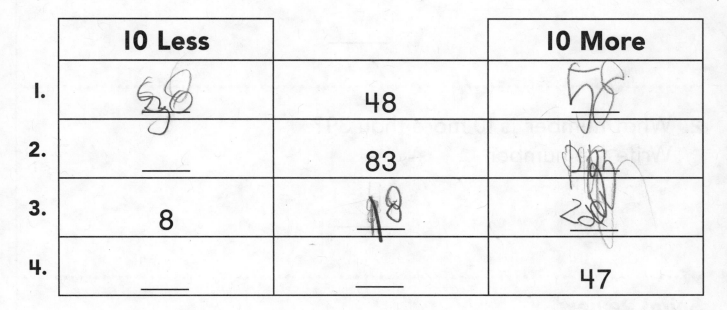

	10 Less		**10 More**
1.	38	48	58
2.	___	83	___
3.	8	18	___
4.	___	___	47

Problem Solving Real World

Choose a way to solve. Draw or write to show your work.

5. Jim has 16 books. Doug has 10 fewer books than Jim. How many books does Doug have?

_____ books

6. WRITE Math Choose a number from 10 to 90. Draw and write to show the numbers that are 10 less and 10 more than your number.

Lesson Check

1. What number is 10 less than 67?
Write the number.

57

2. What number is 10 more than 39?
Write the number.

49

Spiral Review

3. How many tens and ones
make this number?
Write how many.

 __1__ ten __8__ ones

18
eighteen

4. What number does the model show?
Write the number.

__7__ tens = __70__

FOR MORE PRACTICE
GO TO THE
Personal Math Trainer

✓ Chapter 7 Review/Test

Personal Math Trainer
Online Assessment and Intervention

1. Compare. Is the math sentence true?
Choose Yes or No.

54 is greater than 45.   ● Yes   ○ No

37 is greater than 29.   ● Yes   ○ No

29 > 43   ○ Yes   ● No

55 > 45   ○ Yes   ○ No

2. Choose all the numbers that are less than 71.

● 62   ○ 80   ● 70   ● 49

3. Circle the symbol that makes the math sentence true.

46   >   58
     <
     =

4. Megan has these number cards. Write each number in the box to show **less than** 33 or **greater than** 33.

| 37 | 34 | 31 | 35 | 32 |

less than 33	greater than 33
31 32	34 37 35

5. Use mental math. Complete the chart.

10 Less		10 More
23	33	43
47	57	67

6. Write a number that is less than 30.

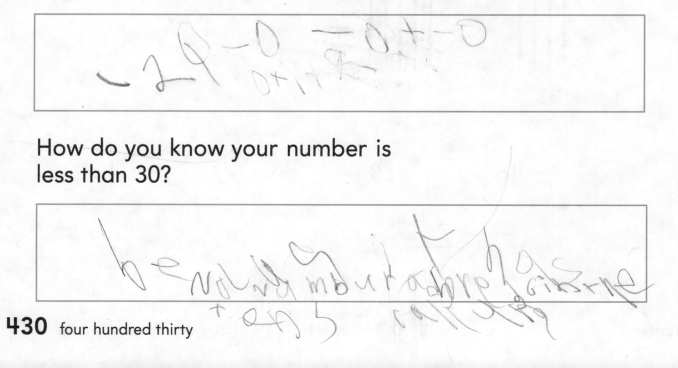

How do you know your number is less than 30?

7. Choose all the math sentences that are true.

- $35 < 47$
- $24 = 39$
- $14 > 41$
- $48 = 48$
- $23 > 21$

---

8. James circles the numbers that are **less than** 87 or **greater than** 91. Which numbers does James circle?

86   88   89   90   92

James circles ____ and ____.

Personal Math Trainer

9. **THINK SMARTER** Draw a quick picture to show a number that is 10 more than the model.

10. Compare. Is the math sentence true?
Choose Yes or No.

49 is greater than 57. ○ Yes ☒ No

54 is greater than 53. ☒ Yes ○ No

60 > 50 ☒ Yes ○ No

72 > 68 ☒ Yes ○ No

11. **GO DEEPER** Write <, >, or = to compare the numbers.

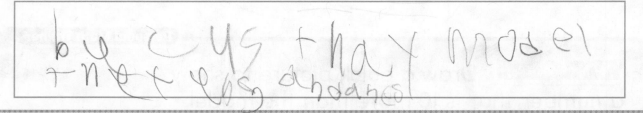

48 __>__ 36

How do the drawings help you compare
the numbers?

by cys thay model
+ not yesg ahdaned

12. Circle the words that make the sentence true.

88 is | greater than / (less than) / equal to | 90.

Two-Digit Addition and Subtraction

Curious About Math with

Curious George

There are 4 boxes of oranges
on a table. Each box holds
10 oranges. How many
oranges are there?

Name _____

Personal Math Trainer
Online Assessment
and Intervention

Add and Subtract

Use ■▪ and ▪■ to add. Write the sum.
Break apart ▪■ to subtract.
Write the difference.

1.

$4 + 1 =$ _____

$5 - 1 =$ _____

Count Groups to 20

Circle groups of 10. Write how many.

2.   ___

3. ___

Use a Hundred Chart to Count

Touch and count. Shade the last
number counted.

4. Start at 1 and count to 20.

5. Start at 30 and count to 56.

6. Start at 77 and count to 93.

1	2	3	4	5	6	7	8	9	10
11	12	13	14	15	16	17	18	19	20
21	22	23	24	25	26	27	28	29	30
31	32	33	34	35	36	37	38	39	40
41	42	43	44	45	46	47	48	49	50
51	52	53	54	55	56	57	58	59	60
61	62	63	64	65	66	67	68	69	70
71	72	73	74	75	76	77	78	79	80
81	82	83	84	85	86	87	88	89	90
91	92	93	94	95	96	97	98	99	100

This page checks understanding of important skills needed
for success in Chapter 8.

Vocabulary Builder

Review Words
add
subtract
sum
difference

Visualize It

Sort the review words from the box.

Put Together

_____

_____

_____

Take Apart

_____

_____

_____

Understand Vocabulary

Use a review word to complete each sentence.

1. 8 is the _____ for $17 - 9$.

2. 17 is the _____ for $8 + 9$.

3. When you _____ 4 to 8,
   you find the sum.

4. When you _____ 4 from 8,
   you find the difference.

Materials

- 👥👥 · 🌀 · 9🔲 · 9🔲 · 9🔲

Play with a partner.

1. Put your 🧍 on START.
2. Spin the 🌀. Move that number of spaces.
3. Make a ten to help you find the sum.
4. The other player uses 🔲🔲🔲 to check.
5. If you are not correct, you lose a turn.
6. The first player to get to END wins.

2 4 +8	Move ahead one space.	4 9 +6	4 4 +6	9 1 +6	END
4 6 +3	5 3 +7	9 7 +1	Move back one space.	3 7 +7	5 8 +5
					6 6 +4
START	2 4 +8	Move ahead one space.	6 1 +9	8 8 +2	

add

sumar

1

addition sentence

enunciado de suma

3

difference

diferencia

13

fewer

menos

19

more

más

38

subtract

restar

52

subtraction sentence

enunciado de resta

53

sum

suma o total

54

4 + 2 = 6

is an **addition sentence.**

3 + 2 = 5

3 **fewer**

9 − 4 = 5

The **difference** is 5.

5 − 2 = 3

5 − 3 = 2

There are **more** ★.

2 plus 1 is equal to 3.
The **sum** is 3.

9 − 5 = 4

is a **subtraction sentence.**

Game

Bingo

Materials
- 1 set of word cards
- 18 ●

How to Play
Play with a partner.
1. Mix the cards. Put the cards in a pile with the blank side up.
2. Take a card. Read the word.
3. Find the matching word on your bingo board. Cover the word with a ●. Put the card at the bottom of the pile.
4. The other player takes a turn.
5. The first player to cover 3 spaces in a line wins. The line may go across or down.

Word Box

add
addition
   sentence
difference
fewer
more
subtract
subtraction
   sentence
sum

Player 1

fewer	add	more
addition sentence	BINGO	sum
subtraction sentence	difference	subtract

Player 2

subtraction sentence	addition sentence	fewer
add	BINGO	difference
subtract	more	sum

The Write Way

Reflect

Choose one idea. Draw and write about it.

- Write sentences that include at least two of these terms.

  add   subtract   addition sentence   subtraction sentence

- Explain how you would solve this problem.

$$53 + 20 = \text{\_\_\_\_\_}$$

Name _____

Add and Subtract Within 20

Essential Question What strategies can you use to add and subtract?

Learning Objective You will use strategies to add and subtract within 20.

Listen and Draw Real World

What is 5 + 4?
Use a strategy to solve the addition
fact. Draw to show your work.

5 + 4 = ___

Math Talk

Math Processes and Practices 3

Apply What strategy did
you use to find the answer?

FOR THE TEACHER • Have children choose and
model a strategy to solve the addition fact. Then
have them draw to show their work.

Model and Draw

Think of a strategy you can use
to add or subtract.

What is 14 − 6?

I can use a
related fact.

$\underline{6} \oplus \underline{8} = 14$

So, $14 - 6 = \underline{8}$.

Share and Show [MATH BOARD]

Add or subtract.

1. $5 + 3 = \underline{8}$ 2. $10 - 5 = \underline{5}$ 3. $3 + 6 = \underline{9}$

4. $12 - 5 = \underline{7}$ 5. $15 - 9 = \underline{6}$ 6. $5 + 7 = \underline{12}$

7. $8 + 7 = \underline{16}$ 8. $9 - 7 = \underline{2}$ 9. $5 + 5 = \underline{10}$

10. $12 - 7 = \underline{5}$ 11. $18 - 9 = \underline{9}$ 12. $9 + 4 = \underline{13}$

13. $2 + 7 = \underline{9}$ 14. $5 - 1 = \underline{4}$ 15. $9 + 1 = \underline{10}$

16. $7 - 6 = \underline{1}$ ⊘17. $13 - 4 = \underline{17}$ ⊘18. $2 + 6 = \underline{8}$

Name _____

On Your Own

Math Processes and Practices ③ **Apply** Add or subtract.

19. 14
      − 5
      ___
      9

20.   2
      +10
      ___
      12

21.   3
      +3
      ___
      6

22. 14
      − 8
      ___
      6

23.   8
      +9
      ___
      17

24.   6
      −3
      ___
      3

25.   6
      −5
      ___
      1

26.   2
      +8
      ___
      0

27.   0
      +5
      ___
      5

28. 10
      − 2
      ___
      8

29.   9
      +9
      ___
      18

30.   5
      −4
      ___
      1

31.   8
      −8
      ___
      0

32. 10
      + 1
      ___
      11

33.   4
      +7
      ___
      11

34.   9
      −3
      ___
      6

35.   1
      +8
      ___
      9

36. 17
      − 9
      ___
      8

37. 13
      − 7
      ___
      6

38.   6
      +5
      ___
      11

39. 10
      + 2
      ___
      12

40. 14
      − 9
      ___
      5

41. 10
      +10
      ___
      20

42. 11
      − 3
      ___
      8

43. THINK SMARTER Jamal thinks of an addition fact. The sum is 15. One addend is 8. What is a fact Jamal could be thinking of?

$8 \oplus 7 = 15$

$7 \oplus \underline{} = 15$

Problem Solving • Applications [Real World] [WRITE] Math

Solve. Write or draw to explain.

44. **THINK SMARTER** There are 9 ants on a rock. Some more ants get on the rock. Now there are 18 ants on the rock. How many more ants got on the rock?

_____ more ants

45. **GO DEEPER** Fill in the blanks. Write a number sentence to solve.

Lin sees _____ bees. Some bees flew away. Now there are _____ bees. How many bees flew away?

__ ◯ __ ◯ __

_____ bees

46. **THINK SMARTER** Write each addition or subtraction problem in the box below the sum or difference.

$7 + 9$ $6 + 1$ $17 - 8$ $14 - 7$ $8 + 8$

7	9	16

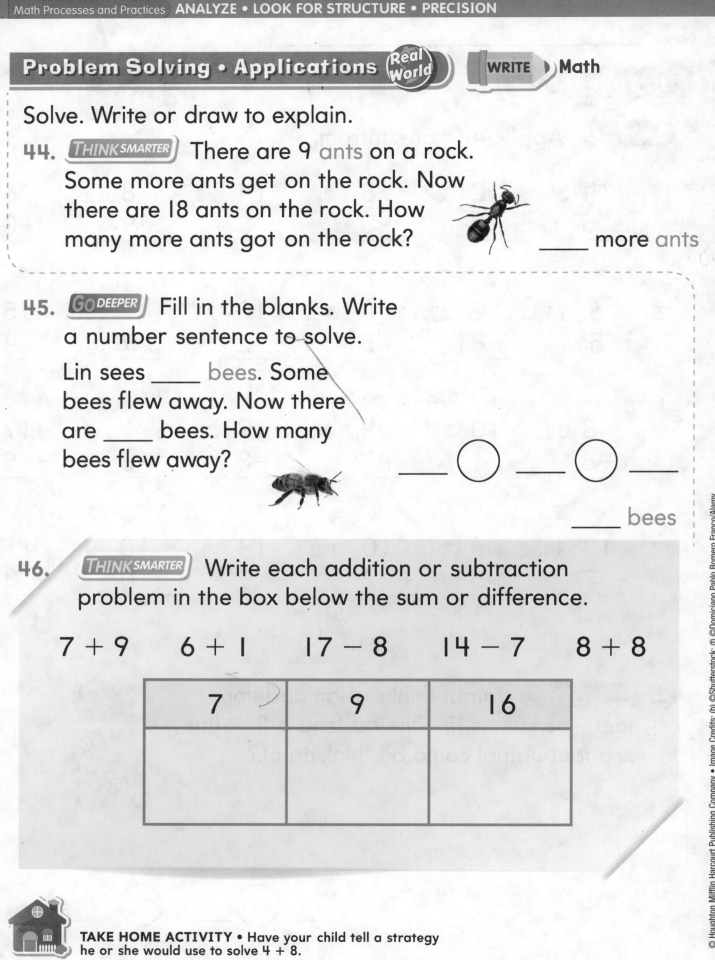

TAKE HOME ACTIVITY • Have your child tell a strategy he or she would use to solve $4 + 8$.

Name _Zach_

Add and Subtract Within 20

Learning Objective You will use strategies to add and subtract within 20.

Add or subtract.

1. C
6
+0
6

2. C
11
− 2
9

3. C
4
+5
9

4. C
9
+8
17

5. C
4
+10
14

6. C
14
− 9
5

7. C
7
+4
11

8. C
8
−5
3

9. C
10
−10
0

10. C
6
+7
13

11.
18
− 9
9

12. C
15
− 6
9

Problem Solving *Real World*

Solve. Draw or write to explain.

13. Jesse has 4 shells. He finds some more. Now he has 12 shells. How many more shells did Jesse find?

_____ more shells

14. WRITE Math Write an addition or subtraction fact. Then write a strategy you could use to add or subtract.

_____
_____
_____
_____

Lesson Check

1. What is the sum?
   Write the number.

$$8 + 5 = \underline{}$$

2. What is the difference?
   Write the number.

$$11 - 4 = \underline{}$$

Spiral Review

3.

Circle the greater number.	Did tens or ones help you decide?	Write the numbers.
43 　 (46)	tens 　 (ones)	2̶¢̶ is greater than 4̶1̶.

4.

Circle the number that is less.	Did tens or ones help you decide?	Write the numbers.
(69) 　 84	(tens) 　 ones	8̶4̶ is less than 8̶4̶. 64 < 8̶4̶

FOR MORE PRACTICE
GO TO THE
Personal Math Trainer

Name _____

Add Tens

Essential Question How can you add tens?

Learning Objective You will draw a model to add tens.

Listen and Draw (Real World)

Choose a way to show the problem.
Draw a quick picture to show your work.

FOR THE TEACHER • Read the following problems. Barb has 20 baseball cards. Ed has 30 baseball cards. How many baseball cards do they have? Kyle has 40 baseball cards. Kim has 50 baseball cards. How many baseball cards do they have?

Math Talk Math Processes and Practices ②

Reasoning Why will there be no ones in your answer when you add 20 + 30?

Chapter 8

four hundred forty-three **443**

How can you find 30 + 40?

30 + 40 = _70_

|||| ||||

_7_ tens

Share and Show MATH BOARD

Use ▭▭▭▭ ▪. Draw to show tens.
Write the sum. Write how many tens.

1. 20 + 40 = _60_

____ tens

2. 30 + 30 = _60_

____ tens

✓3. 40 + 50 = _90_

_9_ tens

✓4. 50 + 30 = _80_

_8_ tens

On Your Own

Math Processes and Practices ② **Represent a Problem** Draw to show tens.
Write the sum. Write how many tens.

5. 40 + 40 = _80_

4 + 4

___ 8 tens

6. 70 + 20 = _90_

4

___ tens

7. 10 + 80 = _90_

___ 4 tens

8. 60 + 30 = _90_

___ 4 tens

9. **GO DEEPER** Draw two groups of tens you can add to
get a sum of 50. Write the number sentence.

⊘ + ⊘ ⊘ = 50

Problem Solving • Applications (Real World)   WRITE Math

10. **THINK SMARTER** Complete the web.
Write the missing addend to
get a sum of 90.

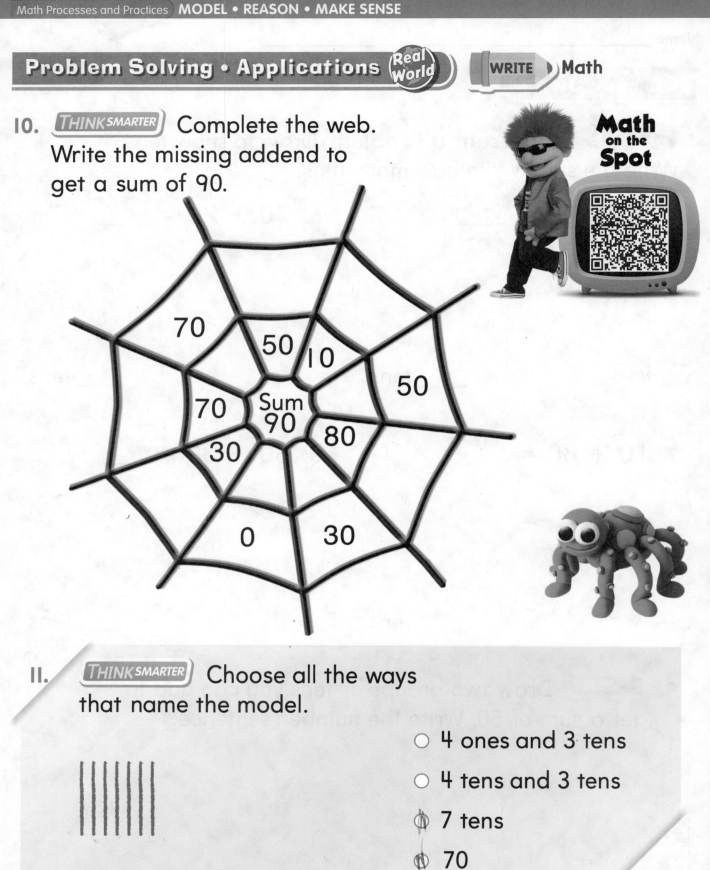

Math on the Spot

11. **THINK SMARTER** Choose all the ways
that name the model.

○ 4 ones and 3 tens

○ 4 tens and 3 tens

⦶ 7 tens

⦶ 70

🏠 **TAKE HOME ACTIVITY** • Ask your child to explain
how to use tens to find 20 + 70.

Add Tens

Learning Objective You will draw a model to add tens.

Draw to show tens. Write the sum.
Write how many tens.

1. $10 + 30 =$ 40

___4___ tens

2. $30 + 30 =$ 60

___6___ tens

3. $60 + 10 =$ 70

___7___ tens

4. $10 + 70 =$ 80

___8___ tens

Problem Solving Real World

Draw tens to solve.

5. Drew makes 20 posters. Tia makes 30 posters. How many posters do they make?

___50___ posters

6. Regina read 40 pages. Alice read 50 pages. How many pages did they read?

___90___ pages

7. WRITE Math Choose an addition problem from the spider web on page 446. Draw a quick picture and write the number sentence.

|||| ||| − | + |||| |= ||||||||||

50

$-10 + 50 = 90$

Chapter 8

Lesson Check

1. What is the sum?
   Write the number.

$$20 + 30 = \underline{}$$

2. What is the sum?
   Write the number.

$$30 + 10 = \underline{}$$

Spiral Review

3. Write a doubles fact that can help you solve $6 + 5 = 11$.

$$\underline{} + \underline{} = \underline{}$$

4. Circle the number sentences that are true.
   Cross out the number sentences that are false.

$$30 > 10 \qquad 30 < 10 \qquad 10 > 30 \qquad 10 < 30$$

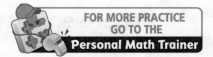

FOR MORE PRACTICE
GO TO THE
Personal Math Trainer

Name _____

Subtract Tens

Essential Question How can you subtract tens?

Learning Objective You will draw a model to subtract tens.

Listen and Draw (Real World)

Choose a way to show the problem.
Draw a quick picture to show your work.

Math Talk Math Processes and Practices ④

Represent How does your picture show the first problem?

FOR THE TEACHER • Read the following problems. Tara has 30 seashells. 20 shells are big. The rest are small. How many small shells does she have? Sammy has 50 shells. He gives 30 shells to his friend. How many shells does Sammy have now?

Chapter 8

four hundred forty-nine **449**

How can you find 80 − 30?

$$80 - 30 = \underline{50}$$

_____ tens 5

Share and Show MATH BOARD

Use ▭▭▭. Draw to show tens.
Write the difference. Write how many tens.

1. 60 − 20 = __40__

Teng
N=4

__4__ tens

2. 70 − 30 = __40__

Tens
N=4

__4__ tens

3. 80 − 20 = __60__

Teng

__6__ tens

4. 90 − 40 = __50__

teht

__5__ tens

On Your Own

Math Processes and Practices ⑥ **Make Connections** Draw to show tens.
Write the difference. Write how many tens.

5. 80 – 40 = __4__

Tens
N = 4

__4__ tens

6. 90 – 70 = __29__

Tens
N = 2

__2__ tens

7. 70 – 50 = __20__

Tens
N = 2

___ tens

8. 30 – 30 = __0__

Tens
N = 0

___ tens

THINK SMARTER Solve.

9. Jeff has 40 pennies. He gives some to Jill. He has 10 pennies left. How many pennies does Jeff give to Jill?

Math on the Spot

__30__ pennies

🏠 **TAKE HOME ACTIVITY** • Ask your child to explain how to use tens to find 90 – 70.

Name _____

✓ Mid-Chapter Checkpoint

Concepts and Skills

Add or subtract.

1. 4
   +8

2. 15
   − 7

3. 9
   −6

4. 3
   +1

5. 10
   + 6

6. 11
   − 2

Use ▭. Draw to show tens.
Write the sum. Write how many tens.

7. 30 + 50 = ____

8. 40 + 20 = ____

____ tens

____ tens

Use ▭. Draw to show tens.
Write the difference. Write how many tens.

9. 90 − 20 = ____

10. 60 − 40 = ____

____ tens

____ tens

11. THINK SMARTER   Mike has 60 marbles.
He gives 20 to Kathy. How many
marbles does Mike have left?
Show your work.

_____ marbles

Subtract Tens

Learning Objective You will draw a model to subtract tens.

Draw to show tens. Write the difference. Write how many tens.

1. $40 - 10 = $ ___

_____ tens

2. $80 - 40 = $ ___

_____ tens

Problem Solving Real World

Draw tens to solve.

3. Mario has 70 baseball cards.
He gives 30 to Lisa.
How many baseball cards
does Mario have left?

_____ baseball cards

4. [WRITE] Math Draw a picture to show how to solve $50 - 40$.

Lesson Check

1. What is the difference?
   Write the number.

   $$60 - 20 = \underline{}$$

2. What is the difference?
   Write the number.

   $$70 - 30 = \underline{}$$

Spiral Review

3. Use ○ ● and a ten frame. Show
   both addends. Draw to make ten.
   Then write a new fact. Add.

   $$\begin{array}{r} 9 \\ + 4 \\ \hline \end{array}$$

4. Bo crosses out the number cards that are
   less than 33 or greater than 38.
   What number cards are left?

   | 30 | 32 | 36 | 37 | 39 |

   Number cards ____ and ____ are left.

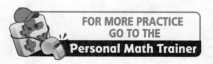

FOR MORE PRACTICE
GO TO THE
Personal Math Trainer

Name _____

Use a Hundred Chart to Add

Essential Question How can you use a hundred chart to count on by ones or tens?

Learning Objective You will use a hundred chart to count on by ones or tens.

Use the hundred chart to solve the problems.

1	2	3	4	5	6	7	8	9	10
11	12	13	14	15	16	17	18	19	20
21	22	23	24	25	26	27	28	29	30
31	32	33	34	35	36	37	38	39	40
41	42	43	44	45	46	47	48	49	50
51	52	53	54	55	56	57	58	59	60
61	62	63	64	65	66	67	68	69	70
71	72	73	74	75	76	77	78	79	80
81	82	83	84	85	86	87	88	89	90
91	92	93	94	95	96	97	98	99	100

FOR THE TEACHER • Read the following problems. Alice picks 12 flowers. Then she picks 4 more flowers. How many flowers does Alice pick? Ella picks 10 strawberries. Then she picks 20 more strawberries. How many strawberries does Ella pick?

Math Talk Math Processes and Practices 6

Explain how you can use a hundred chart to find each sum.

Chapter 8

Count on a hundred chart to find a sum.

Start at **24.**
Count on four ones.
25, 26, 27, 28

1	2	3	4	5	6	7	8	9	10
11	12	13	14	15	16	17	18	19	20
21	22	23	24	25	26	27	28	29	30
31	32	33	34	35	36	37	38	39	40
41	42	43	44	45	46	47	48	49	50
51	52	53	54	55	56	57	58	59	60
61	62	63	64	65	66	67	68	69	70
71	72	73	74	75	76	77	78	79	80
81	82	83	84	85	86	87	88	89	90
91	92	93	94	95	96	97	98	99	100

$24 + 4 = \underline{28}$

Start at **31.**
Count on four tens.
41, 51, 61, 71

$31 + 40 = \underline{71}$

Share and Show

Use the hundred chart to add.
Count on by ones or tens.

1. $42 + 7 = \underline{}$

2. $57 + 30 = \underline{}$

☑ 3. $91 + 5 = \underline{}$

☑ 4. $18 + 50 = \underline{}$

On Your Own

1	2	3	4	5	6	7	8	9	10
11	12	13	14	15	16	17	18	19	20
21	22	23	24	25	26	27	28	29	30
31	32	33	34	35	36	37	38	39	40
41	42	43	44	45	46	47	48	49	50
51	52	53	54	55	56	57	58	59	60
61	62	63	64	65	66	67	68	69	70
71	72	73	74	75	76	77	78	79	80
81	82	83	84	85	86	87	88	89	90
91	92	93	94	95	96	97	98	99	100

How can you use the hundred chart to find each sum?

$32 + 5 =$ ___

$48 + 30 =$ ___

Math Processes and Practices 5 **Use Appropriate Tools**

Use the hundred chart to add.
Count on by ones or tens.

5. $13 + 70 =$ ___

6. $22 + 6 =$ ___

7. $71 + 3 =$ ___

8. $49 + 50 =$ ___

9. $53 + 4 =$ ___

10. $25 + 40 =$ ___

11. **GO DEEPER** Solve. Show your work.

$31 + 20 + 40 =$ ___

Problem Solving • Applications WRITE Math

Choose a way to solve. Draw or
write to show your work.

12. **THINK SMARTER** Rae put 20 books away.
She put 20 more books away,
then 11 more. How many
books did Rae put away?

_____ books

13. **THINK SMARTER +** Use
the hundred chart
to add. Count on
by ones or tens.

$$62 + 9 = \underline{\hspace{1cm}}$$

1	2	3	4	5	6	7	8	9	10
11	12	13	14	15	16	17	18	19	20
21	22	23	24	25	26	27	28	29	30
31	32	33	34	35	36	37	38	39	40
41	42	43	44	45	46	47	48	49	50
51	52	53	54	55	56	57	58	59	60
61	62	63	64	65	66	67	68	69	70
71	72	73	74	75	76	77	78	79	80
81	82	83	84	85	86	87	88	89	90
91	92	93	94	95	96	97	98	99	100

Personal Math Trainer

Explain how you used the chart to find the sum.

 TAKE HOME ACTIVITY • On a piece of paper, write 36 + 40.
Ask your child to explain how to use the hundred chart to
count on by tens to find the sum.

Use a Hundred Chart to Add

Use the hundred chart to add.
Count on by ones or tens.

Learning Objective You will use a hundred chart to count on by ones or tens.

1	2	3	4	5	6	7	8	9	10
11	12	13	14	15	16	17	18	19	20
21	22	23	24	25	26	27	28	29	30
31	32	33	34	35	36	37	38	39	40
41	42	43	44	45	46	47	48	49	50
51	52	53	54	55	56	57	58	59	60
61	62	63	64	65	66	67	68	69	70
71	72	73	74	75	76	77	78	79	80
81	82	83	84	85	86	87	88	89	90
91	92	93	94	95	96	97	98	99	100

1. $47 + 2 =$ _____

2. $26 + 50 =$ _____

3. $22 + 5 =$ _____

4. $4 + 85 =$ _____

Problem Solving Real World

Choose a way to solve. Draw or write to show your work.

5. 17 children are on the bus. Then 20 more children get on the bus. How many children are on the bus now?

_____ children

6. WRITE Math Write a number sentence to add 6 ones to 21. Write a number sentence to add 6 tens to 21.

_____

_____

_____

Lesson Check

1. What is the sum?
Write the number.

$$42 + 50 = \underline{}$$

1	2	3	4	5	6	7	8	9	10
11	12	13	14	15	16	17	18	19	20
21	22	23	24	25	26	27	28	29	30
31	32	33	34	35	36	37	38	39	40
41	42	43	44	45	46	47	48	49	50
51	52	53	54	55	56	57	58	59	60
61	62	63	64	65	66	67	68	69	70
71	72	73	74	75	76	77	78	79	80
81	82	83	84	85	86	87	88	89	90
91	92	93	94	95	96	97	98	99	100

2. What is the sum?
Write the number.

$$11 + 8 = \underline{}$$

Spiral Review

3. Use mental math.
What number is ten less than 52?
Write the number.

$$\underline{}$$

4. Write an addition fact that helps
you solve $16 - 9$.

$$\underline{} + \underline{} = \underline{}$$

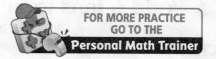

FOR MORE PRACTICE
GO TO THE
Personal Math Trainer

Name _____

Use Models to Add

Essential Question How can models help you add ones or tens to a two-digit number?

Learning Objective You will use models to help you add ones or tens to a two-digit number.

Listen and Draw Real World

Draw to show how you can find the sum.

$$14 + 5 = \underline{\quad}$$

Math Talk   Math Processes and Practices ④

Model Explain how you found the sum.

🍎 **FOR THE TEACHER** • Read the following problem. Amir counts 14 cars as they go by. Then he counts 5 more cars. How many cars does Amir count?

Chapter 8

four hundred sixty-one **461**

Model and Draw

Add ones to a two-digit number.

$$32 \quad + \quad 4 \quad = \quad \underline{36}$$

Add tens to a two-digit number.

$$32 \quad + \quad 40 \quad = \quad \underline{72}$$

Share and Show MATH BOARD

Use ▭ ▫. Draw to show how to add the ones. Write the sum.

1. $27 + 2 = $ ____

2. $41 + 5 = $ ____

Use ▭ ▫. Draw to show how to add the tens. Write the sum.

3. $13 + 50 = $ ____

4. $28 + 30 = $ ____

On Your Own

Math Processes and Practices ④ Use Models

Use ▭▭▭▭▭ ▪ and your MathBoard.
Add the ones or tens. Write the sum.

5. $65 + 3 =$ _____

6. $81 + 8 =$ _____

7. $54 + 20 =$ _____

8. $32 + 10 =$ _____

9. $95 + 2 =$ _____

10. $25 + 60 =$ _____

11. $2 + 54 =$ _____

12. $70 + 29 =$ _____

GO DEEPER Make a sum of 45. Draw a quick
picture. Write the number sentence.

13. Add ones to a two-digit number.

_____ + _____ = 45

14. Add tens to a two-digit number.

_____ + _____ = 45

Problem Solving • Applications

Choose a way to solve. Draw or write to show your work.

15. Rita picks 63 strawberries. Then she picks 30 more. How many strawberries does Rita pick?

_____ strawberries

16. **THINK SMARTER** Kenny planted two rows of corn. He used 20 seeds in each row. He has 18 seeds left. How many seeds of corn did Kenny have?

_____ seeds

17. There are 7 oak trees and 32 pine trees in the park. How many trees are in the park?

_____ trees

18. **THINK SMARTER** Use the model. Draw to show how to add the tens.

42   +   20   =

TAKE HOME ACTIVITY • Give your child the addition problems 25 + 3 and 25 + 30. Ask your child to explain how to solve each problem.

© Houghton Mifflin Harcourt Publishing Company • Image Credits: (b) ©Alamy; (t) ©PhotoAlto/Getty Images

Use Models to Add

Learning Objective You will use models to help you add ones or tens to a two-digit number.

Use ⬚⬚⬚⬚⬚⬚ ⬚ and your MathBoard.
Add the ones or tens. Write the sum.

1. $44 + 5 = $ _49_

2. $16 + 70 = $ _86_

3. $78 + 20 = $ _98_

4. $52 + 7 = $ _59_

5. $2 + 13 = $ _15_

6. $73 + 4 = $ _77_

7. $65 + 3 = $ ___

8. $20 + 25 = $ _45_

9. $49 + 30 = $ _79_

10. $81 + 8 = $ _89_

Problem Solving Real World

Solve. Draw or write to explain.

11. Maria has 21 marbles.
    She buys a bag of 20 marbles.
    How many marbles does
    Maria have now?

    _41_ marbles

12. **WRITE Math** Write a story
    problem about 40 apples
    and 17 pears.

    there are 40 apples
    some other things
    how much has 17 pears

Lesson Check

1. What is the sum?
Write the number.

$$62 + 30 = \underline{\quad}$$

2. What is the sum?
Write the number.

$$37 + 2 = \underline{\quad}$$

Spiral Review

3. Write two ways to make 15.

$$\underline{\quad} + \underline{\quad} = 15$$

$$\underline{\quad} + \underline{\quad} = 15$$

4. What number does the model show?

   $\underline{\quad}$

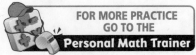

Name _____

Make Ten to Add

Essential Question How can making a ten help you add a two-digit number and a one-digit number?

Learning Objective You will make a ten to add a two-digit number and a one-digit number.

Listen and Draw Real World Hands On

Use ▭▭▭▭▭ ▪. Draw to show how you can find the sum.

$$21 + 6 = \_\_\_.$$

FOR THE TEACHER • Read the following problem. Sally has 21 stickers in her sticker book. She gets 6 more stickers. How many stickers does Sally have now?

Math Talk

Math Processes and Practices ⑤

Use Tools Explain how your model shows the sum of 21 + 6.

Chapter 8

four hundred sixty-seven **467**

Make a ten to find 37 + 8.

What can I add to 7 to make 10?

37 + 8   37 + 3 + 5   40 + 5

$$\underline{40} + \underline{5} = \underline{45}$$

So, 37 + 8 = $\underline{45}$.

Share and Show MATH BOARD

Use ▭▭▭ ▪. Draw to show how you make a ten. Find the sum.

✔1. 49 + 3 = ?

_____ + _____ = _____

So, 49 + 3 = _____.

Name _____

On Your Own

Math Processes and Practices 5 Use a Concrete Model
Use ▮. Draw to show how
you make a ten. Find the sum.

2. $39 + 7 =$ ___

3. $72 + 9 =$ ___

4. $58 + 5 =$ ___

THINK SMARTER Solve. Write the numbers.

5. 46 + 7

    46 + ☐ + 3

        ☐ + 3

    So, 46 + 7 = ____.

6. 53 + 8

    53 + ☐ + 1

        ☐ + 1

    So, 53 + 8 = ____.

© Houghton Mifflin Harcourt Publishing Company

Problem Solving • Applications Real World **WRITE** ▸ **Math**

Choose a way to solve. Draw
or write to show your work.

7. **THINK SMARTER** Koby puts 24 daisies
and 8 tulips in a vase. How many
flowers are in the vase?

_____ flowers

8. **GO DEEPER** There are 27 ducklings
in the water. 20 of them come
out of the water. How
many ducklings are
still in the water?

_____ ducklings

9. Write the missing addend.

$$46 + \boxed{} = 52$$

10. **THINK SMARTER** Use the model. Draw to
show how to make a ten.

34 + 8 = _____

TAKE HOME ACTIVITY • Ask your child to explain how to
find the sum for 25 + 9.

470 four hundred seventy

Make Ten to Add

Learning Objective You will make a ten to add a two-digit number and a one-digit number.

Use 🔲 🔲. Draw to show how you make a ten. Find the sum.

1. $26 + 5 =$ _____

2. $68 + 4 =$ _____

Problem Solving Real World

Choose a way to solve. Draw or write to show your work.

3. Debbie has 27 markers. Sal has 9 markers. How many markers do they have?

_____ markers

4. WRITE Math Use words or pictures to explain how to solve $44 + 7$.

Lesson Check

1. What is the sum?
Write the number.

$$47 + 6 = \underline{\hspace{2cm}}$$

. . . .

2. What is the sum?
Write the number.

$$84 + 8 = \underline{\hspace{2cm}}$$

. . . .

Spiral Review

3. What number does the model show?
Write the number.

\|\|\|\|\|\|\|\|\| o o o o   \underline{\hspace{1.5cm}}

. . . .

4. Write a number to make the sentence true.

$$5 + 4 = 10 - \underline{\hspace{2cm}}$$

FOR MORE PRACTICE
GO TO THE
Personal Math Trainer

Name _____

Use Place Value to Add

Essential Question How can you model tens and ones to help you add two-digit numbers?

Learning Objective You will model tens and ones to help you add two-digit numbers.

Listen and Draw Real World   Hands On

Model the problem with .
Draw a quick picture to show your work.

Tens	Ones

Math Talk Math Processes and Practices ①

Describe How many tens? How many ones? How many in all?

FOR THE TEACHER • Read the following problem. Cameron has 30 old stamps and 25 new stamps. How many stamps does Cameron have?

Chapter 8

four hundred seventy-three **473**

How can you use tens and ones to add?

35
+38

Tens	Ones

3 tens + 5 ones
3 tens + 8 ones
_____
__6__ tens + __13__ ones

60 + 13 = 73

35
+38
73

Share and Show MATH BOARD

Draw a quick picture.
Use tens and ones to add.

1.

Tens	Ones

81
+14

8 tens + 1 one
1 ten + 4 ones
_____
___ tens + ___ ones

___ + ___ = ___

81
+14

Name _____

Math Processes and Practices 6 **Make Connections**

Draw a quick picture. Use tens and ones to add.

2.

43
+37

Tens	Ones

4 tens + 3 ones
3 tens + 7 ones
_____
____ tens + ____ ones

____ ____ + ____ ____ = ____

43
+37

3.

62
+23

Tens	Ones

6 tens + 2 ones
2 tens + 3 ones
_____
____ tens + ____ ones

____ ____ + ____ ____ = ____

62
+23

THINK SMARTER Solve.

4. 28 + 17

28 + ____ + 15

____ + 15 = ____

So, 28 + 17 = ____.

5. 59 + 13

59 + ____ + 12

____ + 12 = ____

So, 59 + 13 = ____.

6. **THINK SMARTER** Draw a quick picture to solve. Han has 37 shells. Jonah has 15 shells. How many shells do they have?

Tens	Ones

____

Problem Solving • Applications Real World   WRITE Math

7. **THINK SMARTER** Draw a quick picture to solve. Kim has 24 marbles. Al has 47 marbles. How many marbles do they have?

_____ marbles

Tens	Ones

8. **GO DEEPER** Choose two addends from 11 to 49. Draw them. Add in any order to solve.

Addend   **Addend**

___ + ___ = ___

___ + ___ = ___

9. **THINK SMARTER** Write the addition that the model shows. Solve.

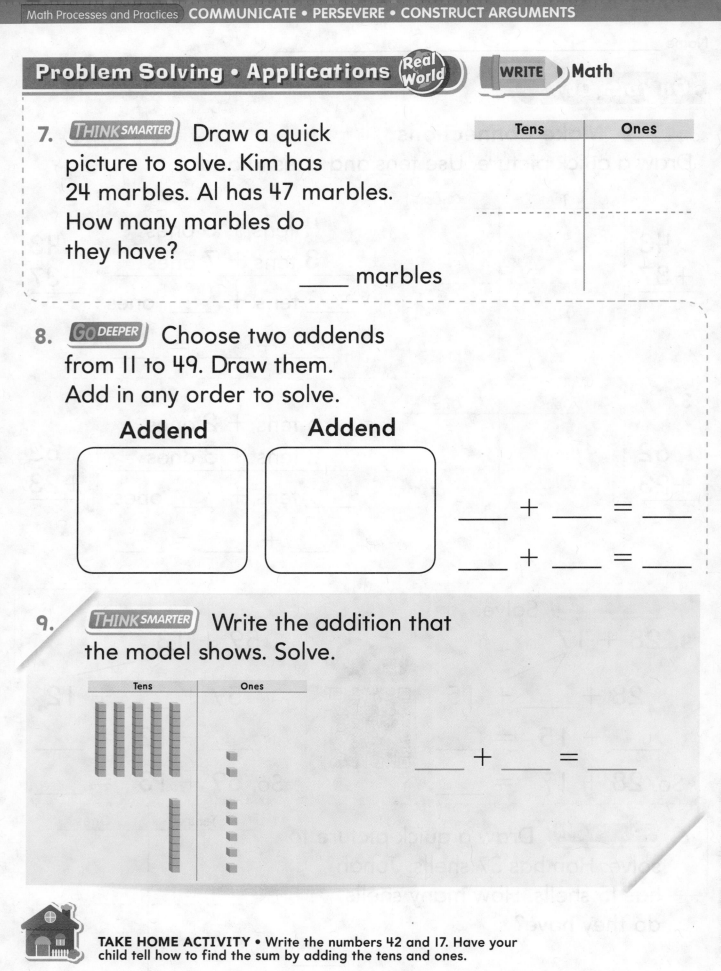

Tens	Ones

___ + ___ = ___

TAKE HOME ACTIVITY • Write the numbers 42 and 17. Have your child tell how to find the sum by adding the tens and ones.

Use Place Value to Add

Learning Objective You will model tens and ones to help you add two-digit numbers.

Draw a quick picture. Use tens and ones to add.

1.
```
  31
+ 26
```

Tens	Ones

3 tens + 1 one
2 tens + 6 ones

____ tens + ____ ones

____ + ____ = ____

```
  31
+ 26
```

2.
```
  54
+ 34
```

Tens	Ones

5 tens + 4 ones
3 tens + 4 ones

____ tens + ____ ones

____ + ____ = ____

```
  54
+ 34
```

Problem Solving Real World

3. Write two addition sentences you can use to find the sum. Then solve.

Addend   **Addend**

____ + ____ = ____

____ + ____ = ____

4. WRITE Math Write and solve a story problem to add 12 and 18.

_____

_____

Lesson Check

1. What is the sum?
   Write the number.

$$
\begin{array}{r}
42 \\
+\ 31 \\
\hline
\end{array}
$$

2. What is the sum?
   Write the number.

$$
\begin{array}{r}
23 \\
+\ 12 \\
\hline
\end{array}
$$

Spiral Review

3. I have 28 cubes. How many tens and ones can I make?

_____ tens _____ ones

_____ ten _____ ones

4. What is the sum?
   Write the number.

$$
\begin{array}{r}
5 \\
+\ 5 \\
\hline
\end{array}
$$

FOR MORE PRACTICE
GO TO THE
Personal Math Trainer

Name _____

Problem Solving •
Addition Word Problems

Essential Question How can drawing a picture help you explain how to solve an addition problem?

Learning Objective You will use the strategy *draw a picture* to solve and explain real-world two-digit addition problems.

Kelly gets 6 new toy cars.
He already has 18 toy cars.
How many does he have now?

Unlock the Problem

What do I need to find?

how many ___toy cars___
Kelly has now

What information do I need to use?

Kelly has ___18___ cars.

He gets ___6___ more cars.

Show how to solve the problem.

_____

_ _ _ _ _ _ _ _ _ _ _ _ _ _ _ _ _ _ _

_____

HOME CONNECTION • Being able to show and explain how to solve a problem helps your child build on their understanding of addition.

Draw and write to solve.
Explain your reasoning.

1. Aisha picks 60 blueberries to make a pie. Then she picks 12 more to eat. How many blueberries does Aisha pick?

_____ blueberries

_____

_____

_____

2. Yuri collects 21 cans for the school food drive. Leo collects 36 cans. How many cans do Yuri and Leo collect?

_____ cans

_____

_____

_____

Math Talk

Math Processes and Practices 6

Explain the addition strategy you used to solve Exercise 1.

Name _____

Math Processes and Practices ② **Use Reasoning**

Draw and write to solve.

3. Tyra sees 48 geese in the field. Then she sees 17 more geese in the sky. How many geese does Tyra see?

_____ geese

_____

– – – – – – – – – – – – – – – – – – –

_____

4. Jade paints 35 circles and 45 triangles in art class. How many shapes does Jade paint?

_____ shapes

_____

– – – – – – – – – – – – – – – – – – –

_____

5. **THINK SMARTER** It takes 10 hops to get across the yard. How many hops does it take to get across the yard and back?

_____ hops

_____

– – – – – – – – – – – – – – – – – – –

_____

On Your Own

Choose a way to solve. Draw or write to explain.

6. **THINK SMARTER** Julian sells 3 books of tickets for the school fair. Each book has 20 tickets. How many tickets does Julian sell?

_____ tickets

7. **GO DEEPER** I have some red roses and pink roses. I have 14 red roses. I have 8 more pink roses than red roses. How many roses do I have?

_____ roses

Personal Math Trainer

8. **THINK SMARTER +** Ella sees 27 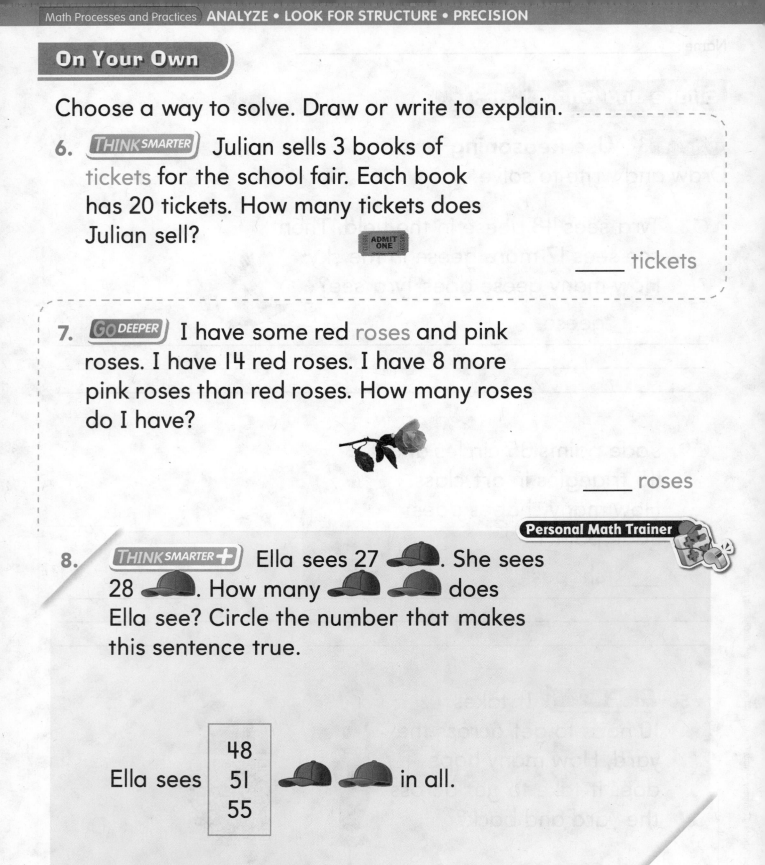. She sees 28 . How many does Ella see? Circle the number that makes this sentence true.

Ella sees
| 48 |
| 51 |
| 55 |

 in all.

TAKE HOME ACTIVITY • Ask your child to solve 16 + 7, 30 + 68, and 53 + 24. Ask him or her to explain how they solved each problem.

Problem Solving • Addition Word Problems

Learning Objective You will use the strategy *draw a picture* to solve and explain real-world two-digit addition problems.

Draw and write to solve. Explain your reasoning.

1. Jean has 10 fish. She gets 4 more fish. How many fish does she have now?

   _____

   _ _ _ _ _ _ _ _ _ _ _ _ _ _ _ _

   _____ fish

2. Courtney buys 2 bags of apples. Each bag has 20 apples. How many apples does she buy?

   _____

   _ _ _ _ _ _ _ _ _ _ _ _ _ _ _ _

   _____ apples

3. John bakes 18 blueberry muffins and 12 banana muffins for the bake sale. How many muffins does he bake?

   _____

   _ _ _ _ _ _ _ _ _ _ _ _ _ _ _ _

   _____ muffins

4. **WRITE** **Math** Draw a picture to show how to find $12 + 37$.

Lesson Check

1. Amy has 9 books about dogs.
She has 13 books about cats.
How many books does she
have about dogs and cats?
Solve. Show your work. Write the number. _____ books

Spiral Review

2. What is the sum for 4 + 2 + 4?
Write the number.

_____

3. Solve. Use the ten frame to make a
ten to help you subtract. Ray has
14 pens. 8 are black. The rest
are blue. How many pens are blue?   _____ blue pens

© Houghton Mifflin Harcourt Publishing Company

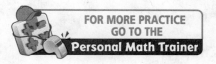

FOR MORE PRACTICE
GO TO THE
Personal Math Trainer

Related Addition and Subtraction

Essential Question How can you use a hundred chart to show the relationship between addition and subtraction?

Learning Objective You will use a hundred chart to find sums and differences.

Listen and Draw (Real World)

Use the hundred chart to solve the problems.

1	2	3	4	5	6	7	8	9	10
11	12	13	14	15	16	17	18	19	20
21	22	23	24	25	26	27	28	29	30
31	32	33	34	35	36	37	38	39	40
41	42	43	44	45	46	47	48	49	50
51	52	53	54	55	56	57	58	59	60
61	62	63	64	65	66	67	68	69	70
71	72	73	74	75	76	77	78	79	80
81	82	83	84	85	86	87	88	89	90
91	92	93	94	95	96	97	98	99	100

Math Talk Math Processes and Practices ③

Apply Describe how you can use a hundred chart to find the sum and the difference.

FOR THE TEACHER • Read the following problems. Trevor collects 38 acorns. He collects 10 more acorns. How many acorns does Trevor have now? Trevor has 48 acorns. He gives 10 acorns to his brother. How many acorns does Trevor have now?

Chapter 8

Model and Draw

You can use a hundred chart to find a sum and a difference.

> Start at **29**. Count on four tens.
> **39, 49, 59, 69**

$$29 + 40 = \underline{69}$$

> Start at **69**. Count back four tens.
> **59, 49, 39, 29**

$$69 - 40 = \underline{29}$$

1	2	3	4	5	6	7	8	9	10
11	12	13	14	15	16	17	18	19	20
21	22	23	24	25	26	27	28	29	30
31	32	33	34	35	36	37	38	39	40
41	42	43	44	45	46	47	48	49	50
51	52	53	54	55	56	57	58	59	60
61	62	63	64	65	66	67	68	69	70
71	72	73	74	75	76	77	78	79	80
81	82	83	84	85	86	87	88	89	90
91	92	93	94	95	96	97	98	99	100

Share and Show MATH BOARD

Use the hundred chart to add and subtract. Count on and back by tens.

☑ 1. $56 + 20 = \underline{}$

☑ 2. $48 + 50 = \underline{}$

$76 - 20 = \underline{}$

$98 - 50 = \underline{}$

Name _ZACH_

1	2	3	4	5	6	7	8	9	10
11	12	13	14	15	16	17	18	19	20
21	22	23	24	25	26	27	28	29	30
31	32	33	34	35	36	37	38	39	40
41	42	43	44	45	46	47	48	49	50
51	52	53	54	55	56	57	58	59	60
61	62	63	64	65	66	67	68	69	70
71	72	73	74	75	76	77	78	79	80
81	82	83	84	85	86	87	88	89	90
91	92	93	94	95	96	97	98	99	100

How can you use the hundred chart to find the sum and the difference?

$28 + 60 =$ ___

$88 - 60 =$ ___

Math Processes and Practices **7** **Look for a Pattern** Use the hundred chart to add and subtract. Count on and back by tens.

3. $36 + 30 =$ ___

$66 - 30 =$ ___

4. $73 + 10 =$ ___

$83 - 10 =$ ___

5. $25 + 70 =$ ___

$95 - 70 =$ ___

6. $18 + 40 =$ ___

$58 - 40 =$ ___

7. **THINK SMARTER** Solve.

There are 73 bees in a hive. 10 bees fly away. Then 10 more bees fly into the hive. How many bees are in the hive now?

___ bees

Problem Solving • Applications   WRITE ▸ Math

Solve. Draw or write to show
your work.

8. **THINK SMARTER** There are 38 ants on a
rock. 10 move to the grass. 10 walk
up a tree. How many ants are on the
rock now?

_____ ants

9. **GO DEEPER** There are 27 birds
at the park. 50 more birds
come. Then 50 fly away.
How many birds are at the
park now?

_____ birds

10. **THINK SMARTER** Match the math sentences
that count on and back by tens.

$$25 + 40 = ? \quad 65 + 20 = ? \quad 45 + 30 = ?$$

•   •   •

•   •   •

$$65 - 40 = ? \quad 75 - 30 = ? \quad 85 - 20 = ?$$

TAKE HOME ACTIVITY • On slips of paper, write 36 + 40 and
76 − 40. Ask your child to explain how to use the hundred chart
to count on and back by tens to find the sum and the difference.

Name _____

Related Addition and Subtraction

Learning Objective You will use a hundred chart to find sums and differences.

Use the hundred chart to add and subtract. Count on and back by tens.

1. $16 + 60 =$ _____

   $76 - 60 =$ _____

2. $61 + 30 =$ _____

   $91 - 30 =$ _____

3. $64 + 20 =$ _____

   $84 - 20 =$ _____

1	2	3	4	5	6	7	8	9	10
11	12	13	14	15	16	17	18	19	20
21	22	23	24	25	26	27	28	29	30
31	32	33	34	35	36	37	38	39	40
41	42	43	44	45	46	47	48	49	50
51	52	53	54	55	56	57	58	59	60
61	62	63	64	65	66	67	68	69	70
71	72	73	74	75	76	77	78	79	80
81	82	83	84	85	86	87	88	89	90
91	92	93	94	95	96	97	98	99	100

Problem Solving Real World

Choose a way to solve. Draw or write to show your work.

4. There are 53 leaves in a tree. 20 leaves blow away. How many leaves are left in the tree?

   _____ leaves

5. **WRITE Math** Write a number sentence to subtract 3 tens from 93.

   _____

   _____

Lesson Check

1. What is 78 − 20?
Write the number.

_____

1	2	3	4	5	6	7	8	9	10
11	12	13	14	15	16	17	18	19	20
21	22	23	24	25	26	27	28	29	30
31	32	33	34	35	36	37	38	39	40
41	42	43	44	45	46	47	48	49	50
51	52	53	54	55	56	57	58	59	60
61	62	63	64	65	66	67	68	69	70
71	72	73	74	75	76	77	78	79	80
81	82	83	84	85	86	87	88	89	90
91	92	93	94	95	96	97	98	99	100

2. What is 37 + 50?
Write the number.

_____

Spiral Review

3. Use the model.
What is the difference of 7 − 3?
Write the number.

7 − 3 = _____

4. What is the sum for 0 + 7?
Write the number.

_____

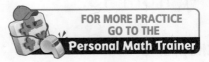
FOR MORE PRACTICE
GO TO THE
Personal Math Trainer

Name _____

Practice Addition and Subtraction

Essential Question What different ways can you use to add and subtract?

Learning Objective You will add and subtract within 100.

Listen and Draw Real World

Draw to show the problem.
Then solve.

Math Talk

Math Processes and Practices ①

Describe How did you solve the problem?

FOR THE TEACHER • Read the following problem. The class collects paper bags for an art project. Ron brings 7 more bags than Ben. Ben brings 35 bags. How many bags does Ron bring?

Chapter 8

What ways have you learned to
add and subtract?

$5 + 9 = \underline{14}$

THINK
9 + 5 is the same
as 10 + $\underline{4}$?

$50 - 30 = \underline{20}$

THINK
5 tens − 3 tens.

$51 + 21 = \underline{72}$

THINK
5 tens + 2 tens.
1 one + 1 one.

Share and Show MATH BOARD

Add or subtract.

1. $30 + 60 = \underline{90}$ 2. $73 + 5 = \underline{78}$ 3. $10 - 4 = \underline{6}$

4. $29 + 4 = \underline{33}$ 5. $9 + 9 = \underline{18}$ 6. $5 + 6 = \underline{11}$

7. $25 + 54 = \underline{79}$ 8. $15 - 8 = \underline{7}$ 9. $40 + 10 = \underline{50}$

10. $40 - 10 = \underline{20}$ 11. $14 - 7 = \underline{7}$ 12. $90 - 70 = \underline{20}$

13. $86 + 12 = \underline{98}$ 14. $1 + 9 = \underline{10}$ 15. $6 + 7 = \underline{13}$

16. $9 - 2 = \underline{7}$ 17. $8 + 31 = \underline{39}$ 18. $50 + 11 = \underline{61}$

On Your Own

Math Processes and Practices ⑧ **Use Repeated Reasoning** Add or subtract.

19.
$$\begin{array}{r} 12 \\ -\ 3 \\ \hline \end{array}$$
9

20.
$$\begin{array}{r} 10 \\ +10 \\ \hline \end{array}$$
20

21.
$$\begin{array}{r} 7 \\ +42 \\ \hline \end{array}$$
44

22.
$$\begin{array}{r} 41 \\ +36 \\ \hline \end{array}$$
77

23.
$$\begin{array}{r} 8 \\ +10 \\ \hline \end{array}$$

24.
$$\begin{array}{r} 16 \\ +\ 7 \\ \hline \end{array}$$
23

25.
$$\begin{array}{r} 6 \\ -6 \\ \hline \end{array}$$
0

26.
$$\begin{array}{r} 3 \\ +8 \\ \hline \end{array}$$
11

27.
$$\begin{array}{r} 64 \\ +\ 3 \\ \hline \end{array}$$
67

28.
$$\begin{array}{r} 60 \\ -30 \\ \hline \end{array}$$
30

29.
$$\begin{array}{r} 2 \\ +7 \\ \hline \end{array}$$
9

30.
$$\begin{array}{r} 5 \\ -1 \\ \hline \end{array}$$
4

31.
$$\begin{array}{r} 13 \\ -\ 5 \\ \hline \end{array}$$
8

32.
$$\begin{array}{r} 52 \\ +40 \\ \hline \end{array}$$

33.
$$\begin{array}{r} 3 \\ +2 \\ \hline \end{array}$$
5

34.
$$\begin{array}{r} 30 \\ +50 \\ \hline \end{array}$$
80

Solve. Write or draw to explain.

35. **THINK SMARTER** Lara collects 8 more stamps than Samson. Samson collects 39 stamps. How many stamps does Lara collect?

$8 + 39 = 47$

47

_____ stamps

Problem Solving • Applications

Real World

WRITE • Math

Solve. Write or draw to explain.

36. THINK SMARTER Jane drew some stars. Then she drew 9 more stars. Now there are 19 stars. How many stars did Jane draw first?

★

____ stars

37. THINK SMARTER Adel drew 10 more stars than Charlie. Charlie drew 24 stars. How many stars did Adel draw?

____ stars

38. GO DEEPER Write three ways to get a sum of 49.

____ ◯ ____ = 49

____ ◯ ____ = 49

____ ◯ ____ = 49

39. THINK SMARTER Find the sum of 23 and 30. Use any way to add.

$$23 + 30 = \underline{\quad}$$

Explain how you solved the problem.

TAKE HOME ACTIVITY • Have your child explain how he or she solved Exercise 36.

Practice Addition and Subtraction

Learning Objective You will add and subtract within 100.

Add or subtract.

1. 20 + 20 **40**	2. 90 − 30 **60**	3. 52 + 4 **56**	4. 62 + 21 **83**	5. 39 − 10 **29**
6. 8 + 2 **10**	7. 47 + 34 **76**	8. 4 − 0 **4**	9. 49 − 6 **43**	10. 64 + 30 **94**

Problem Solving Real World

Solve. Write or draw to explain.

11. Andrew read 17 pages of his book before dinner. He read 9 more pages after dinner. How many pages did he read?

$17 + 9 = 26$

___26___ pages

12. WRITE Math Write two ways you could use to find 5 + 8.

_____

_____

_____

_____

Lesson Check

1. What is the sum of 20 + 18?
    Write the sum.

    $$20 + 18 = \underline{38}$$

2. What is the difference of 90 − 50?
    Write the difference.

    $$90 - 50 = \underline{103}$$

Spiral Review

3. Use the model. What number
    sentence does this model show?
    Write the number sentence that
    the model shows.

    $$\underline{10} + \underline{3} = \underline{13}$$

4. Solve. Mo had some toys. He gave 6 away.
    Now he has 6 toys. How many toys did
    Mo start with?

    _____ toys $\underline{12}$

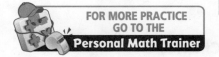

FOR MORE PRACTICE
GO TO THE
Personal Math Trainer

✓ Chapter 8 Review/Test

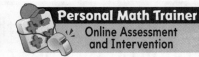

1. Write each addition or subtraction problem in the box below the answer.

7 + 2	3 + 3	15 − 9	8 + 6	14 − 5

6	9	14
	2 +2	

2. Choose all the ways that name the model.

‖ ‖‖

○ 2 tens and 3 tens
○ 20 + 30
○ 5
○ 50

3. Sasha has 70 stickers. She uses 40 of them. How many stickers are left? Show your work.

30 stickers

4. **THINK SMARTER +** Use the hundred chart to add.
Count on by ones or tens.

$37 + 5 = \underline{42}$

Explain how you used the chart to find the sum.

I COUNTED 5 PACES
FROM 37 – 5 more.

1	2	3	4	5	6	7	8	9	10
11	12	13	14	15	16	17	18	19	20
21	22	23	24	25	26	27	28	29	30
31	32	33	34	35	36	37	38	39	40
41	42	43	44	45	46	47	48	49	50
51	52	53	54	55	56	57	58	59	60
61	62	63	64	65	66	67	68	69	70
71	72	73	74	75	76	77	78	79	80
81	82	83	84	85	86	87	88	89	90
91	92	93	94	95	96	97	98	99	100

5. Use the model. Draw to show how to add the tens.

$33 + 20 = \underline{\hspace{2cm}}$

Name _____

6. Use the model. Draw to show how to make a ten.

26 + 7 = _____

7. Write the addition sentence that the model shows. Solve.

Tens	Ones

$\underline{47} + \underline{52} = 79$

8. What is the difference?

15
− 7
——

○ 7   ○ 8   ○ 10   ○ 12

9. What is the sum?

40
+ 50
——

○ 10   ○ 70   ○ 80   ✳ 90

10. Luis has 16 🍂 .

He has 38 🍂 .

How many leaves does Luis have? Circle the number that makes the sentence true.

Luis has | 48
54
59 | leaves.

11. Match the math sentences that count on and back by tens.

$$38 + 30 = ?$$ $$48 + 40 = ?$$ $$38 + 20 = ?$$

●   ●   ●

●   ●   ●

$$58 - 20 = ?$$ $$68 - 30 = ?$$ $$88 - 40 = ?$$

12. GO DEEPER Find the sum of 62 and 15. Use any way to add.

$$62 + 15 = \underline{\quad\quad}$$

Explain how you solved the problem.

All Kinds of

Weather

written by Margie Sigman

BIG IDEA Measure using non-standard units and develop a conceptual understanding of time. Represent data in picture graphs, bar graphs, and tally charts.

In rainy weather,

We play together.

Things We Use for Rainy Weather

raincoats

umbrellas

Use ● to complete the graph.

How many raincoats do you see? _____

How many umbrellas do you see? _____

SCIENCE

Describe rainy weather.

In sunny weather,

We play together.

Things We Use for Sunny Weather

sun hats

sunglasses

❀ Use ⬤ to complete the graph.

How many sunglasses do you see? ____

How many sun hats do you see? ____

SCIENCE

Describe sunny weather.

505

Whatever the weather,

We play together.

SCIENCE

Describe the weather shown here.

Write About the Story

Use 🔵. Show some sun hats and sunglasses in each category on the graph.

Vocabulary Review
category
classify
graph

Things We Use for Sunny Weather

sun hats

sunglasses

WRITE ▸ Math Write a sentence telling how many sun hats there are. Write a sentence telling how many sunglasses there are.

_____

_____

_____

_____

_____

_____

_____

_____

More or Fewer?

1. Show more raincoats than umbrellas.
   Use ⬤ in each category.

Things We Use for Rainy Weather

raincoats

umbrellas

2. Show fewer raincoats than umbrellas.
   Use ⬤ in each category.

Things We Use for Rainy Weather

raincoats

umbrellas

Write a story problem about raincoats and umbrellas. Tell how to classify each item in the correct category.

Chapter 9

Measurement

Curious About Math with Curious George

What objects in the picture are shorter than the arch?

Name _____

Bigger and Smaller

Circle the bigger object.

Circle the smaller object.

1.

2.

Compare Length

Circle the longer object.
Draw a line under the shorter object.

3.

4.

Numbers 1 to 10

Write each number in order to 10.

5.

1 ☐ ☐ ☐ ☐ ☐ ☐ ☐ ☐ 10

This page checks understanding of important skills needed for success in Chapter 9.

Name _____

Vocabulary Builder

Visualize It

Sort the review words from the box.

length

long

_____

_____

_____

sort

numbers

nine

_____

_____

_____

Understand Vocabulary

Complete the sentences with the correct word.

1. A crayon is _____ than a marker.

2. A toothbrush is _____ than a paper clip.

Write the name below the number.

3.   9   10   11   12

_____   _____   _____   _____

GO DIGITAL • Interactive Student Edition
• Multimedia eGlossary

Game Measure UP!

Materials

- 12 ● ○
- 2 (eraser)
- 2 (marker)
- 2 (pencil)
- 2 (crayon)
- 2 (scissors)
- 2 (paintbrush)

Play with a partner.

1 Put 👥 on START.

2 Spin the 🔄. Move your 👤 that many spaces. Take that object.

3 Your partner spins, moves, and takes that object.

4 Compare the lengths of the two objects.

5 The player with the longer object places a ● on the space. If both objects are the same length, both players put a ● on the board.

6 Keep playing until one person gets to END. The player with the most ● wins.

START

END

half hour

media hora

23

hour

hora

27

hour hand

horario

28

longest

el más largo

33

minute hand

minutero

36

minutes

minutos

37

more

más

38

shortest

el más corto

48

An **hour** has 60 minutes.

A **half hour** has 30 minutes.

longest

hour hand

An hour has 60 **minutes**.

minute hand

shortest

$5 - 3 = 2$

There are **more** ⭐.

Going to a Weather Station

Word Box
half hour
hour
hour hand
longest
minute hand
minutes
more
shortest

Materials

- 1
- 1
- 1

How to Play

1. Each player puts a 🔲 on START.
2. Toss the 🎲 to take a turn. Move your 🔲 that many spaces.
3. Follow these directions for the space where you land.

   White Space Read the math word or term. Tell its meaning. If you are correct, jump ahead to the next space with the same term.

   Green Space Follow the directions. If there are no directions, stay where you are.
4. The first player to reach FINISH wins.

Game

HOW TO PLAY

1. Put your on START.

2. Toss the and move your that many spaces.

3. If you land on one of these spaces:

White Space Explain the math word or term, or use it in a sentence. If your answer is correct, jump ahead to the next space with that word or term.

Green Space Follow the directions in the space. If there are no directions, don't move.

4. The first player to reach FINISH wins.

MATERIALS
• 1 • 1 • 1

FINISH

| minute hand | longest | hour hand | hour |

| minute hand | minutes | more | | shortest |

| longest | hour hand | Go back to | hour | half hour |

| hour hand | longest | minute hand | minutes | more |

| hour | half hour | shortest | | minutes |

START

| half hour | hour | half hand | longest |

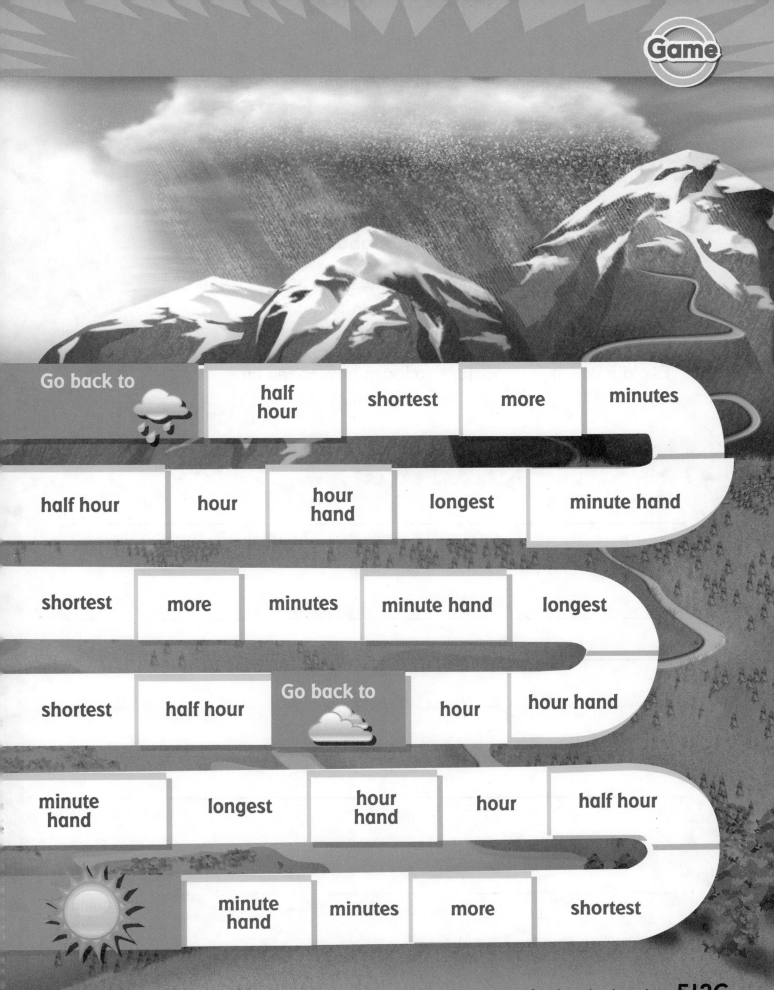

Go back to

half hour

shortest

more

minutes

half hour

hour

hour hand

longest

minute hand

shortest

more

minutes

minute hand

longest

shortest

half hour

Go back to

hour

hour hand

minute hand

longest

hour hand

hour

half hour

minute hand

minutes

more

shortest

The Write Way

Reflect

Choose one idea. Draw and write about it.

- Julia has to measure an object. She does not have a ruler. Tell what Julia could do to solve her problem.

- Explain why it is important to learn how to tell time.

Name _____

Order Length

Essential Question How do you order objects by length?

Learning Objective You will order objects by length.

Listen and Draw Real World   Hands On

Use objects to show the problem. Draw to show your work.

Math Talk   Math Processes and Practices ③

FOR THE TEACHER • Read the problem. Have children use classroom objects to act it out. Rosa has something that is longer than the drinking straw. She has another object that is shorter than the key. What objects might she have?

Compare the straw and the key. Which is longer? Which is shorter? How do you know?

Model and Draw

Order three pieces of yarn from **shortest** to **longest**. Draw the missing piece of yarn.

shortest | ━━━━━━━━━ |

| |

longest | ━━━━━━━━━━━━━━━━━ |

Share and Show MATH BOARD

Draw three lines in order from **shortest** to **longest**.

1. shortest |

2. |

3. longest |

Draw three lines in order from **longest** to **shortest**.

4. longest |

5. |

6. shortest |

514 five hundred fourteen

© Houghton Mifflin Harcourt Publishing Company

On Your Own

Math Processes and Practices ③   **Compare Representations**

Draw three crayons in order from **shortest** to **longest**.

7. **shortest**

8.

9. **longest**

Draw three crayons in order from **longest** to **shortest**.

10. **longest**

11.

12. **shortest**

13. *THINK SMARTER*   Complete each sentence.

The _____ yarn is the shortest.

The _____ yarn and the _____ yarn
are the same length.

Problem Solving • Applications Real World WRITE Math

Solve.

14. **GO DEEPER** Draw four objects in order from shortest to longest.

Objects

15. **THINK SMARTER** The string is shorter than the ribbon. The chain is shorter than the ribbon. Circle the longest object.

string

ribbon

chain

16. **THINK SMARTER** Match each word on the left to a drawing on the right.

shortest •

longest •

🏠 **TAKE HOME ACTIVITY** • Show your child three different lengths of objects, such as three pencils or spoons. Ask him or her to order the objects from shortest to longest.

Name _____

Order Length

Learning Objective You will order objects by length.

Draw three markers in order from longest to shortest.

1. longest

2.

3. shortest

Problem Solving Real World

Solve.

4. Fred has the shortest toothbrush in the bathroom. Circle Fred's toothbrush.

5. WRITE Math Draw three different lines in order from shortest to longest. Label the shortest line and the longest line.

Lesson Check

1. Draw three crayons in order
from longest to shortest.

2. Draw three paint brushes in
order from shortest to longest.

Spiral Review

3. Use 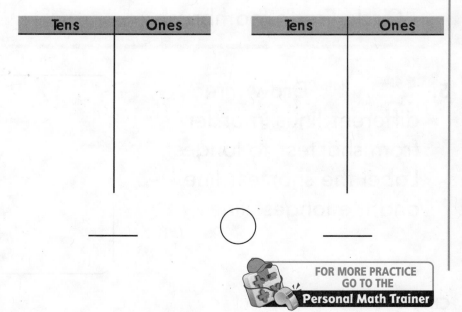 to show 22 two different ways.
Draw both ways.

Tens	Ones

Tens	Ones

FOR MORE PRACTICE
GO TO THE
Personal Math Trainer

Name _____

Indirect Measurement

Essential Question How can you compare lengths of three objects to put them in order?

Learning Objective You will explain how to compare lengths of three objects to put them in order.

Listen and Draw (Real World)

Clue 1: A yellow string is shorter than a blue string.

Clue 2: The blue string is shorter than a red string.

Clue 3: The yellow string is shorter than the red string.

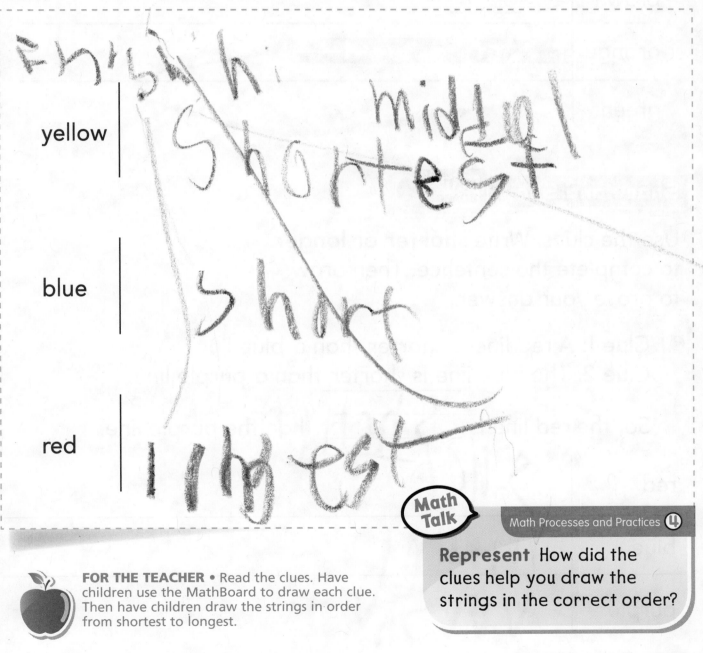

yellow

blue

red

Math Talk

Math Processes and Practices ④

FOR THE TEACHER • Read the clues. Have children use the MathBoard to draw each clue. Then have children draw the strings in order from shortest to longest.

Represent How did the clues help you draw the strings in the correct order?

Chapter 9

Model and Draw

Use the clues. Write **shorter** or **longer** to complete the sentence. Then draw to prove your answer.

Clue 1: A green pencil is longer than an orange pencil.

Clue 2: The orange pencil is longer than a brown pencil.

So, the green pencil is ___longer___ than the brown pencil.

brown

orange

green

Share and Show MATH BOARD

Use the clues. Write **shorter** or **longer** to complete the sentence. Then draw to prove your answer.

☑ 1. Clue 1: A red line is shorter than a blue line.
   Clue 2: The blue line is shorter than a purple line.

So, the red line is ___shorter___ than the purple line.

red

blue

purple

Name _____

Math Processes and Practices ① **Analyze Relationships** Use the clues. Write **shorter** or **longer** to complete the sentence. Then draw to prove your answer.

2. Clue 1: A green line is shorter than a pink line.
   Clue 2: The pink line is shorter than a blue line.

   So, the green line is _____ than the blue line.

   | green |
   | pink |
   | blue |

3. Clue 1: An orange line is longer than a yellow line.
   Clue 2: The yellow line is longer than a red line.

   So, the orange line is _____ than the red line.

   | red |
   | yellow |
   | orange |

Problem Solving • Applications (Real World)   WRITE ▸ Math

4. **THINK SMARTER** The ribbon is longer than the yarn. The yarn is longer than the string. The yarn and the pencil are the same length. Draw the lengths of the objects next to their labels.

ribbon	
yarn	
pencil	
string	

5. **THINK SMARTER** Is the first line longer than the second line? Choose Yes or No.

● Yes   ○ No

○ Yes   ○ No

○ Yes   ● No

TAKE HOME ACTIVITY • Show your child the length of one object. Then show your child an object that is longer and an object that is shorter than the first object.

Indirect Measurement

Learning Objective You will explain how to compare lengths of three objects to put them in order.

Read the clues. Write shorter or longer to complete the sentence. Then draw to prove your answer.

1. Clue 1: A piece of yarn is longer than a ribbon.

   Clue 2: The ribbon is longer than a crayon.

   So, the yarn is ___longer___ than the crayon.

yarn	
ribbon	
crayon	

Problem Solving Real World

Solve. Draw or write to explain.

2. Megan's pencil is shorter than Tasha's pencil.

   Tasha's pencil is shorter than Kim's pencil.

   Is Megan's pencil shorter or longer than Kim's pencil?

   shorter

3. **WRITE** Math Use different colors to draw 3 lines that are different lengths. Then write a sentence comparing their lengths.

Lesson Check

1. A black line is longer than a gray line. The gray line is longer than a white line. Is the black line shorter or longer than the white line? Draw to prove your answer.

longer

· ·

Spiral Review

2. What is the sum? Write the number.

$$42 + 20 = 62$$

524 five hundred twenty-four

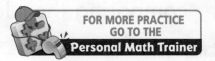

FOR MORE PRACTICE GO TO THE Personal Math Trainer

Name _____

Use Nonstandard Units to Measure Length

Essential Question How do you measure length using nonstandard units?

Learning Objective You will measure length by using nonstandard units.

 Listen and Draw Real World **Hands On**

Use ▪. Draw to show the problem.

Math Talk Math Processes and Practices ②

Reasoning How do you draw the boat to be the right length?

FOR THE TEACHER • Read the problem. Jimmy sees that his boat is about 6 color tiles long. Draw Jimmy's boat. Draw the color tiles to show how you measured.

Model and Draw

You can use ▪ to measure length.
Write how many.

about _____ ▪

Share and Show MATH BOARD

Use real objects. Use ▪ to measure.

1.

about _____ ▪

2.

about _____ ▪

☑ 3.

about _____ ▪

☑ 4.

about _____ ▪

Name _____

Use real objects. Use to measure.

5.

about _____ ◼

6.

about _____ ◼

7.

about _____ ◼

8.

about _____ ◼

9. THINK SMARTER The green yarn is about 2 ◼ long.
About how long is the blue yarn?

about _____ ◼

Problem Solving • Applications Real World WRITE Math

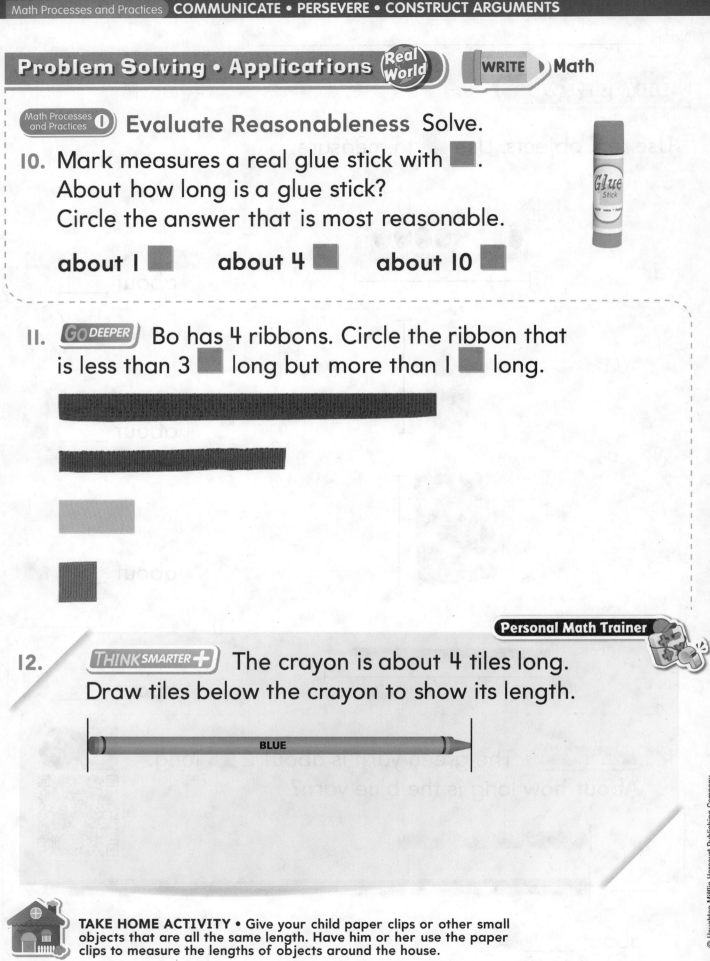

Math Processes and Practices ① **Evaluate Reasonableness** Solve.

10. Mark measures a real glue stick with ■.
About how long is a glue stick?
Circle the answer that is most reasonable.

about 1 ■   about 4 ■   about 10 ■

11. GO DEEPER Bo has 4 ribbons. Circle the ribbon that
is less than 3 ■ long but more than 1 ■ long.

12. THINK SMARTER ＋   The crayon is about 4 tiles long.
Draw tiles below the crayon to show its length.

BLUE

Personal Math Trainer

🏠 **TAKE HOME ACTIVITY •** Give your child paper clips or other small
objects that are all the same length. Have him or her use the paper
clips to measure the lengths of objects around the house.

Use Nonstandard Units to Measure Length

Learning Objective You will measure length by using nonstandard units.

Use real objects. Use **to measure.**

1. MATH

   about _____ ▪

2. glue stick

   about _____ ▪

3. CRAYONS

   about _____ ▪

Problem Solving Real World

Solve.

4. Don measures his desk with ▪.
   About how long is his desk?

   about _____ ▪

5. WRITE Math Use words or pictures to explain how to measure an index card using color tiles.

Lesson Check

1. Use ■. Kevin measures the ribbon with ■. About how long is the ribbon?

about ____ ■

Spiral Review

2. Draw and write to solve.
I have 27 red flowers and 19 white flowers. How many flowers do I have?

____ flowers

3. Circle the number that is less.	Did tens or ones help you decide?	Write the numbers.
51 50	tens ones	____ is less than ____ ____ < ____

FOR MORE PRACTICE
GO TO THE
Personal Math Trainer

Name _____

Make a Nonstandard Measuring Tool

Essential Question How do you use a nonstandard measuring tool to measure length?

Learning Objective You will make a nonstandard measuring tool and show how to measure length.

 Listen and Draw Real World

Circle the name of the child who measured correctly.

Alli

Mateo

 FOR THE TEACHER • Read the problem. Mateo and Alli measure the same pencil. Mateo says it is about 4 paper clips long. Alli says it is about 3 paper clips long. Circle the name of the child who measured correctly.

Math Talk Math Processes and Practices 5

Use Tools Explain how you know who measured correctly.

Make your own paper clip measuring tool like the one on the shelf. Measure the length of a door. About how long is the door?

about _____ ⌐⊃

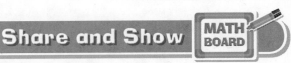

Use real objects and the measuring tool you made.
Measure. Circle the longest object.
Underline the shortest object.

1.

about _____ ⌐⊃

2.

about _____ ⌐⊃

☑ 3.

about _____ ⌐⊃

☑ 4.

about _____ ⌐⊃

Name _____

On Your Own

Math Processes and Practices ⑤ **Use Appropriate Tools**

Use the measuring tool you made.
Measure real objects.

5. 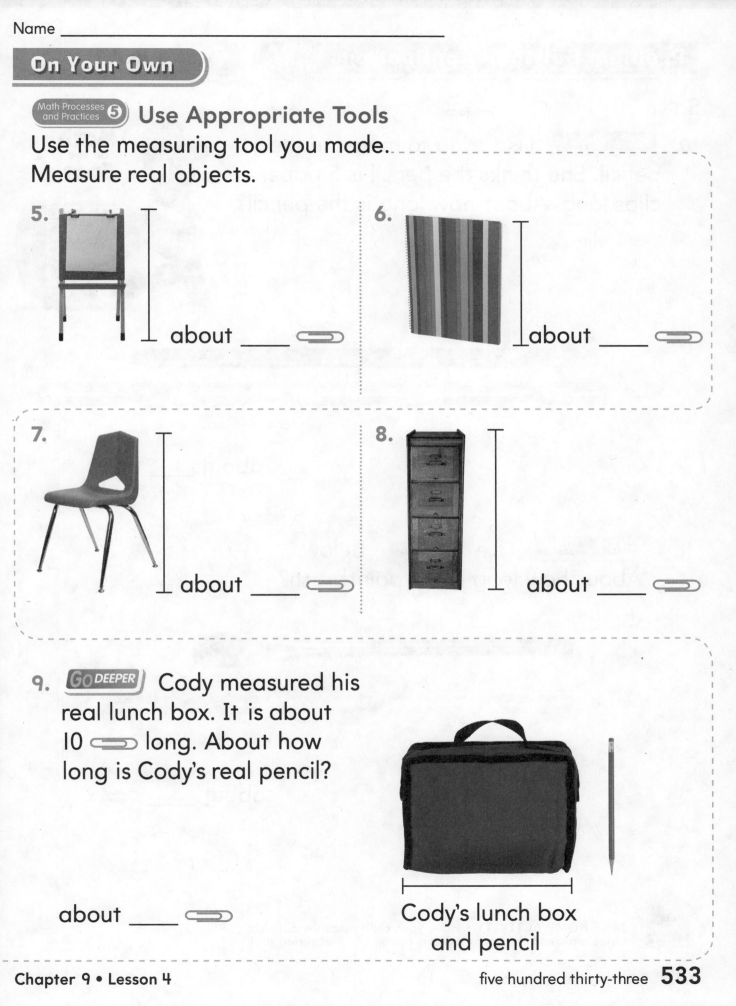 about _____ ⬭

6. about _____ ⬭

7. about _____ ⬭

8. about _____ ⬭

9. **GO DEEPER** Cody measured his
real lunch box. It is about
10 ⬭ long. About how
long is Cody's real pencil?

about _____ ⬭

Cody's lunch box
and pencil

© Houghton Mifflin Harcourt Publishing Company • Image Credits: (cr) ©PhotoDisc/Getty Images

Problem Solving • Applications (Real World) WRITE Math

Solve.

10. **THINK SMARTER** Lisa tried to measure the pencil. She thinks the pencil is 5 paper clips long. About how long is the pencil?

Math on the Spot

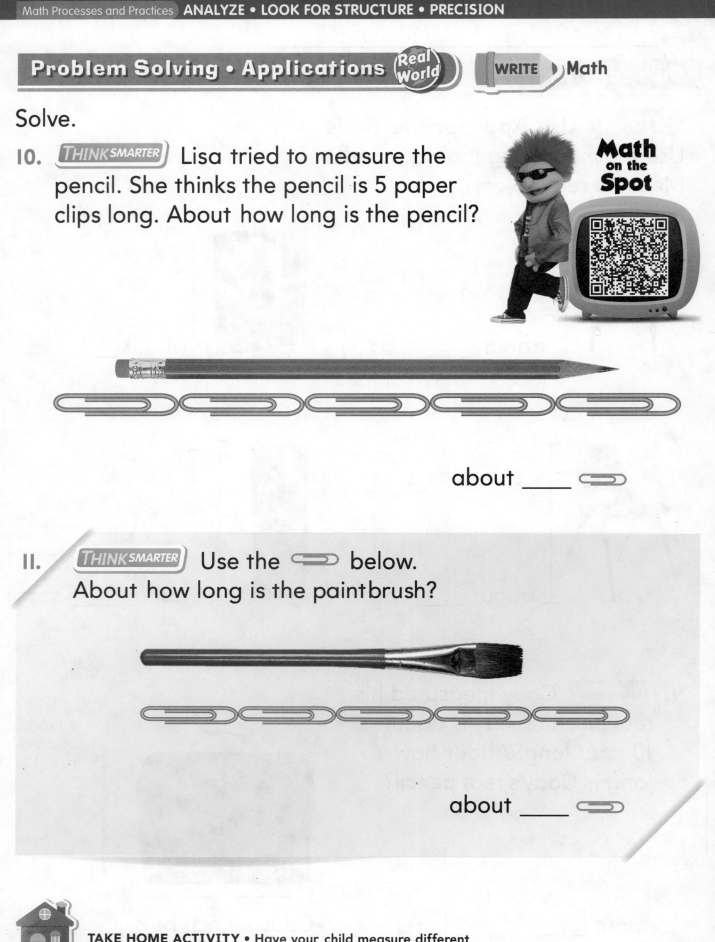

about _____ ◯

11. **THINK SMARTER** Use the ◯ below.
About how long is the paintbrush?

about _____ ◯

🏠 **TAKE HOME ACTIVITY** • Have your child measure different objects around the house using a paper clip measuring tool.

© Houghton Mifflin Harcourt Publishing Company

Make a Nonstandard Measuring Tool

Learning Objective You will make a nonstandard measuring tool and show how to measure length.

Use the measuring tool you made. Measure real objects.

1.

about _____ ⌾

2.

about _____ ⌾

3.

about _____ ⌾

4.

about _____ ⌾

5.

about _____ ⌾

6.

about _____ ⌾

7. **WRITE** Math Use words or pictures to explain how to measure a table using a paper clip measuring tool.

Lesson Check

1. Use the ⚬ below. Circle the string that is about 4 ⚬ long.

Spiral Review

2. Ty crosses out the number cards that are greater than 38 and less than 34. What numbers are left?

33	35	37	39	40

_____ and _____

3. There are 12 books. 4 books are large. The rest are small. Write a number sentence that shows how to find the number of small books.

_____ − _____ = _____

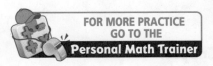

FOR MORE PRACTICE
GO TO THE
Personal Math Trainer

536 five hundred thirty-six

Name _____

Problem Solving • Measure and Compare

Essential Question How can acting it out help you solve measurement problems?

Learning Objective You will use the strategy *act it out* to solve real-world measurement problems by drawing ribbons in order of length.

The blue ribbon is about 4 long. The red ribbon is 1 long. The green ribbon is 2 longer than the red ribbon. Measure and draw the ribbons in order from **shortest** to **longest**.

Unlock the Problem

What do I need to find?

order the ribbons from

 to

What information do I need to use?

Measure the ribbons using paper clips.

Show how to solve the problem.

HOME CONNECTION • Have your child act out a measurement problem by finding the lengths of 3 objects and ordering them from shortest to longest.

© Houghton Mifflin Harcourt Publishing Company

Zack has 3 ribbons. The yellow ribbon is about 4 🖇 long. The orange ribbon is 3 🖇 shorter than the yellow ribbon. The blue ribbon is 2 🖇 longer than the yellow ribbon.

Measure and draw the ribbons in order from **longest** to **shortest**.

- What do I need to find?
- What information do I need to use?

1. about _____ 🖇

2. about _____ 🖇

3. about _____ 🖇

Math Talk

Math Processes and Practices ③

Compare How many paper clips shorter is the orange ribbon than the blue ribbon?

Name _____

Share and Show MATH BOARD

Solve. Draw or write to explain.

☑4. **GO DEEPER** Lisa measures her shoe to be about 5 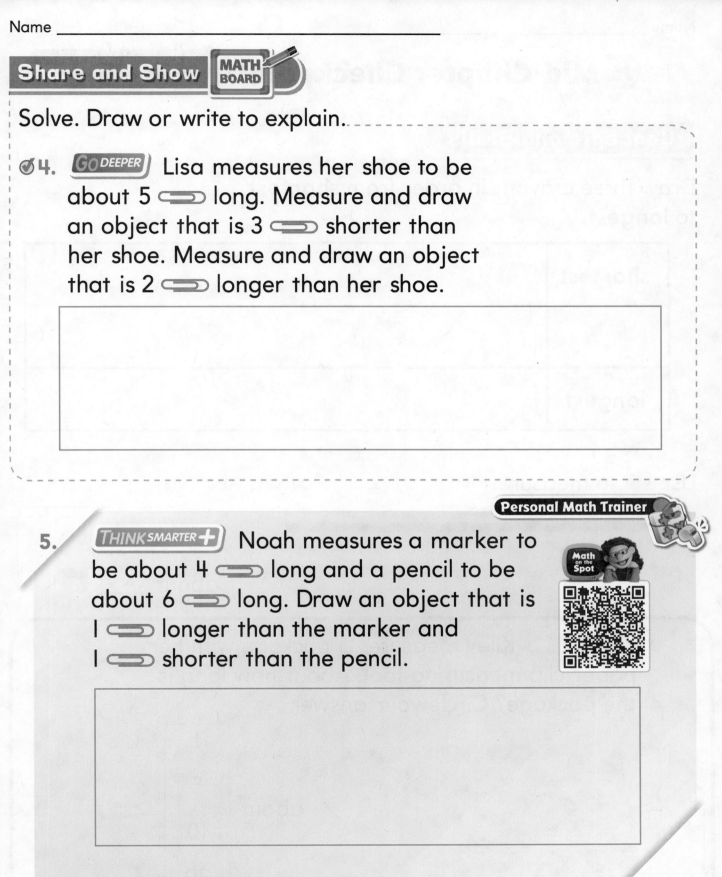 long. Measure and draw an object that is 3 ⊂⊃ shorter than her shoe. Measure and draw an object that is 2 ⊂⊃ longer than her shoe.

Personal Math Trainer

5. **THINK SMARTER +** Noah measures a marker to be about 4 ⊂⊃ long and a pencil to be about 6 ⊂⊃ long. Draw an object that is 1 ⊂⊃ longer than the marker and 1 ⊂⊃ shorter than the pencil.

TAKE HOME ACTIVITY • Have your child explain how he or she solved Exercise 4.

✓ Mid-Chapter Checkpoint

Personal Math Trainer
Online Assessment
and Intervention

Concepts and Skills

Draw three crayons in order from **shortest** to **longest**.

1.

shortest		
longest		

Use to measure.

2. ▬▬▬▬▬▬▬▬▬▬▬▬▬▬▬▬▬▬▬

about _____ ■

3. THINK SMARTER Kiley measures a package with her paper clip measuring tool. About how long is the package? Circle your answer.

about
1
5
10
20

Problem Solving • Measure and Compare

Learning Objective You will use the strategy *act it out* to solve real-world measurement problems by drawing ribbons in order of length.

The blue string is about 3 ⊂⊃ long. The green string is 2 ⊂⊃ longer than the blue string. The red string is 1 ⊂⊃ shorter than the blue string. Measure and draw the strings in order from **longest** to **shortest**.

1. |
   about ____ ⊂⊃

2. |
   about ____ ⊂⊃

3. |
   about ____ ⊂⊃

Problem Solving Real World

4. Sandy has a ribbon about 4 ⊂⊃ long. She cut a new ribbon 2 ⊂⊃ longer. Measure and draw the two ribbons.

   |
   |

   The new ribbon is about ____ ⊂⊃ long.

5. WRITE Math Measure and draw to show a blue crayon and a green crayon that is about 1 paper clip longer.

© Houghton Mifflin Harcourt Publishing Company

Lesson Check

1. Mia measures a stapler with her paper clip ruler. About how long is the stapler?

about _____ ⌐⌐

Spiral Review

2. What is the unknown number? Write the number.

$$4 + \underline{\quad} = 13$$

---

3. Count by tens. What numbers are missing? Write the numbers.

17, 27, _____, _____, 57, 67

542 five hundred forty-two

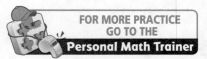

FOR MORE PRACTICE
GO TO THE
Personal Math Trainer

Name _____

Time to the Hour

Essential Question How do you tell time to the hour on a clock that has only an hour hand?

Learning Objective You will tell time to the hour on a clock that has only an hour hand.

Listen and Draw (Real World)

Start at 1.
Write the unknown numbers.

Start

| 1 | 2 | 3 | 4 | 5 | 6 | 7 | 8 | 9 | 10 | 11 | 12 |

FOR THE TEACHER • In the top workspace, have children write the unknown numbers in the squares on the green yarn. In the bottom workspace, have children write the unknown numbers on the clock face.

Math Talk Math Processes and Practices 7

Look for Structure
How are a clock face and ordering numbers alike?

Chapter 9

What does this clock show?

The **hour hand** points to the 3.
It is 3 o'clock.

Say three o'clock.

Write 3:00.

Share and Show MATH BOARD

Look at where the hour hand points.
Write the time.

1.

_9:00_

2.

_1:00_

3.

_____

4.

_____

5.

_____

6.

_____

Name _____

Math Processes and Practices 6 **Make Connections** Look at where the hour hand points. Write the time.

7. 4:00

8. 10:00

9. 6:00

10. 12

11. 1:00

12. 3:00

13. THINKSMARTER On Rae's clock, the hour hand points to the 9. Circle Rae's clock.

11:00

9:00

10:00

Problem Solving • Applications (Real World) ✏️ WRITE ▸ Math

14. THINK SMARTER   Which time is **not** the same? Circle it.

1:00   1 o'clock

15. GO DEEPER   Manny leaves for school at 8 o'clock. Write and draw to show 8 o'clock.

_____

16. THINK SMARTER   Look at the hour hand. What is the time?

○ 7:00

○ 8 o'clock

○ 9 o'clock

○ 12:00

TAKE HOME ACTIVITY • Have your child describe what he or she did in this lesson.

Time to the Hour

Learning Objective You will tell time to the hour on a clock that has only an hour hand.

Look at where the hour hand points.
Write the time.

1. _____

2. _____

3. _____

Problem Solving Real World

Solve.

4. Which time is **not** the same? Circle it.

7:00   7 o'clock

5. WRITE Math Draw a clock to show where the hour hand points for 11:00.

Lesson Check

1. Look at the hour hand. What is the time? Write the time.

_____

2. Look at the hour hand. What is the time? Write the time.

_____ o'clock

Spiral Review

3. What is the sum? Write the number.

$$40 + 30 = \underline{\hspace{2cm}}$$

4. What is the sum? Write the number.

$$53 + 30 = \underline{\hspace{2cm}}$$

548 five hundred forty-eight

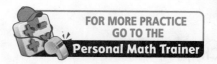

FOR MORE PRACTICE
GO TO THE
Personal Math Trainer

Name _____

Time to the Half Hour

Essential Question How do you tell time to the half hour on a clock that has only an hour hand?

Learning Objective You will tell time to the half hour on a clock that has only an hour hand.

Listen and Draw

Circle **4:00**, **5:00**, or **between 4:00 and 5:00** to describe the time shown on the clock.

4:00

between 4:00 and 5:00

5:00

4:00

between 4:00 and 5:00

5:00

4:00

between 4:00 and 5:00

5:00

Math Talk

Math Processes and Practices ②

Reasoning Use **before** and **after** to describe the time shown on the middle clock.

FOR THE TEACHER • Have children look at the hour hand on each clock to decide which choice best describes the time shown.

Model and Draw

As an **hour** passes, the hour hand moves from one number to the next number.

The hour hand is halfway between the 7 and the 8.

When a **half hour** has passed, the hour hand points halfway between two numbers.

half past 7:00

Share and Show MATH BOARD

Look at where the hour hand points.
Write the time.

1.

_____
- - - - - - - - -
_____

2.

_____
- - - - - - - - -
_____

✓ 3.

_____
- - - - - - - - -
_____

✓ 4.

_____
- - - - - - - - -
_____

© Houghton Mifflin Harcourt Publishing Company

On Your Own

Math Processes and Practices ② **Use Reasoning** Look at where the hour hand points. Write the time.

5.

_____

- - - - - - - - - - - - -

_____

6.

_____

- - - - - - - - - - - - -

_____

7.

_____

- - - - - - - - - - - - -

_____

8.

_____

- - - - - - - - - - - - -

_____

9. THINK SMARTER Maya starts reading at half past 8. Circle the clock that shows the time Maya starts reading.

Problem Solving • Applications (Real World)   WRITE ▸ Math

10. **THINK SMARTER** Tim plays soccer at half past 9:00. He eats lunch at half past 1:00. He sees a movie at half past 2:00.

Look at the clock.
Write what Tim does.

_____

_____

Tim _____.

11. **GO DEEPER** Tyra has a piano lesson at 5:00. The lesson ends at half past 5:00. How much time is Tyra at her lesson? Circle your answer.

half hour

hour

12. **THINK SMARTER** What time is it? Circle the time that makes the sentence true.

The time is

| half past 5:00 |
| 6:00 |
| half past 6:00 |

TAKE HOME ACTIVITY • Say a time, such as half past 10:00.
Ask your child to describe where the hour hand points at this time.

Time to the Half Hour

Learning Objective You will tell time to the half hour on a clock that has only an hour hand.

Look at where the hour hand points. Write the time.

I.

_____

2.

_____

3.

_____

Problem Solving Real World

Solve.

4. Greg rides his bike at half past 4:00. He eats dinner at half past 6:00. He reads a book at half past 8:00.

Look at the clock. Write what Greg does.

_____

_____

Greg _____.

5. WRITE Math Draw clocks to show where the hour hand points for 5:00 and half past 5:00.

Lesson Check

1. Look at the hour hand. What is the time? Write the time.

_____

- - - - - - - - - - - - - - - -

_____

2. Look at the hour hand. What is the time? Write the time.

_____

- - - - - - - - - - - - - - - -

_____

Spiral Review

3. What number does the model show? Write the number.

‖‖‖‖‖‖‖‖‖‖ ∘∘∘

_____

4. How many tens and ones make this number?

14
fourteen

____ ten ____ ones

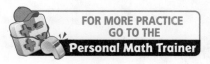

FOR MORE PRACTICE
GO TO THE
Personal Math Trainer

Name _____

Tell Time to the Hour and Half Hour

Essential Question How are the minute hand and hour hand different for time to the hour and time to the half hour?

Learning Objective You will tell time to the hour and time to the half hour.

Listen and Draw

Each clock has an hour hand and a minute hand. Use what you know about the hour hand to write the unknown numbers.

It is 1:00.

The hour hand points to the _____.

The minute hand points to the _____.

It is half past 1:00.

The hour hand points between the _____ and the _____.

The minute hand points to the _____.

Math Talk Math Processes and Practices ⑤

Use Tools Look at the top clock. Explain how you know which is the minute hand.

FOR THE TEACHER • Read the time on the first clock and have children identify where the hour hand and minute hand point. Then repeat for the second clock.

Chapter 9

five hundred fifty-five **555**

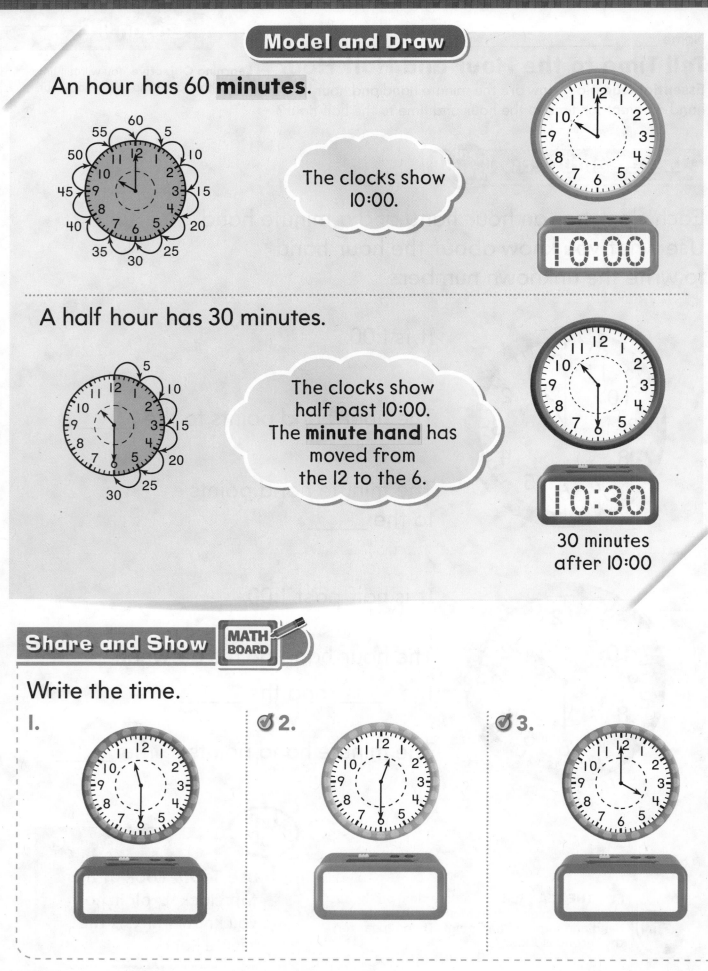

Model and Draw

An hour has 60 **minutes**.

The clocks show 10:00.

A half hour has 30 minutes.

The clocks show half past 10:00. The **minute hand** has moved from the 12 to the 6.

30 minutes after 10:00

Share and Show MATH BOARD

Write the time.

1.

2.

3.

Name _____

Math Processes and Practices **6** **Attend to Precision** Write the time.

4.

5.

6.

7.

8.

9.

Circle your answer.

10. Sara goes to the park when both the hour hand and the minute hand point to the 12. What time does Sara go to the park?

    1:00   12:00   12:30

11. THINK SMARTER Mel goes to the park when the hour hand points between the 3 and 4 and the minute hand points to the 6. What time does Mel go to the park?

    3:00   3:30   6:00

Math on the Spot

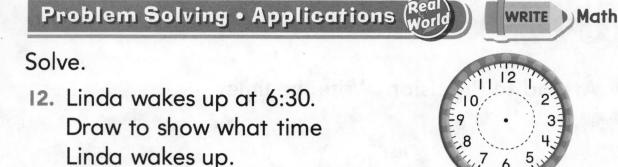

Problem Solving • Applications (Real World)   WRITE ▶ Math

Solve.

12. Linda wakes up at 6:30. Draw to show what time Linda wakes up.

13. David left school at 3:30. Circle the clock that shows 3:30.

14. [GO DEEPER] The hour hand points halfway between the 2 and 3. Draw the hour hand and the minute hand. Write the time.

15. [THINK SMARTER] Choose all the ways that name the time on the clock.

- ○ half past 7:00
- ○ half past 6:00
- ○ 8:30
- ○ 7:30

TAKE HOME ACTIVITY • At times on the half hour, have your child show you the minute hand and the hour hand on a clock and tell what time it is.

Tell Time to the Hour and Half Hour

Write the time.

1.

2.

3.

4.

5.

6.

Problem Solving Real World

Solve.

7. Lulu walks her dog at 7 o'clock. Bill walks his dog 30 minutes later. Draw to show what time Bill walks his dog.

8. WRITE Math Draw a clock to show the time 1:30.

Lesson Check

1. What time is it?
Write the time.

_____

2. What time is it?
Write the time.

_____

Spiral Review

3. What is the sum?
Write the number.

$$48 + 20 = \underline{}$$

4. How many tens and ones
are in the sum? Write the
numbers. Write the sum.

$$\begin{array}{r} 67 \\ + 25 \\ \hline \end{array}$$

____ tens ____ ones

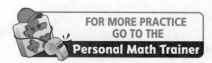

FOR MORE PRACTICE
GO TO THE
Personal Math Trainer

Name _____

Practice Time to the Hour and Half Hour

Essential Question How do you know whether to draw and write time to the hour or half hour?

Learning Objective You will use the hour hand to draw and write times on analog and digital clocks.

Circle the clock that matches the problem.

FOR THE TEACHER • Read the following problems. Barbara goes to the store at 8:00. Circle the clock that shows 8:00. Have children use the top workspace to solve. Then have children solve this problem: Barbara takes Ria for a walk at 1:30. Circle the clock that shows 1:30.

Math Talk Math Processes and Practices ⑧

Generalize Describe how you know which clock shows 1:30.

Chapter 9

five hundred sixty-one **561**

Where should you draw the minute hand to show the time?

9:00

9:30

Share and Show   MATH BOARD

Use the hour hand to write the time.
Draw the minute hand.

1.

2.

3.

4.

⊘ 5.

⊘ 6.

Name _____

Math Processes and Practices ④ **Use Diagrams** Use the hour hand to write the time. Draw the minute hand.

7.

8.

9.

10.

11.

12.

13. **THINK SMARTER** **What is the error?**
Zoey tried to show 6:00. Explain how to change the clock to show 6:00.

_____

_____

_____

_____

Problem Solving • Applications (Real World) WRITE Math

Solve.

14. Vince goes to a baseball game at 4:30. Draw to show what time Vince goes to a baseball game.

15. **GO DEEPER** Brandon has lunch at 1 o'clock. Write and draw to show what time Brandon has lunch.

16. **THINK SMARTER** Juan tried to show 8:30. He made a mistake.

What did Juan do wrong? Explain his mistake.

TAKE HOME ACTIVITY • Show your child a time to the hour or half hour on a clock. Ask him or her what time it will be in 30 minutes.

564 five hundred sixty-four

© Houghton Mifflin Harcourt Publishing Company

Practice Time to the Hour and Half Hour

Learning Objective You will use the hour hand to draw and write times on analog and digital clocks.

Use the hour hand to write the time. Draw the minute hand.

1.

2.

3.

Problem Solving Real World

Solve.

4. Billy played outside for a half hour. Write how many minutes Billy played outside.

_____ minutes

5. WRITE Math Draw a clock to show a time to the hour. Draw another clock to show a time to the half hour. Write each time.

Lesson Check

1. Write the time.

_____

···

Spiral Review

2. What is the difference?
Write the number.

$$80 - 30 = \rule{2em}{0.4pt}$$

···

3. Use . Amy measures the eraser with ■.
About how long is the eraser?

about ____ ■ long

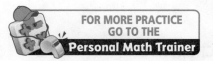
FOR MORE PRACTICE
GO TO THE
Personal Math Trainer

✓ Chapter 9 Review/Test

Personal Math Trainer
Online Assessment
and Intervention

1. Match each word on the left to a drawing on the right.

shortest •

longest •

• ☐

• ☐

• ☐

---

2. Is the first line shorter than the second line? Choose Yes or No.

○ Yes   ○ No

○ Yes   ○ No

○ Yes   ○ No

---

3. The crayon is about 5 tiles long. Draw tiles below the crayon to show its length.

Crayon

4. Use the ⬭ below. About how long is the 🪱 ?

about _____ ⬭

5. Measure the ▬. Use ⬭ .

about _____ ⬭

about _____ ⬭

about _____ ⬭

6. Look at the hour hand. What is the time?

○ 9:00

○ 10 o'clock

○ 11 o'clock

○ 12:00

---

7. What time is it? Circle the time that makes the sentence true.

The time is .

1:30

2:00

2:30

---

8. Choose all the ways that name the time on the clock.

○ half past 6:00

○ half past 11:00

○ 6:00

○ 11:30

9. Draw the hand on the clock to show 9:30.

10. **GO DEEPER** Lucy tried to show 5:00. She made a mistake.

Draw hands on the clock to show 5:00.

What did Lucy do wrong? Explain her mistake.

11. **THINK SMARTER** The ——— is shorter than the ——————— .
The ——————————— is longer than the ——————— .
Draw the length of the ——————— .

——	
———————	
———————	

Represent Data

Curious About Math with
Curious George

How many days will it
snow or rain this week
where you live? How
can you find out?

Name _____

Make a Concrete Graph

Sort a handful of ■ and ▢. Make a concrete graph.

Square Colors							
■							
▢							

1. How many ■ are there? _____

More, Fewer

2. Shade to show a set of fewer.

Draw Equal Groups

3. Draw a ◯ below each picture to show
the same number of objects.

This page checks understanding of important skills needed
for success in Chapter 10.

Vocabulary Builder

Review Words

graph
more
fewer
most
fewest

Visualize It

Complete the chart.
Mark each row with a ✔.

Word	I Know	Sounds Familiar	I Do Not Know
graph			
more			
fewer			
most			
fewest			

Understand Vocabulary

Use the review words. Label the groups.

1.

_____   _____

2.

_____   _____

Game

Graph Game

Materials 🕐 •16 🔲 •16 🔲 •16 🔲

Play with a partner.

1. Spin the 🕐.

2. Put 1 cube of that color in the correct row of your graph.

3. Take turns. Play until each partner has 5 turns.

4. The player who went last spins again to get a color.

5. The player with more cubes of that color wins. Spin again if you both have the same number of cubes of that color.

Player 1

Player 2

bar graph

gráfica de barras

4

fewer

menos

19

longest

el más largo

33

more

más

38

picture graph

gráfica con dibujos

41

shortest

el más corto

48

tally chart

tabla de conteo

55

tally mark

marca de conteo

56

3 fewer 🐦

Flowers in the Garden

Kinds of Flowers							
daisies	■	■	■	■	■		
sunflowers							

Number of Flowers
0 1 2 3 4 5 6 7

$5 - 3 = 2$

There are **more** ⭐.

| longest

| shortest

Our Favorite Activity at the Fair

🐴 animals	👤	👤	👤	👤	👤		
🎠 rides	👤	👤	👤	👤	👤	👤	👤

Each 👤 stands for 1 child.

Each **tally mark |** stands for 1. 卌 stands for 5.

Boys and Girls in Our Class		Total
boys	卌 ||||	9
girls	卌		6

Picture It

Word Box

bar graph
fewer
longest
more
picture graph
shortest
tally chart
tally mark

Materials

timer

How to Play

Play with two other players.

1. Choose a secret word from the Word Box. Do not tell the other players.

2. Set the timer.

3. Draw pictures to show clues for the secret word.

4. The first player to guess the word before time runs out gets 1 point.

5. Take turns.

6. The first player to score 5 points wins.

The Write Way

Reflect

Choose one idea. Draw and write about it.

- Tell the difference between a picture graph and a bar graph.

- Explain how to read a tally chart.

Name _____

Read Picture Graphs

Essential Question What do the pictures in a picture graph show?

Learning Objective You will learn to compare information shown in a picture graph where each symbol represents one child.

Listen and Draw Real World   Hands On

Use . Draw to show the cubes.
Write how many more .

_____ more

FOR THE TEACHER • Read the following problem. There are 2 green cubes and 4 blue cubes. How many more blue cubes are there than green cubes?

Math Talk Math Processes and Practices ④

Represent Describe how you can use your picture to compare the cubes.

Chapter 10

Children at the Playground

swings	♀	♀	♀	♀	
slide	♀	♀			

Each ♀ stands for I child.

A **picture graph** uses pictures to show information.

There are ___4___ children on the 🛝.

There are ____ children on the 🛝.

There are more children on the _____.

Our Favorite Activity at the Fair

animals	♀	♀	♀	♀	♀		
rides	♀	♀	♀	♀	♀	♀	♀

Each ♀ stands for I child.

Use the picture graph to answer the question.

I. Which activity did more children choose? Circle.

2. How many children chose 🐴?   ____ children

3. How many children chose 🎡?   ____ children

4. How many fewer children chose 🐴 than 🎡?   ____ fewer children

576 five hundred seventy-six

On Your Own

What We Drink for Lunch									
milk	☆	☆	☆	☆	☆	☆	☆	☆
juice	☆	☆	☆					
water	☆	☆	☆	☆	☆			

Each ☆ stands for 1 child.

Use the picture graph to answer the question.

5. How many children drink 🥛?

_____ children

6. How many children in all drink 🧃 and 💧?

_____ children

7. How many fewer children drink 💧 than 🥛?

_____ fewer children

8. How many more children drink 🥛 than 🧃?

_____ more children

9. THINK SMARTER How many children in all drink 🥛, 🧃, and 💧?

_____ children

10. GO DEEPER 4 new children join the class. They drink 🧃 at lunch. Now, how many more children drink 🧃 than 💧?

_____ more children

Problem Solving • Applications (Real World)   WRITE Math

Our Favorite Animal at the Zoo								
🦓 zebras	⚲	⚲	⚲	⚲	⚲			
🦁 lions	⚲	⚲	⚲	⚲	⚲	⚲	⚲	⚲
🦭 seals	⚲							

Each ⚲ stands for 1 child.

(Math Processes and Practices 4) **Write an Equation** Write a number sentence to solve the problem.

11. How many children chose 🦓 and 🦭 altogether?

___ ◯ ___ ◯ ___

___ children

12. How many more children chose 🦁 than 🦭?

___ ◯ ___ ◯ ___

___ more children

13. GO DEEPER How many more children chose 🦁 than 🦓 and 🦭 altogether?

___ ◯ ___ ◯ ___

___ more children

14. THINK SMARTER Use the graph at the top. How many children chose 🦁?

☐

🏠 **TAKE HOME ACTIVITY** • Keep track of the weather for one week by drawing a picture each day to show if it is sunny, cloudy, or rainy. At the end of the week, ask your child what the weather was like for most of the week.

578 five hundred seventy-eight

Name _____

Read Picture Graphs

Learning Objective You will learn to compare information shown in a picture graph where each symbol represents one child.

Our Favorite Outdoor Activity

🚲 biking	♀	♀	♀	♀	♀	♀	♀	♀
🛹 skating	♀	♀						
🏃 running	♀	♀	♀	♀				

Each ♀ stands for 1 child.

Use the picture graph to answer the question.

1. How many children chose 🚲 ?

_____ children

2. How many children chose 🛹 and 🏃 altogether?

_____ children

Problem Solving Real World

Write a number sentence to solve the problem.
Use the picture graph at the top of the page.

3. How many more children chose 🚲 than 🏃 ?

_____ more children

____ ◯ ____ ◯ ____

4. WRITE Math Use numbers and pictures to show why a row with 6 smiley faces has one more than a row with 5 smiley faces.

Lesson Check

Use the picture graph to answer the question.

Do you do chores at home?								
yes	☺	☺	☺	☺	☺	☺	☺	☺
no	☺	☺	☺	☺	☺	☺		

Each ☺ stands for I child.

1. How many children do chores at home?
   Write the number.

   _____ children

2. How many more children answered yes
   than no? Write a number sentence to
   solve the problem.

   _____ more children   ___ ◯ ___ ◯ ___

Spiral Review

3. What number is ten less than 82?
   Circle the number. Then write the
   number sentence.

   92   83   81   72

   ___ − 10 ___

4. Count forward. What number is missing?
   Write the number.

   110, 111, 112, _____, 114

FOR MORE PRACTICE
GO TO THE
Personal Math Trainer

Name _____

Make Picture Graphs

Essential Question How do you make a picture graph to answer a question?

Learning Objective You will make a picture graph to answer a question.

Listen and Draw Real World

Use ⬤ to solve the problem.
Draw to show your work.

Which has more?

Math Talk

Math Processes and Practices ③

Compare Describe what the picture graph shows.

FOR THE TEACHER • Read the following problem. Asaf has 6 baseballs. He has 4 bats. Does he have more baseballs or bats? Have children draw circles to show the baseballs and bats. Then have them circle the object with more.

Are there more black or white sheep in the picture? Make a picture graph to find out.

Sheep in the Meadow

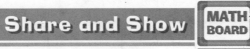 black	◯				
white					

Each ◯ stands for 1 sheep.

There are more _____ sheep.

Share and Show MATH BOARD

Do more children like cats or dogs?
Ask 10 friends which pet they like better.
Draw 1 circle for each child's answer.

Our Favorite Pet

cats										
dogs										

Each ◯ stands for 1 child.

Use the picture graph to answer each question.

1. How many children chose 🐱?   ____ children

✓ 2. How many children chose 🐕?   ____ children

✓ 3. Which pet did more children choose? Circle.

Name _____

Which activity do the most children like best?
Ask 10 friends. Draw 1 circle for each child's answer.

Our Favorite Activity										
📖 reading										
💻 computer										
⚽ sports										

Each ◯ stands for 1 child.

Math Processes and Practices 4 **Use Graphs** Use the picture graph
to answer the question.

4. How many children
   chose 📖?

   _____ children

5. How many children
   chose 💻 and ⚽?

   _____ children

6. Which activity did the most
   children choose? Circle.

   📖   💻   ⚽

7. Did all your classmates make
   picture graphs that look the
   same? Circle **yes** or **no**.

8. **THINK SMARTER** Write your own question about
   the graph.

   _____

9. **GO DEEPER** Look at the question you wrote.
   Answer your question.

   _____

Problem Solving • Applications Real World   WRITE Math

Matt made this picture graph to show the paint colors his friends like best.

Favorite Paint Color					
blue	○	○	○	○	○
red	○	○	○		
green	○	○			

Each ○ stands for 1 child.

10. How many children chose a paint color?

_____ children

11. How many fewer children chose 🔴 than 🔵?

_____ fewer children

Personal Math Trainer

12. THINK SMARTER ✛ Complete the picture graph to show the number of flowers.

Flowers in the Vase					
🌷					
🌷					

Each ○ stands for 1 flower.

TAKE HOME ACTIVITY • Ask your child to make a picture graph showing how many glasses of water each family member drinks in a day. Discuss how to find who drinks the most water.

Make Picture Graphs

Learning Objective You will make a picture graph to answer a question.

Which dinosaur do the most children like best? Ask 10 friends.
Draw 1 circle for each child's answer.

Our Favorite Dinosaur										
🦖 Tyrannosaurus										
🦕 Triceratops										
🦕 Apatosaurus										

Each ○ stands for 1 child.

Use the picture graph to answer the question.

1. How many children chose 🦖 ?

   _____ children

2. Which dinosaur did the most children choose? Circle.

   🦖   🦕   🦕

Problem Solving Real World

3. Write your own question about the graph.

   _____

   _____

   _____

4. WRITE Math Write a question that can be answered by making a picture graph.

   _____

   _____

   _____

Lesson Check

Use the picture graph to answer the question.

Which Hand Do You Use to Eat?								
left	○	○	○					
right	○	○	○	○	○	○	○	○

Each ○ stands for 1 child.

1. How many children use their right hand?
   Write the answer.

   _____ children

2. How many more children use their right
   hand than their left? Write a number
   sentence to solve the problem.

   _____ more children

   _____ ○ _____ ○ _____

Spiral Review

3. Write the sum.

   $$6 + 3 = \underline{\hphantom{00}}$$

4. Write the difference. Write how many tens.

   $$60 - 20 = \underline{\hphantom{00}}$$

   _____ tens

© Houghton Mifflin Harcourt Publishing Company

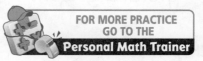

FOR MORE PRACTICE
GO TO THE
Personal Math Trainer

Name _____

Read Bar Graphs

Essential Question How can you read a bar graph to find the number that a bar shows?

Learning Objective You will learn to read, compare, and interpret information shown in a bar graph.

 Listen Real World Hands On

Write a question about the graph.
Use ⬤ to help solve the problem.

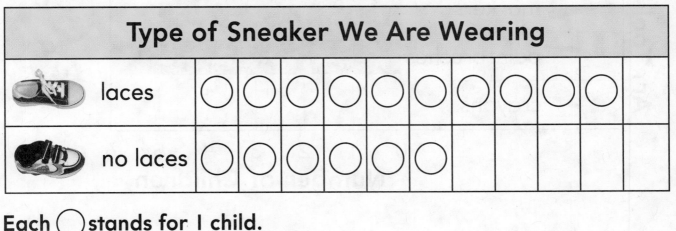

Type of Sneaker We Are Wearing											
👟 laces	◯	◯	◯	◯	◯	◯	◯	◯	◯	◯	
👟 no laces	◯	◯	◯	◯	◯	◯					

Each ◯ stands for 1 child.

_____

_____

_____

_____

_____

_____

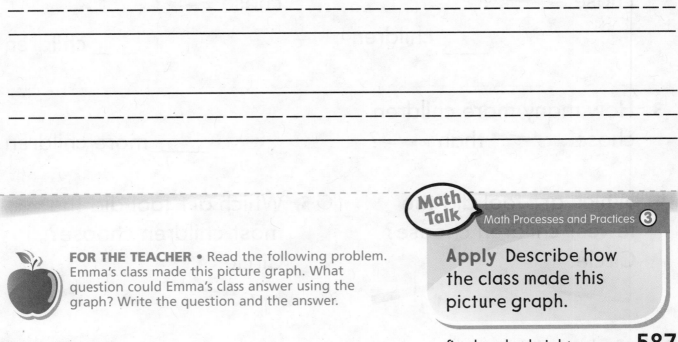

FOR THE TEACHER • Read the following problem. Emma's class made this picture graph. What question could Emma's class answer using the graph? Write the question and the answer.

Math Talk Math Processes and Practices ③

Apply Describe how the class made this picture graph.

Model and Draw

In a **bar graph,** each bar shows information. You can compare the lengths of the bars.

What title describes this graph?

> Touch the end of a bar. Look down to see the number of children.

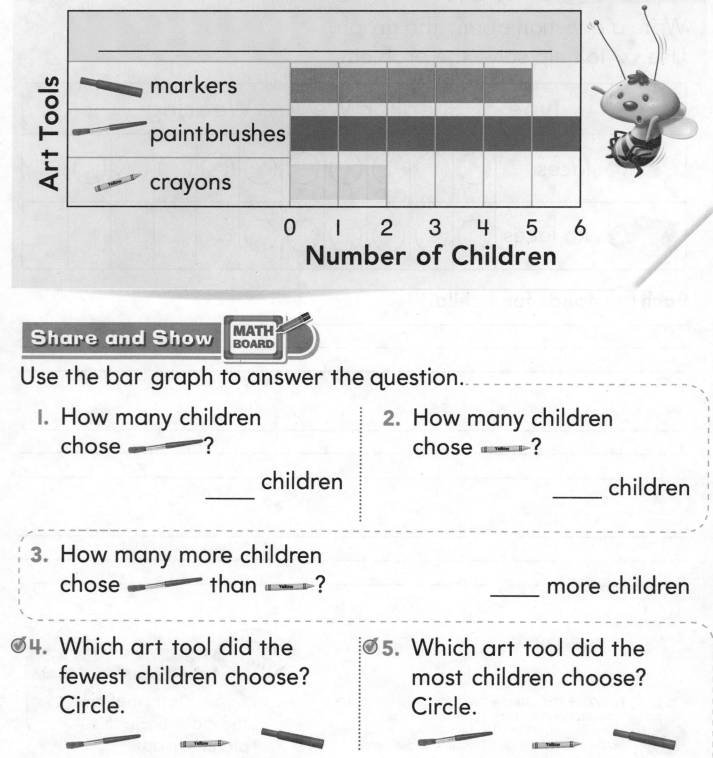

Art Tools

markers

paintbrushes

crayons

0 1 2 3 4 5 6
Number of Children

Share and Show   MATH BOARD

Use the bar graph to answer the question.

1. How many children chose ____?

   _____ children

2. How many children chose ____?

   _____ children

3. How many more children chose ____ than ____?

   _____ more children

4. Which art tool did the fewest children choose? Circle.

5. Which art tool did the most children choose? Circle.

© Houghton Mifflin Harcourt Publishing Company

Name _____

Math Processes and Practices ④ **Use Graphs** Use the bar graph to answer the question.

6. How many children chose 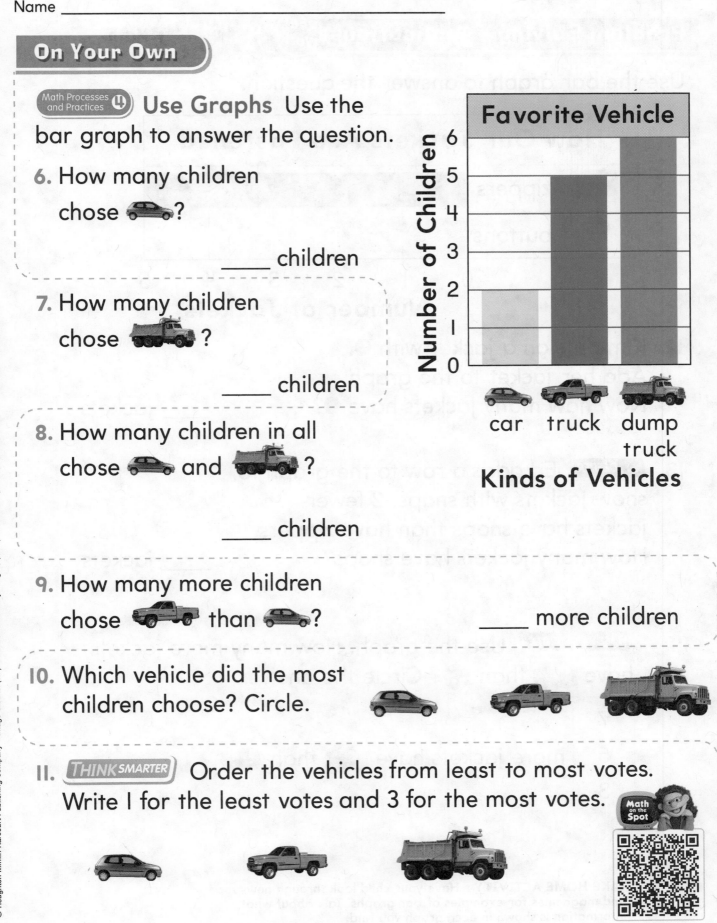?

_____ children

7. How many children chose 🚛 ?

_____ children

8. How many children in all chose 🚗 and 🚛 ?

_____ children

9. How many more children chose 🛻 than 🚗?

_____ more children

10. Which vehicle did the most children choose? Circle.

11. *THINK SMARTER* Order the vehicles from least to most votes. Write 1 for the least votes and 3 for the most votes.

_____   _____   _____

© Houghton Mifflin Harcourt Publishing Company • Image Credits: (car) ©Dave Rudkin/Getty Images; (truck) ©Stuart Kelly/Alamy; (yellow truck) ©Darryl Brooks/Alamy

Problem Solving • Applications WRITE Math

Use the bar graph to answer the question.

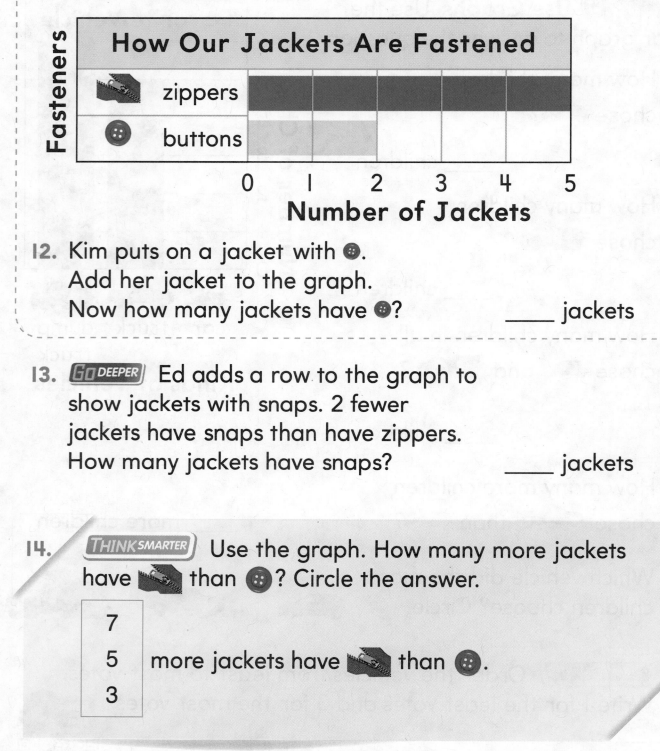

12. Kim puts on a jacket with ⚫.
Add her jacket to the graph.
Now how many jackets have ⚫? _____ jackets

13. GO DEEPER Ed adds a row to the graph to
show jackets with snaps. 2 fewer
jackets have snaps than have zippers.
How many jackets have snaps? _____ jackets

14. THINK SMARTER Use the graph. How many more jackets
have 🤐 than ⚫? Circle the answer.

7

5   more jackets have 🤐 than ⚫.

3

 TAKE HOME ACTIVITY • Have your child look through newspapers
and magazines for examples of bar graphs. Talk about what
information is shown in each graph you find.

Read Bar Graphs

Learning Objective You will learn to read, compare, and interpret information shown in a bar graph.

Use the bar graph to answer the question.

1. How many children chose ◯?

   _____ children

2. How many more children chose 🥞 than ◯?

   _____ more children

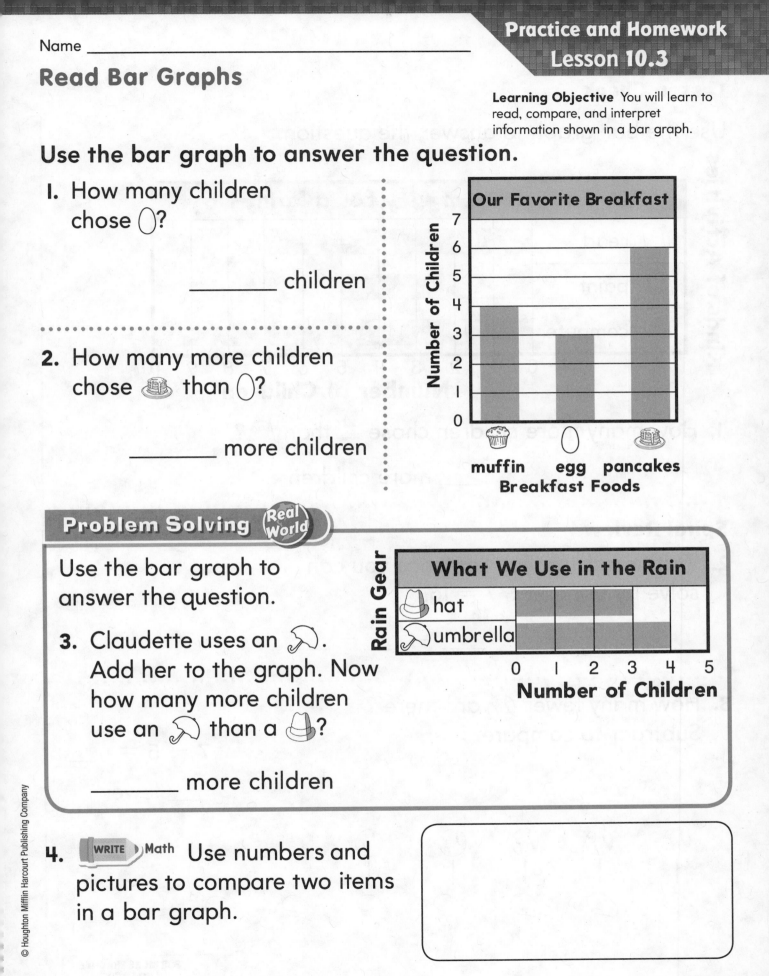

Our Favorite Breakfast

Number of Children

muffin   egg   pancakes
Breakfast Foods

Problem Solving Real World

Use the bar graph to answer the question.

3. Claudette uses an ☂. Add her to the graph. Now how many more children use an ☂ than a 🎩?

   _____ more children

What We Use in the Rain

Rain Gear

🎩 hat
☂ umbrella

0   1   2   3   4   5
Number of Children

4. WRITE Math Use numbers and pictures to compare two items in a bar graph.

Lesson Check

Use the bar graph to answer the question.

Kinds of Activities

Our Favorite Activity for a Rainy Day

read

paint

computer

0 1 2 3 4 5 6 7 8 9 10

Number of Children

1. How many more children chose [computer] than [paint]?

   _____ more children

Spiral Review

2. Write a subtraction sentence you can solve by using $9 + 7 = 16$.

   _____ − _____ = _____

3. How many fewer [baseball] are there?
   Subtract to compare.

   $7 - 5 =$ _____

   _____ fewer

FOR MORE PRACTICE
GO TO THE
Personal Math Trainer

Name _____

Make Bar Graphs

Essential Question How does a bar graph help you compare information?

Learning Objective You will make a bar graph, compare, and interpret information in the bar graph.

Listen and Draw Real World Hands On

Use ▣ to model the problem.
Color 1 box for each food item
to complete the graph.

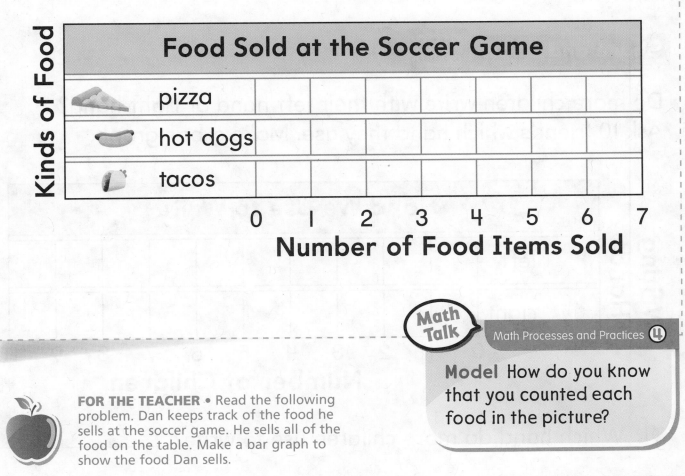

Kinds of Food	Food Sold at the Soccer Game							
pizza								
hot dogs								
tacos								
	0	1	2	3	4	5	6	7

Number of Food Items Sold

Math Talk

Math Processes and Practices ④

Model How do you know that you counted each food in the picture?

© Houghton Mifflin Harcourt Publishing Company

FOR THE TEACHER • Read the following problem. Dan keeps track of the food he sells at the soccer game. He sells all of the food on the table. Make a bar graph to show the food Dan sells.

Chapter 10

five hundred ninety-three **593**

Model and Draw

Are there more or 🌻 in the garden?
Make a bar graph to find out.
Shade 1 box for each flower in the picture.

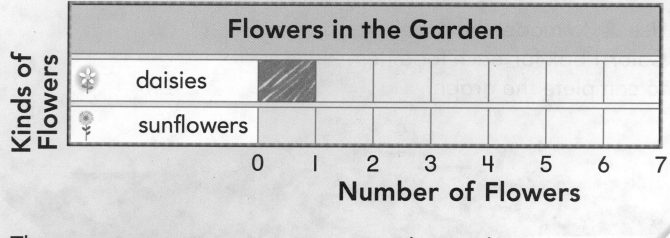

Flowers in the Garden

Kinds of Flowers		0	1	2	3	4	5	6	7
🌼	daisies								
🌻	sunflowers								

Number of Flowers

There are more _____ in the garden.

Share and Show MATH BOARD

Do more children write with their left hand or right hand?
Ask 10 friends which hand they use. Make a bar graph.

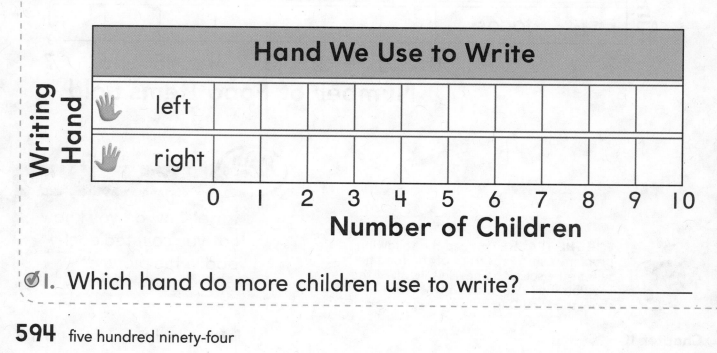

Hand We Use to Write

Writing Hand		0	1	2	3	4	5	6	7	8	9	10
🖐	left											
🖐	right											

Number of Children

✓1. Which hand do more children use to write? _____

Name _____

Math Processes and Practices 8 **Draw Conclusions**

Do children like 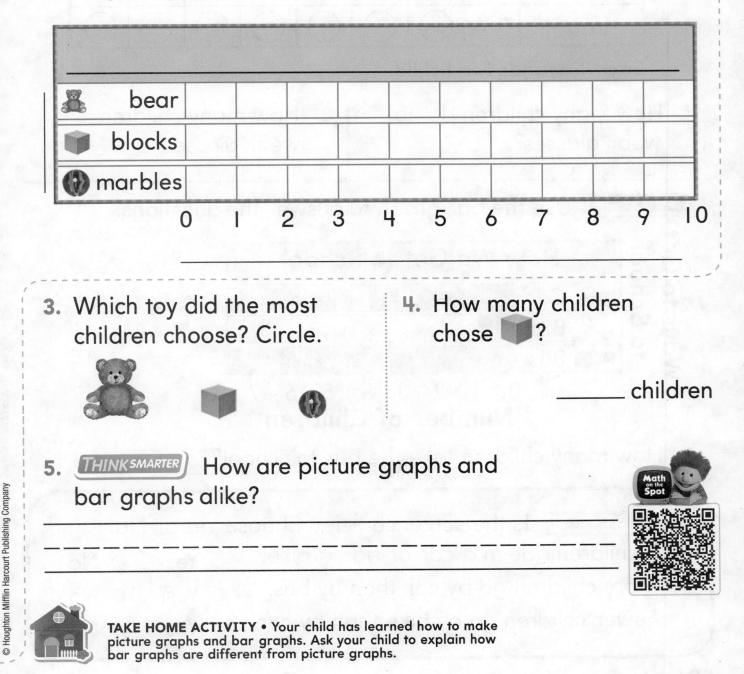, , or best?
Ask 10 friends which toy they like best.

2. Make a bar graph. Write a title and labels
   for your graph.

bear												
blocks												
marbles												
	0	1	2	3	4	5	6	7	8	9	10	

3. Which toy did the most
   children choose? Circle.

4. How many children
   chose ?

   _____ children

5. THINK SMARTER How are picture graphs and
   bar graphs alike?

_____

_____

_____

Math on the Spot

🏠 **TAKE HOME ACTIVITY** • Your child has learned how to make
picture graphs and bar graphs. Ask your child to explain how
bar graphs are different from picture graphs.

© Houghton Mifflin Harcourt Publishing Company

Name _____

✓ Mid-Chapter Checkpoint

Concepts and Skills

Use the picture graph to answer the questions.

Do you wear glasses?								
yes	◯	◯	◯					
no	◯	◯	◯	◯	◯	◯	◯	◯

Each ◯ stands for 1 child.

1. How many children do not wear glasses? _____

2. How many children wear glasses? _____

THINK SMARTER Use the bar graph to answer the questions.

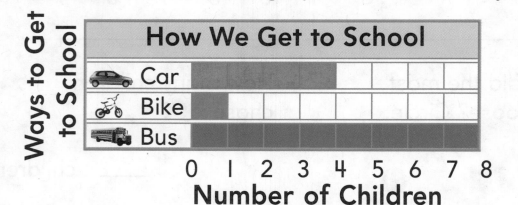

How We Get to School

Ways to Get to School

Car
Bike
Bus

0 1 2 3 4 5 6 7 8
Number of Children

3. How many children take the bus to school? _____

4. THINK SMARTER Is the sentence true? Choose Yes or No.

5 children ride in a car or ride a bike. ◯ Yes ◯ No

More children go by car than by bus. ◯ Yes ◯ No

Fewer children go by bike than by car. ◯ Yes ◯ No

Make Bar Graphs

Learning Objective You will make a bar graph, compare, and interpret information in the bar graph.

Which is your favorite meal?

1. Ask 10 friends which meal they like best. Make a bar graph.

2. How many children chose breakfast?

_____ children

3. Which meal was chosen by the most children?

_____

Problem Solving Real World

4. What if 10 children chose breakfast? How many children could choose lunch or dinner?

_____ children

5. ✏️ WRITE ▸ Math Use words and pictures to show how to make a bar graph about favorite storybooks.

Lesson Check

Use the bar graph to answer the question.

1. How many more children chose ✈ than 🚂?

   _____ more children

Spiral Review

2. Write the number sentence that
   completes the related facts.

   $$7 + 8 = 15 \qquad 15 - 8 = 7$$
   $$8 + 7 = 15$$

   $\boxed{} - \boxed{} = \boxed{}$

3. What is the sum? Use tens
   and ones to add.

   $$\begin{array}{r} 43 \\ +\ 21 \\ \hline \end{array}$$

   4 tens + 3 ones

   2 tens + 1 one

   _____ tens + _____ ones

   _____ + _____ = _____

FOR MORE PRACTICE
GO TO THE
Personal Math Trainer

Name _____

Read Tally Charts

Essential Question How do you count the tallies on a tally chart?

Learning Objective You will learn to read, count tallies, and compare information on a tally chart.

Listen and Draw *Real World* *Hands On*

Use ⬤ to solve the problem.
Draw to show your work.
Write how many.

_____ _____

Math Talk Math Processes and Practices ②

Reasoning How did you sort the counters?

FOR THE TEACHER • Read the following problem. Jane is sorting her crayons. Draw to show how she can sort the crayons into two groups.

Chapter 10

Model and Draw

Do more children like chicken or pizza better?

Food We Like		Total
chicken	III	3
pizza	HHH III	

You can use a **tally chart** to collect information.

Each I is a **tally mark.**
It stands for I child.
HHH stands for 5 children.
More children like __pizza__.

Share and Show MATH BOARD

Complete the tally chart.

Boys and Girls in Our Class		Total
boys	HHH IIII	
girls	HHH I	

Use the tally chart to answer each question.

1. How many girls are in the class? _____ girls

2. How many boys are in the class? _____ boys

3. How many children are in the class in all? _____ children

4. Are there more boys or girls in the class? _____

Name _____

Complete the tally chart.

Our Favorite Sport		Total
🏐 t-ball	IIII	
⚽ soccer	IIII II	
🥏 swimming	III	

Use the tally chart to answer the question.

5. How many children chose ⚽? _____ children

6. How many more children chose 🏐 than 🥏? _____ more children

7. Which sport did the most children choose? Circle.

8. **THINK SMARTER** Write your own question about the tally chart.

_____

_____

_____

9. **GO DEEPER** Sam asked some other children which sport they like. They all chose 🥏. Now the most children chose 🥏. How many children did Sam ask? _____ children

Problem Solving • Applications (Real World)   WRITE Math

Our Favorite Season		Total
❄ winter	||||	
☀ summer	卌 卌	
🍁 fall	||||	

Remember to write the total.

Math Processes and Practices ② Connect Symbols and Words

Complete each sentence about the tally chart.
Write **greater than, less than,** or **equal to.**

10. The number of tallies for ☀ is _____
    the number of tallies for ❄.

11. The number of tallies for ❄ is _____
    the number of tallies for 🍁.

12. The number of tallies for 🍁 is _____
    the number of tallies for ☀.

13. **GO DEEPER** The number of tallies for ☀ is _____
    the number of tallies for both ❄ and 🍁.

14. **THINK SMARTER** Look at the chart. How many tallies in all?

   ○ 卌 \|\|\| ○ 卌 卌 \|\|\|\|

   ○ 卌 卌   ○ 卌 卌 卌 \|\|\|

TAKE HOME ACTIVITY • Together with your child, make a tally chart showing how many times you all say the word "eat" during a meal. Then have your child write the number.

Name _____

Read Tally Charts

Learning Objective You will learn to read, count tallies, and compare information on a tally chart.

Complete the tally chart.

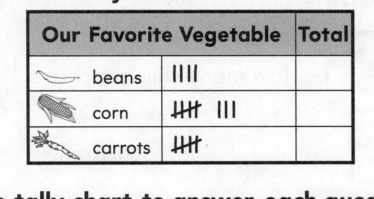

Our Favorite Vegetable		Total
beans	IIII	
corn	HHH III	
carrots	HHH	

Use the tally chart to answer each question.

1. How many children chose ?   ____ children

2. How many more children chose 🌽 than 🥕 ?   ____ more children

Problem Solving Real World

Complete each sentence about the tally chart.
Write **greater than**, **less than**, or **equal to**.

3. The number of children who chose 🫛 is
_____ the number who chose 🥕 .

4. The number of children who chose 🌽 is
_____ the number who chose 🫛 .

5. WRITE Math Use words, numbers, or pictures to show how to group and count tally marks for the number 8.

Lesson Check

Use the tally chart to answer each question.

Our Favorite Pet	
🐕 dog	ⵌ II
🐈 cat	ⵌ
🐟 fish	II

1. How many children chose 🐈 ?

   _____ children

2. How many more children chose 🐕 than 🐟 ?

   _____ more children

Spiral Review

3. Complete the number sentence.

   There are 8 apples.
   6 apples are red.
   The rest are green.
   How many apples are green?

   $\underline{\quad 8 \quad} \ominus \underline{\quad 6 \quad} \ominus \underline{\qquad}$

4. Write the sum.

   $34 + 40 = \underline{\qquad}$

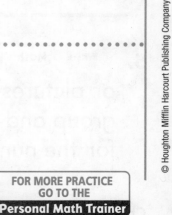

FOR MORE PRACTICE
GO TO THE
Personal Math Trainer

Name _____

Make Tally Charts

Essential Question Why is a tally chart a good way to show information that you have collected?

Learning Objective You will make a tally chart and understand the information you collected.

Listen

Complete the tally chart.

Our Favorite Game		Total
card game	⊦⊦⊦⊦	
puzzle	|||	
board game	⊦⊦⊦⊦ ⊦⊦⊦⊦	

Use the tally chart to answer the question.

Which game did the most children choose? Circle.

Which game did the fewest children choose?
Circle.

Math Talk Math Processes and Practices ①

Analyze How do you know which game is the favorite?

 FOR THE TEACHER • Read the following problem. Ava asks the children in her class which of three games they like the best. She makes a tally mark to show each child's answer. Which game did the most children choose? Which did the fewest children choose?

Chapter 10

Model and Draw

How can you make a tally chart to show the boats at the lake?

Decide if each boat has a sail.

Boats at the Lake		Total
boats with sails	‖	
boats without sails		

Share and Show MATH BOARD

Use the picture to complete the tally chart. Then answer each question.

Fish in the Tank		Total
zebra fish		
angel fish		

1. How many are in the tank?

____ fish

2. How many more than are there?

____ more

3. How many and are in the tank?

____ fish

On Your Own

Which of these snacks do most children like the best?
Ask 10 friends. Make 1 tally mark for each child's answer.

Our Favorite Snack		Total
pretzel		
🍎 apple		
🥛 yogurt		

Use the tally chart to answer each question.

4. How many children chose 🥨?

   _____ children

5. How many children chose 🥛 ?

   _____ children

6. Which snack do most children like best? Circle.

7. **THINK SMARTER** What if 6 children out of the 10 chose 🥨? Which snack would be the favorite? Circle it.

8. **Explain** Write your own question about the tally chart.

_____

_____

© Houghton Mifflin Harcourt Publishing Company • Image Credits: (car) ©FEV/Shutterstock; (pretzel) ©PhotoDisc/Getty Images; (apple) ©Artville/Getty Images

Problem Solving • Applications WRITE Math

Math Processes and Practices ❶ Analyze Relationships Jenna asked 10 friends to choose their favorite subject. She will ask 10 more children.

Our Favorite School Subject		Total
math	ЖЖ I	
reading	II	
science	II	

9. Predict. Which subject will children most likely choose? _____

10. Predict. Which subject will children least likely choose? _____

11. **THINK SMARTER** How can you prove if your prediction is good? Try it.

_____

12. **THINK SMARTER** Complete the tally chart to show the number of votes.

Fruit We Like		Total
🍎 apple	IIII	4
🍌 banana		5
🍇 grapes		2

 TAKE HOME ACTIVITY • With your child, survey friends and family to find out their favorite food. Draw tally marks to record the results and then prepare the food.

608 six hundred eight

Make Tally Charts

Learning Objective You will make a tally chart and understand the information you collected.

Which color do most children like best? Ask 10 friends. Make 1 tally mark for each child's answer.

Favorite Color		Total
red		
blue		

1. How many children chose red?

_____ **children**

2. How many children chose blue?

_____ **children**

Problem Solving Real World

Jason asked 10 friends to choose their favorite game. He will ask 10 more children.

Our Favorite Game	
tag	I
kickball	⦀⦀ II
hopscotch	II

3. Predict. Which game will children most likely choose?

_____

4. Predict. Which game will children least likely choose?

_____

5. [WRITE] Math Write a question that can be answered by making a tally chart.

_____
_____

Lesson Check

1. Which insect did the most children choose?
   Circle the answer.

Our Favorite Insect		Total
ladybug	III	3
bee	I	I
butterfly	Ⅲ II	7

Spiral Review

2. Circle the number that is greater than 54.
   Write the number.

   45   50   54   57

   _____ is greater than 54.

   _____ > 54

3. Use the model. Write the number
   three different ways.

   _____ ten _____ ones

   _____ + _____

   _____

FOR MORE PRACTICE
GO TO THE
Personal Math Trainer

Name _____

Problem Solving • Represent Data

Essential Question How can showing information in a graph help you solve problems?

Learning Objective You will use the strategy *make a graph* to solve real-world problems by making bar graphs and a tally chart.

Brad sees many animals at the park. How can you find how many animals Brad sees?

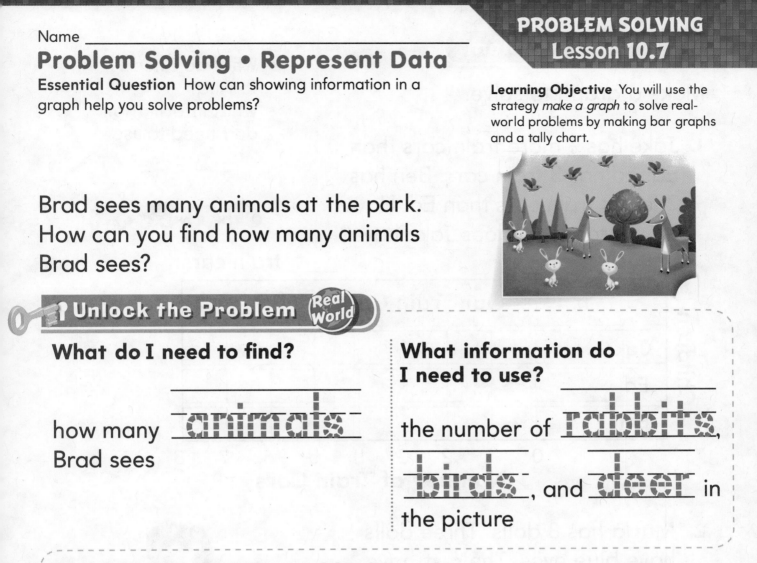

🔑 Unlock the Problem Real World

What do I need to find?

how many ⎯⎯⎯**animals**⎯⎯⎯ Brad sees

What information do I need to use?

the number of **rabbits**, **birds**, and **deer** in the picture

Show how to solve the problem.

Animals Brad Sees							
🐰 rabbit							
🐦 bird							
🦌 deer							

Animals

0   1   2   3   4   5   6   7
Number of Animals

____ + ____ + ____ = ____ animals

HOME CONNECTION • Your child learned how to represent data from a picture in a bar graph. Have your child explain why it is easier to use data in a bar graph than in a picture.

Chapter 10

Try Another Problem

Make a graph to solve.

- What do I need to find?
- What information do I need to use?

1. Jake has 4 more train cars than Ed. Ed has 3 train cars. Ben has 2 fewer train cars than Ed. How many train cars does Jake have?

_____ train cars

Our Train Cars

Children									
Jake									
Ed									
Ben									

0 1 2 3 4 5 6 7 8
Number of Train Cars

2. Marla has 8 dolls. Three dolls have blue eyes. The rest have brown. How many dolls have brown eyes?

_____ dolls

Dolls Marla Has

Eye Color								
blue eyes								
brown eyes								

0 1 2 3 4 5 6 7 8
Number of Dolls

Math Talk

Math Processes and Practices ⑤

Use Tools Describe how the bar graph helps you solve Exercise 2.

© Houghton Mifflin Harcourt Publishing Company • Image Credits: (tr) ©Denkou Images/Alamy

Share and Show

Math Processes and Practices **6** **Make Connections** Find out about the eye color of your classmates.

3. Write a question you can ask your friends.

_____

☑**4.** Ask 10 friends your question. Make a tally chart.

		Total

5. THINK SMARTER Use the tally chart to make a bar graph.

0   1   2   3   4   5   6   7   8

6. Explain What did you learn from the graph?

_____

On Your Own **WRITE** Math

What is your favorite fruit? Nina asked 20 children this question. Then she made a bar graph. But Nina spilled paint on the graph.

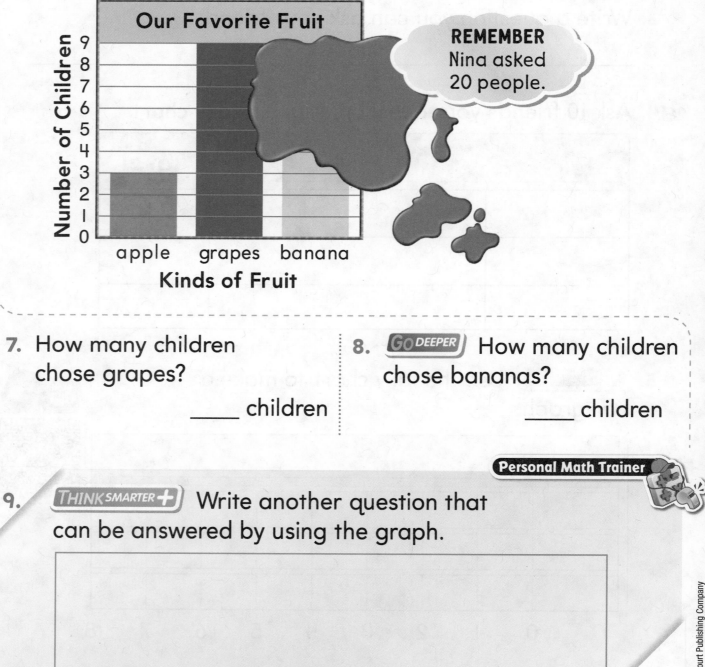

REMEMBER
Nina asked 20 people.

7. How many children chose grapes?

_____ children

8. GO DEEPER How many children chose bananas?

_____ children

Personal Math Trainer

9. THINK SMARTER+ Write another question that can be answered by using the graph.

TAKE HOME ACTIVITY • Work with your child to make a tally chart and a bar graph showing the favorite color of 10 family members or friends. Talk about the results.

Name _____

Problem Solving • Represent Data

Learning Objective You will use the strategy *make a graph* to solve real-world problems by making bar graphs and a tally chart.

Bella made a tally chart to show the favorite sport of 10 friends.

Our Favorite Sport	
Soccer	ⅢⅠ Ⅰ
Basketball	ⅠⅠⅠ
Baseball	Ⅰ

Use the tally chart to make a bar graph.

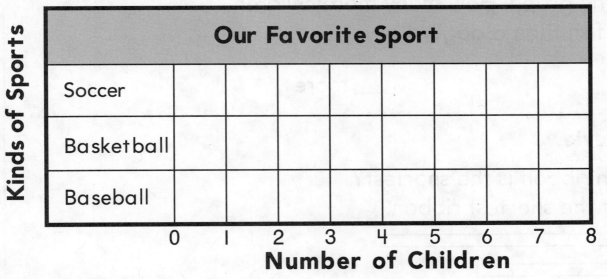

Kinds of Sports

Our Favorite Sport

Soccer

Basketball

Baseball

0   1   2   3   4   5   6   7   8
Number of Children

Use the graph to solve.

1. How many friends chose soccer?

   _____ friends

2. How many friends chose soccer or basketball?

   _____ friends

3. **WRITE Math** Write the names of 3 types of animals. Count the letters in each name. Make a bar graph showing the letter for each animal.

Chapter 10

Lesson Check

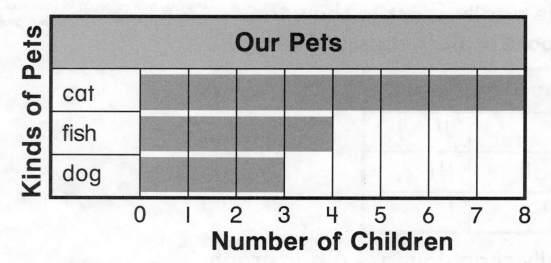

Our Pets

Kinds of Pets

cat

fish

dog

Number of Children

0 1 2 3 4 5 6 7 8

1. Use the graph. How many more children have fish than a dog?

_____ more

Spiral Review

2. Which ribbon is the shortest?
Color the shortest ribbon.

3. Look at the hour hand.
Write the time.

_____

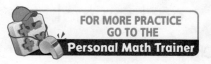

FOR MORE PRACTICE
GO TO THE
Personal Math Trainer

✓ Chapter 10 Review/Test

Use the picture graph to answer the questions.

Color We Like						
🖍 RED red	옷	옷	옷	옷	옷	
🖍 BLUE blue	옷	옷	옷	옷	옷	옷

Each 옷 stands for 1 child.

1. How many children chose 🖍 RED ?

  ☐

2. Is the sentence true? Choose Yes or No.

   More children like blue than red. ○ Yes   ○ No

   5 children like red. ○ Yes   ○ No

   2 more children like blue than red. ○ Yes   ○ No

3. 1 more child gets a 🖍 BLUE . Draw what the blue row looks like now.

| 🖍 BLUE blue | 옷 | 옷 | 옷 | 옷 | 옷 | 옷 | |

 Assessment Options
Chapter Test

Use the bar graph to answer the questions.

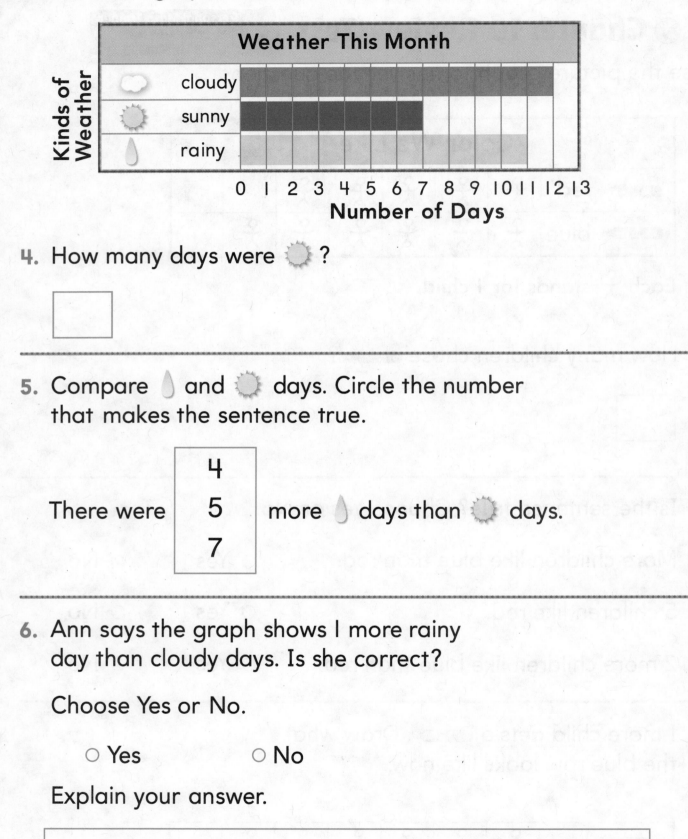

4. How many days were ☀ ?

[ ]

---

5. Compare 💧 and ☀ days. Circle the number
that makes the sentence true.

There were
| 4 |
| 5 |
| 7 |
more 💧 days than ☀ days.

---

6. Ann says the graph shows 1 more rainy
day than cloudy days. Is she correct?

Choose Yes or No.

○ Yes   ○ No

Explain your answer.

[   ]

Name _____

Use the tally chart to answer the questions.

Sam's Cars and Trucks		Total
cars		8
trucks	IIII I	6

7. How many [truck image] does Sam have?

[ ]

8. Draw tally marks for the number of cars that the chart shows.

[ ]

9. Circle the words that make the sentence true.

The number of tally marks for [truck image] is

| greater than |
| less than |
| equal to |

the number of tally marks for [car image] .

10. **THINK SMARTER +** Chung visits the zoo.
He sees 2 🦁. He sees 4 more 🐘 than 🦁.
He sees 3 fewer 🐒 than 🐘. Make a bar graph.

Use the bar graph to answer the question.

11. **GO DEEPER** How many more 🐘 does Chung see than 🦁 and 🐒 altogether?

_____ more 🐘

12. Write another question that can be answered by the bar graph.

Big Idea Geometry

On the Move

written by Jennifer Earnshaw

BIG IDEA Identify, describe, and combine two- and three-dimensional shapes. Develop a conceptual understanding of equal and unequal parts.

The train car waits for the engine.

Name some shapes you see.

Social Studies

What will this train bring?

The big truck travels up the road.

Name some shapes you see.

Social Studies

What will this truck bring?

The ship loads at the dock.

Name some shapes you see.

Social Studies

624

What will this ship bring?

These trucks drive across town.

Name some shapes you see.

Social Studies

What will these trucks bring?

The airplane arrives at the airport.

Name some shapes you see.

Social Studies

What will this airplane bring?

Write About the Story

Think of another kind of truck that takes goods from one place to another. Draw a picture. Use circles, squares, triangles, or rectangles in your drawing.

Vocabulary Review

circle   triangle

square   rectangle

truck

WRITE Math Write about your drawing.

_____

_____

_____

_____

Figure It Out

1. Draw an airplane.
Use some triangles and
circles in your drawing.

2. Draw a train.
Use some rectangles and
circles in your drawing.

Choose two shapes to use to draw
a ship. Draw the ship.

Chapter

11

Three-Dimensional Geometry

Curious About Math with

Curious George

What three-dimensional
shapes do you see in
the sand castle?

✓ **Show What You Know**

Personal Math Trainer
Online Assessment
and Intervention

Alike and Different

Circle the objects that are alike.

1.

2.

Identify Three-Dimensional Shapes

Color the ⬤ blue. Color the ▮ red.
Color the ▬ yellow.

3.

4.

5.

Sort by Size

Mark an X on the object that does not belong.

6.

This page checks understanding of important skills needed
for success in Chapter 11.

Name _____

Vocabulary Builder

Visualize It

Write review words to name the shapes.

sphere

three-dimensional shapes

_____

_____

_____

Understand Vocabulary

Look at the three-dimensional shapes.
Color the sphere . Color the cube .
Color the cylinder 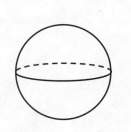.

1.

2.

3.

Game Shape Match Bingo

Materials • 9 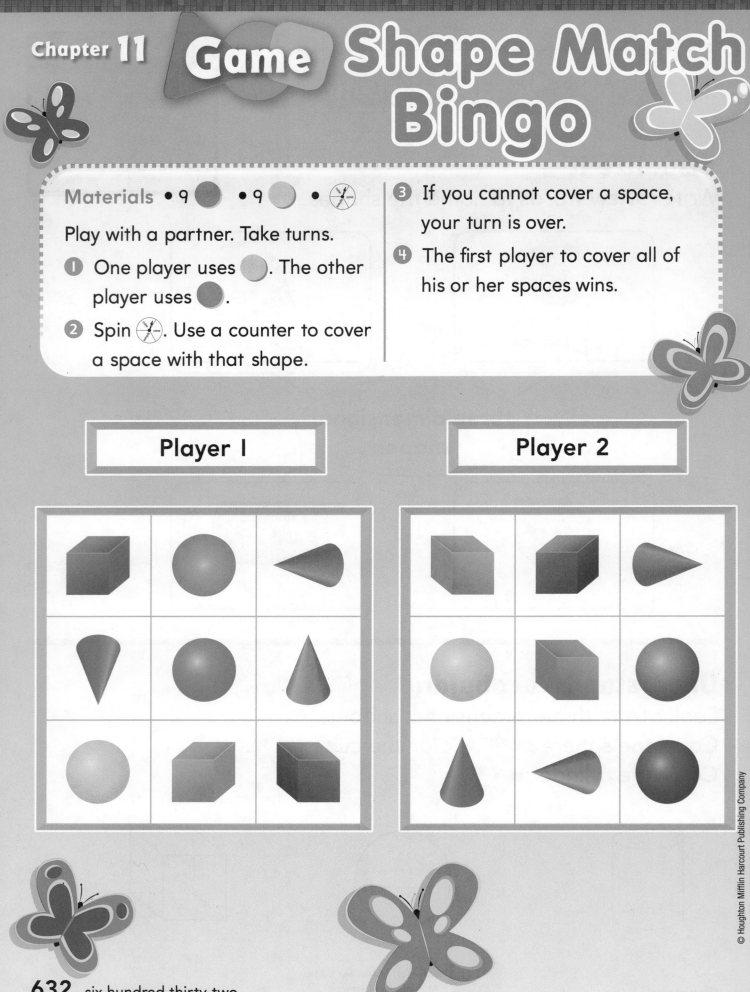 • 9 ◯ • 🌀

Play with a partner. Take turns.

1. One player uses ◯. The other player uses ●.

2. Spin 🌀. Use a counter to cover a space with that shape.

3. If you cannot cover a space, your turn is over.

4. The first player to cover all of his or her spaces wins.

Player 1

Player 2

bar graph

gráfica de barras

4

cone

cono

7

cube

cubo

10

curved surface

superficie curva

11

cylinder

cilindro

12

flat surface

superficie plana

20

rectangular prism

prisma rectangular

46

sphere

esfera

50

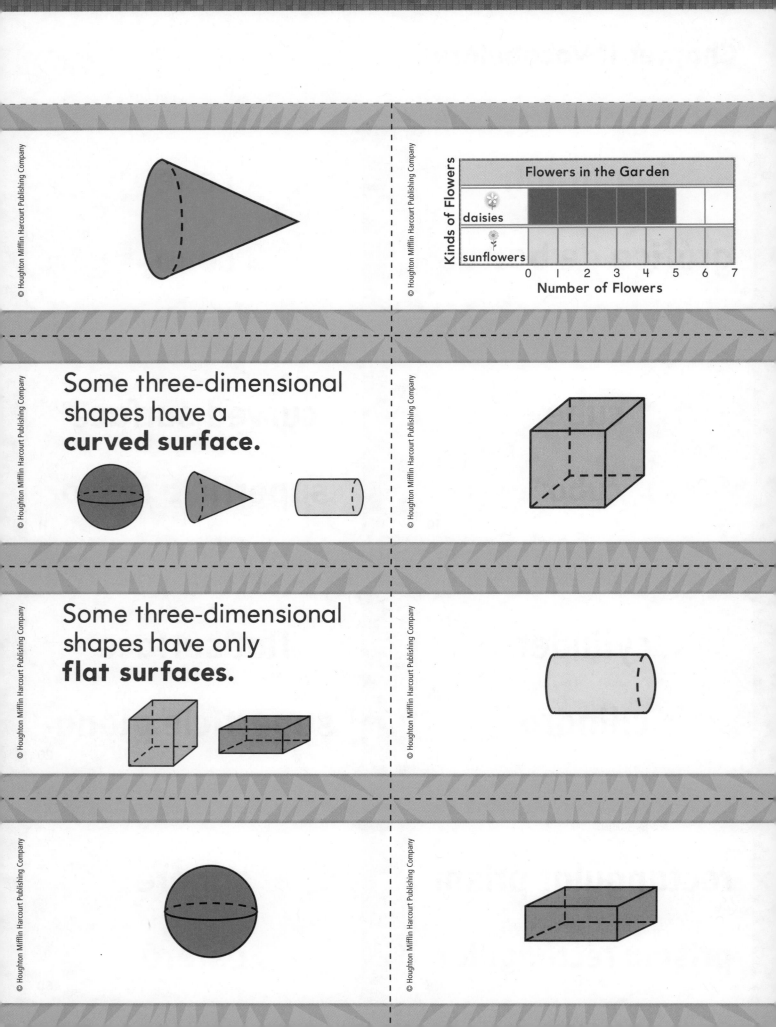

Flowers in the Garden

Kinds of Flowers									
🌼 daisies									
🌻 sunflowers									

Number of Flowers: 0 1 2 3 4 5 6 7

Some three-dimensional shapes have a **curved surface.**

Some three-dimensional shapes have only **flat surfaces.**

Game

Going on a Train Trip

For 2 players

Materials

- 1
- 1
- 1
- Clue Cards

Word Box

bar graph
cone
cube
curved
  surface
cylinder
flat surface
rectangular
  prism
sphere

How to Play

1. Choose a and put it on START.
2. Toss the to take a turn. Move your that many spaces.
3. If you land on these spaces:
   Red Space Take a Clue Card. Answer the question. If you are correct, keep the Clue Card and move ahead 1. If you are not correct, return the Clue Card to the bottom of the pile.
   Blue Space Follow the directions on the space.
4. Collect 5 Clue Cards. Move around the track as many times as you need to. Then, follow the closest center path to reach FINISH.
5. The first player to reach FINISH wins.

TAKE A
CLUE CARD

Ride a high-
speed train.
Move ahead 1.

FINISH

TAKE A
CLUE CARD

You miss your train.
Go back 1.

Your train is late.
Go back 1.

TAKE A
CLUE CARD

New tracks
are put in!
Move ahead 1.

FINISH

TAKE A
CLUE CARD

START ▶

The Write Way

Reflect

Choose one idea. Draw and write about it.

- Tell about **two** of these words.

    cone   cube   cylinder   sphere

- Compare a curved surface to a flat surface.
  Tell how they are alike and how they are different.

Name _____

Three-Dimensional Shapes

Essential Question How can you identify and describe three-dimensional shapes?

Listen and Draw

Draw to sort the three-dimensional shapes.

Math Talk Math Processes and Practices ⑧

Generalize Explain how you sorted the shapes.

FOR THE TEACHER • Have children sort the three-dimensional shapes into two groups. Have them draw around each group to show how they sorted.

Chapter 11

These are three-dimensional shapes.

Why is a cube a special kind of rectangular prism?

sphere | cone | cylinder | rectangular prism | cube

Share and Show MATH BOARD

Use three-dimensional shapes.
Sort the shapes into three groups.
Name and draw the shapes.

1. only flat surfaces

2. only a curved surface

✓ 3. both flat and curved surfaces

Name _____

On Your Own

© Houghton Mifflin Harcourt Publishing Company • Image Credits: (tl) ©Corbis; (bl) ©PhotoDisc/Getty Images (tc) ©Comstock/Getty Images (br) ©Corbis

Math Processes and Practices ④ **Use Models** Use three-dimensional shapes. Write the number of flat surfaces for each shape.

4. A rectangular prism has ___6___ flat surfaces.

5. A cube has _____ flat surfaces.

6. A cylinder has _____ flat surfaces.

7. A sphere has _____ flat surfaces.

Exercises 4–7 can help you write the shape names.

GO DEEPER Write to name each shape.

8. sphere

9. _____

10. _____

11. _____

12. _____

Problem Solving • Applications Real World   WRITE Math

Circle the objects that match the clues.

13. Kelly drew objects that have both flat and curved surfaces.

14. THINK SMARTER Sandy drew some rectangular prisms.

15. THINK SMARTER + Match each shape to the group where it belongs.

| Both flat and curved surfaces | Only flat surfaces | Only a curved surface |

🏠 **TAKE HOME ACTIVITY** • Ask your child to name real objects shaped like a sphere, a rectangular prism, and a cylinder.

636 six hundred thirty-six

Name _____

Three-Dimensional Shapes

**Use three-dimensional shapes.
Write the number of flat surfaces
for each shape.**

1. A cylinder has __ flat surfaces.

2. A rectangular prism has __ flat surfaces.

3. A cone has __ flat surface.

4. A cube has __ flat surfaces.

Problem Solving *Real World*

5. Circle the object that matches the clue.
   Mike finds an object that has only a curved surface.

6. WRITE Math Use pictures or words to describe a cone.

Lesson Check

1. Circle the shape that has both flat and curved surfaces.

2. Circle the shape that has only a curved surface.

Spiral Review

3. Count forward. Write the number that is missing.

109, 110, 111, ____, 113

4. What is the sum of 2 and 3? Write the number sentence.

____ ◯ ____ = ____

638 six hundred thirty-eight

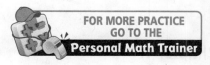

FOR MORE PRACTICE GO TO THE Personal Math Trainer

Name _____

Combine Three-Dimensional Shapes

Essential Question How can you combine three-dimensional shapes to make new shapes?

Learning Objective You will combine three-dimensional shapes to make new shapes.

Listen and Draw Real World

Trace to draw the new shape.
Write to name the new shape.

Mandy

Carl

_____

_ _ _ _ _ _ _ _ _ _ _ _ _ _

_____

_____

_ _ _ _ _ _ _ _ _ _ _ _ _ _

_____

Math Talk Math Processes and Practices ③

Apply Describe the new shapes Mandy and Carl made.

FOR THE TEACHER • Have children trace the shapes to solve the problems. Mandy stacks one cylinder on top of another cylinder. Carl stacks one cube on top of another cube. What new shapes did Mandy and Carl make?

Chapter 11

six hundred thirty-nine **639**

Model and Draw

You can put shapes together to make a new shape.

What other new shapes could you make?

Share and Show MATH BOARD

Use three-dimensional shapes.

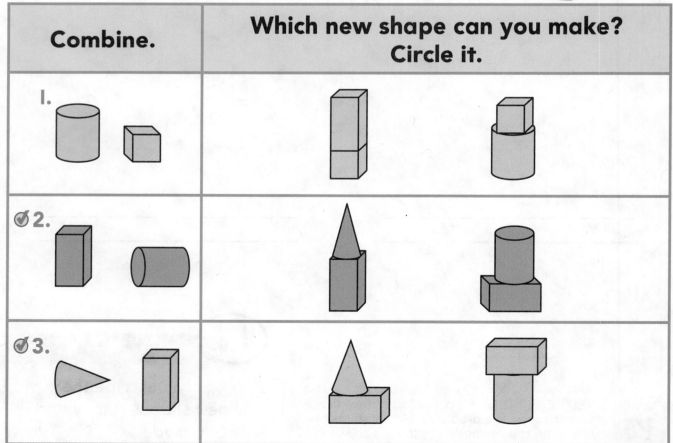

Combine.	Which new shape can you make? Circle it.
1.	
☑ 2.	
☑ 3.	

Name _____

Math Processes and Practices **6** **Attend to Precision**
Use three-dimensional shapes.

Combine.	Which new shape can you make? Circle it.
4. 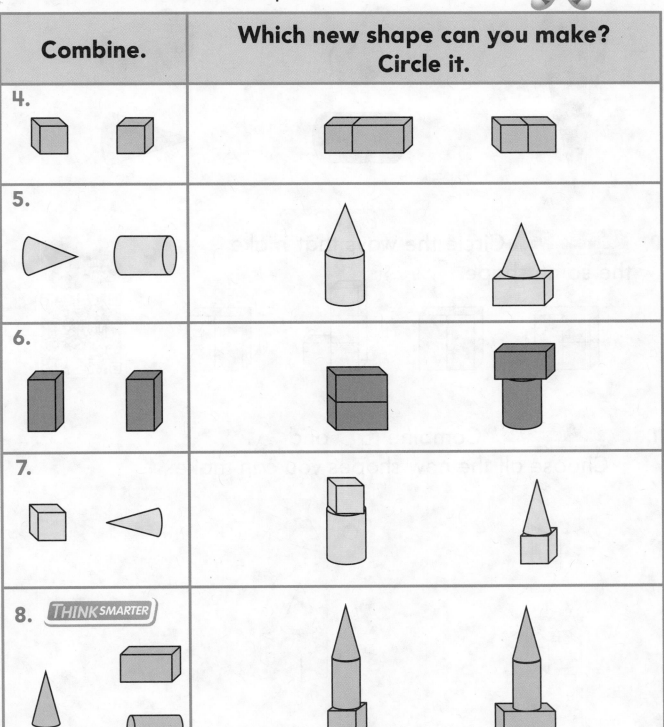	
5.	
6.	
7.	
8. THINK SMARTER	

Problem Solving • Applications (Real World) WRITE Math

GO DEEPER Circle the shapes you could use to model the ice cream cone.

9.

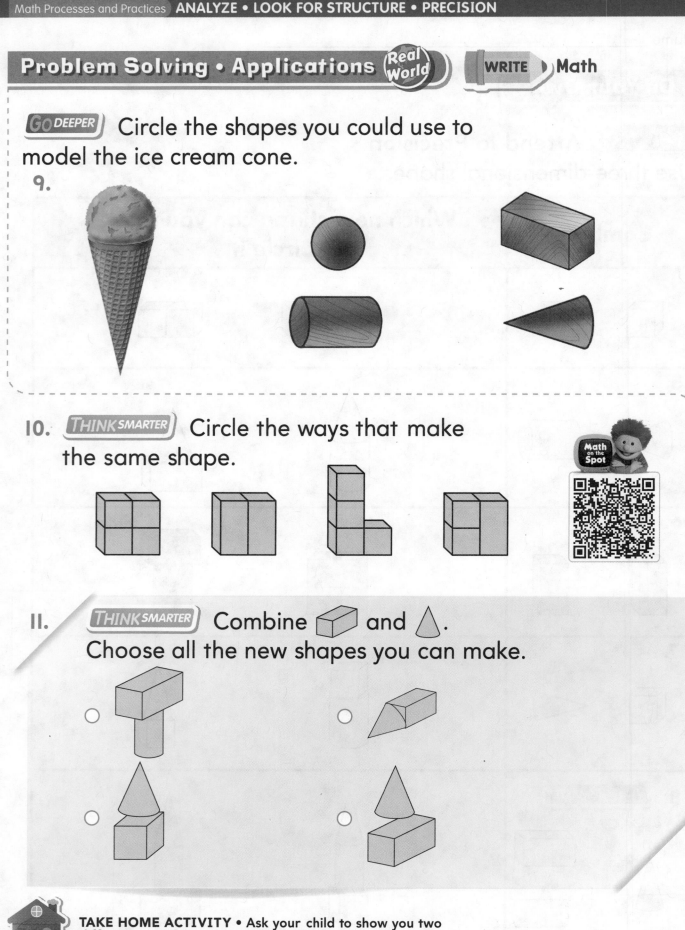

10. **THINK SMARTER** Circle the ways that make the same shape.

11. **THINK SMARTER** Combine ▭ and △. Choose all the new shapes you can make.

TAKE HOME ACTIVITY • Ask your child to show you two different new shapes he or she can make by combining a soup can and a cereal box.

Combine Three-Dimensional Shapes

Learning Objective You will combine three-dimensional shapes to make new shapes.

Use three-dimensional shapes.

Combine.	Which new shape can you make? Circle it.
1.	
2.	

Problem Solving *Real World*

3. Circle the shapes you could use to model the bird feeder.

4. **WRITE** Math Combine two shapes to make a new shape. Describe how you put the shapes together.

_____

_____

_____

_____

Lesson Check

1. Circle the shape that combines ⬭ and △.

Spiral Review

2. Write the sum. Write how many tens.

$$40 + 20 = \underline{\hspace{1cm}}$$

_____ tens

---

3. Emi has 15 crayons.
She gives some crayons to Jo.
Now she has 9 crayons.
How many crayons did
Emi give to Jo?
Use the model to solve.

_____ crayons

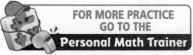

FOR MORE PRACTICE
GO TO THE
Personal Math Trainer

Name _____

Make New Three-Dimensional Shapes

Essential Question How can you use a combined shape to build new shapes?

Learning Objective You will use a combined shape to build a new shape.

Draw to copy the shape.

FOR THE TEACHER • Leila put a box on top of another box. Draw to copy the new shape Leila made.

Math Talk Math Processes and Practices ①

Describe how to draw to copy the new shape.

Chapter 11

© Houghton Mifflin Harcourt Publishing Company

Model and Draw

Step 1
Build.

Step 2
Repeat.

Step 3
Combine.

Circle a new shape you can make. **Explain** why you cannot make the other shape.

Share and Show MATH BOARD

Use three-dimensional shapes.

Build and Repeat.	Combine. Which new shape can you make? Circle it.
1.	
☑ 2.	
☑ 3.	

Name _____

On Your Own

Math Processes and Practices 5 Use a Concrete Model

Use three-dimensional shapes.

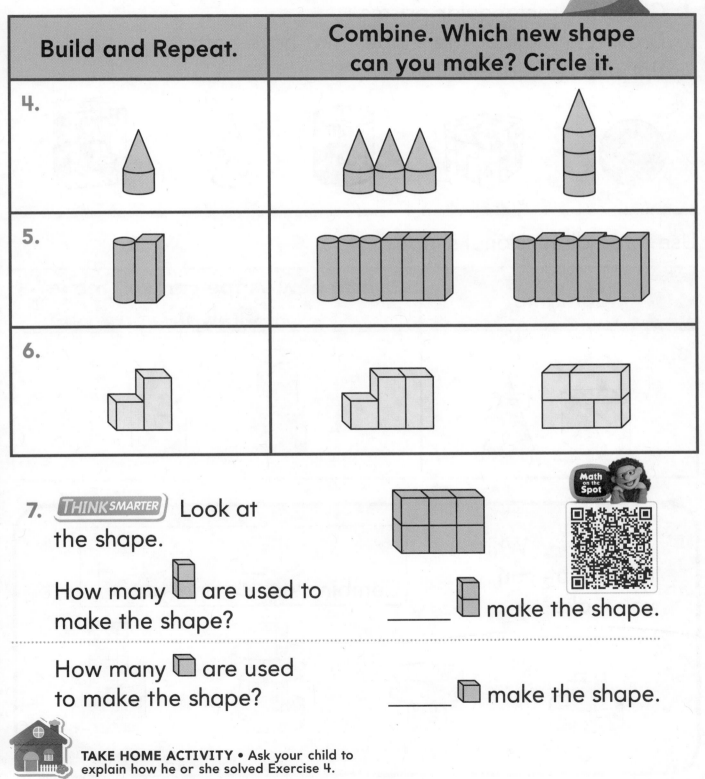

Build and Repeat.	Combine. Which new shape can you make? Circle it.
4.	
5.	
6.	

7. **THINK SMARTER** Look at the shape.

How many ▯ are used to make the shape?

_____ ▯ make the shape.

How many ▢ are used to make the shape?

_____ ▢ make the shape.

TAKE HOME ACTIVITY • Ask your child to explain how he or she solved Exercise 4.

© Houghton Mifflin Harcourt Publishing Company • Image Credits: (t) ©Virinaflora/Shutterstock

Mid-Chapter Checkpoint

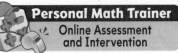
Concepts and Skills

1. Circle the rectangular prisms.
2. Draw a line under the shapes that have both flat and curved surfaces.

Use three-dimensional shapes.

Combine.	Which new shape can you make? Circle it.
3.	

4. **THINK SMARTER** Which new shape can you make?

Combine [cylinder] and [cube].

Make New Three-Dimensional Shapes

Learning Objective You will use a combined shape to build a new shape.

Use three-dimensional shapes.

Build and Repeat.

Combine. Which new shape can you make? Circle it.

1.

2.

Problem Solving Real World

3. Dave builds this shape.
   Then he repeats and combines.
   Draw a shape he can make.

4. WRITE Math Use a cube and a cylinder to build a new shape. Repeat. Draw to show how you can combine these two new shapes to make a larger shape.

Lesson Check

1. Which new shape can you make? Circle the shape.

Combine ▱ and ▱.

· ·

Spiral Review

2. Which addition fact helps you solve $15 - 6 =$ _____?
Write the number sentence.

$$\underline{} + \underline{} = \underline{}$$

· ·

3. Which doubles fact helps you solve $5 + 6 = 11$?
Circle the number sentence.

$3 + 3 = 6$ $4 + 4 = 8$

$5 + 5 = 10$ $7 + 7 = 14$

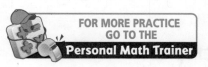

FOR MORE PRACTICE
GO TO THE
Personal Math Trainer

Name _____

Problem Solving • Take Apart Three-Dimensional Shapes

Essential Question How can acting it out help you take apart combined shapes?

Learning Objective You will use the strategy *act it out* to solve real-world problems by taking apart combined shapes.

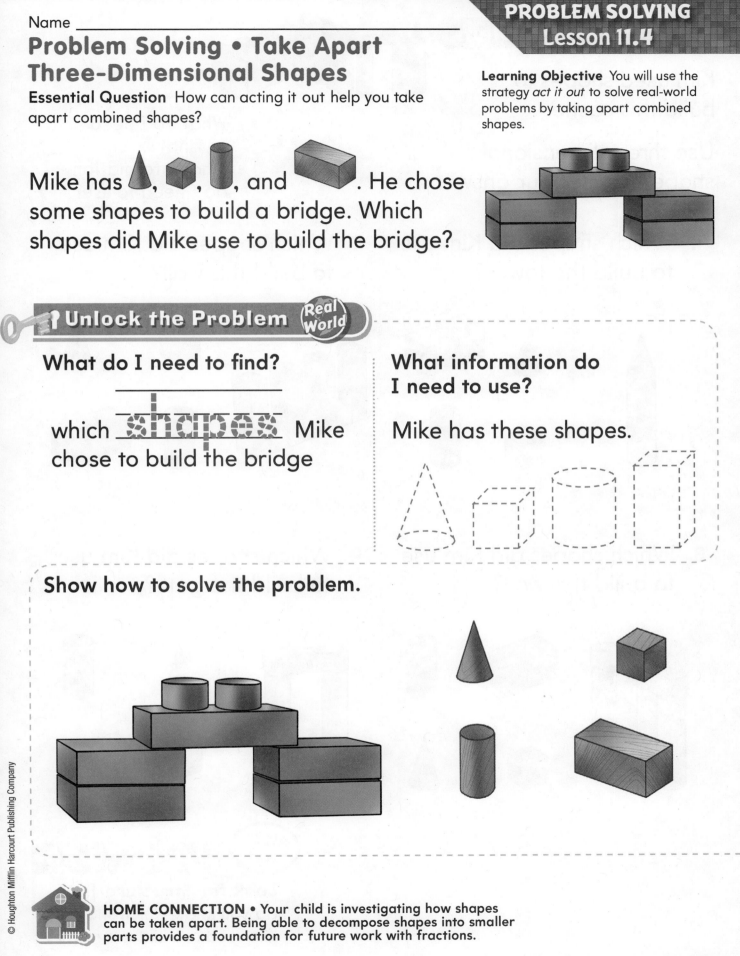

Mike has 🔺, ◼, ⬛, and ▭. He chose some shapes to build a bridge. Which shapes did Mike use to build the bridge?

Unlock the Problem (Real World)

What do I need to find?

which **shapes** Mike chose to build the bridge

What information do I need to use?

Mike has these shapes.

Show how to solve the problem.

HOME CONNECTION • Your child is investigating how shapes can be taken apart. Being able to decompose shapes into smaller parts provides a foundation for future work with fractions.

© Houghton Mifflin Harcourt Publishing Company

Try Another Problem

Kim used shapes to build this castle.

Use three-dimensional shapes. Circle your answer.

- What do I need to find?
- What information do I need to use?

1. Which shapes did Kim use to build the tower?

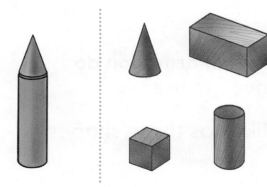

2. Which shapes did Kim use to build this wall?

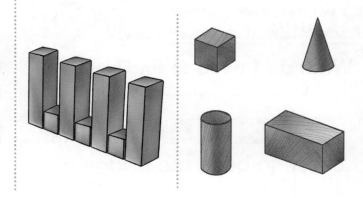

3. Which shapes did Kim use to build this wall?

4. Which shapes did Kim use to build the gate?

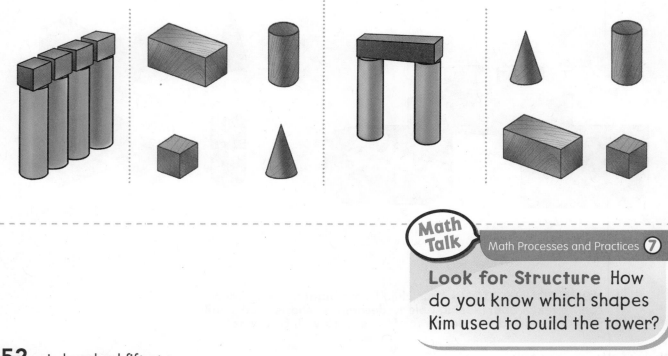

Math Talk

Math Processes and Practices 7

Look for Structure How do you know which shapes Kim used to build the tower?

Name _____

Math Processes and Practices ① **Analyze** Use three-dimensional shapes. Circle your answer.

☑ **5.** Zack used shapes to build this gate. Which shapes did Zack use?

☑ **6.** Chris used shapes to build this wall. Which shapes did Chris use?

7. **THINK SMARTER** Rosa uses ◼, ▲, ▮, and ▬ to build a tower. Draw to show a tower Rosa could build.

Math on the Spot

On Your Own   WRITE Math

GO DEEPER Circle the ways that show the same shape.

8.

9. **THINK SMARTER**

10. **THINK SMARTER** Sharon has many different blocks. She built this shape with her blocks.

Choose all the shapes Sharon used.

○   ○

○   ○

TAKE HOME ACTIVITY • Use real items such as a soup can (cylinder) and a cereal box (rectangular prism) to build a shape. Ask your child to name the shapes you used.

© Houghton Mifflin Harcourt Publishing Company

Problem Solving • Take Apart Three-Dimensional Shapes

Learning Objective You will use the strategy *act it out* to solve real-world problems by taking apart combined shapes.

Use three-dimensional shapes. Circle your answer.

1. Paco used shapes to build this robot. Circle the shapes he used.

Problem Solving Real World

2. Circle the ways that show the same shape.

3. WRITE Math Draw a picture of a house made from shapes. Write the shape names you used.

Lesson Check

1. Lara made this picture frame. Circle the shapes she used to make the frame.

Spiral Review

2. Compare each pair of numbers. Write <, >, or =.

13 ◯ 31   13 ◯ 13   31 ◯ 13   31 ◯ 31

3. Subtract. What is the difference? Write the number.

$$60 - 30 = \underline{\qquad}$$

FOR MORE PRACTICE
GO TO THE
Personal Math Trainer

Name _____

Two-Dimensional Shapes on Three-Dimensional Shapes

Essential Question What two-dimensional shapes do you see on the flat surfaces of three-dimensional shapes?

Learning Objective You will identify two-dimensional shapes on the flat surfaces of three-dimensional shapes.

Use a cone.

FOR THE TEACHER • Read the following problem and have children use the workspace to act it out. Lee places a cone on a piece of paper and draws around its flat surface. What did Lee draw?

Math Talk Math Processes and Practices ①

Analyze What other shape could you use to draw the same kind of picture?

Chapter 11

Model and Draw

Trace around the flat surfaces of the three-dimensional shape to find the two-dimensional shapes.

Share and Show MATH BOARD

Use three-dimensional shapes. Trace around the flat surfaces. Circle the shapes you draw.

1.

2.

3.

On Your Own

Math Processes and Practices ⑥ **Make Connections** Circle the objects you could trace to draw the shape.

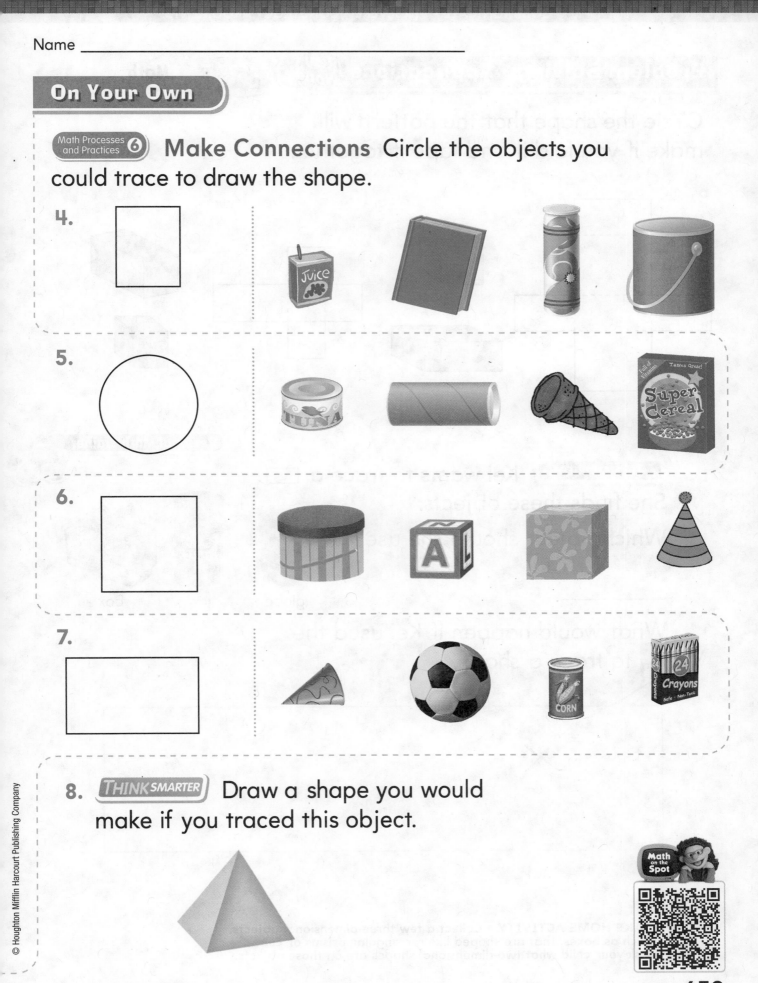

4.

5.

6.

7.

8. **THINK SMARTER** Draw a shape you would make if you traced this object.

Problem Solving • Applications WRITE Math

Circle the shape that the pattern will make if you fold it and tape it together.

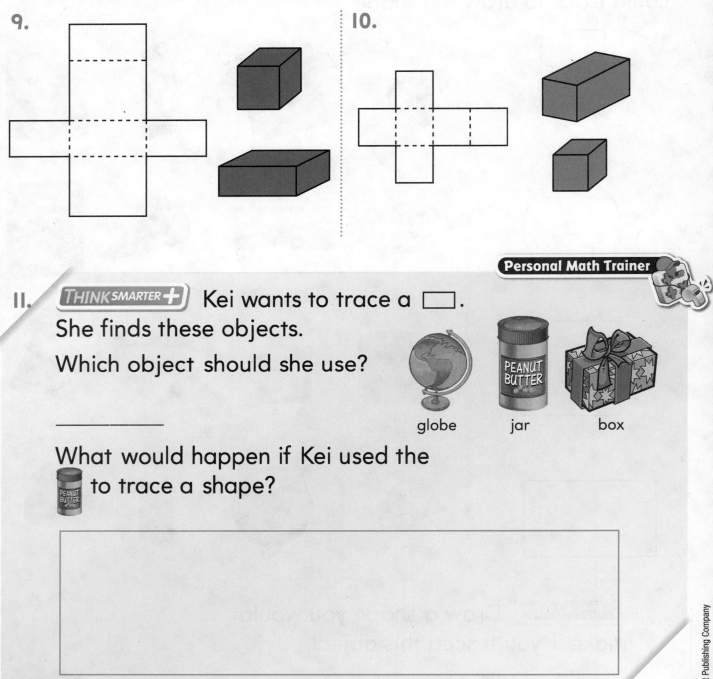

9.

10.

11. THINK SMARTER + Kei wants to trace a ☐.
She finds these objects.
Which object should she use?

globe   jar   box

_____

What would happen if Kei used the
to trace a shape?

Personal Math Trainer

🏠 **TAKE HOME ACTIVITY** • Collect a few three-dimensional objects, such as boxes, that are shaped like rectangular prisms or cubes. Ask your child what two-dimensional shapes are on those objects.

Two-Dimensional Shapes on Three-Dimensional Shapes

Learning Objective You will identify two-dimensional shapes on the flat surfaces of three-dimensional shapes.

Circle the objects you could trace to draw the shape.

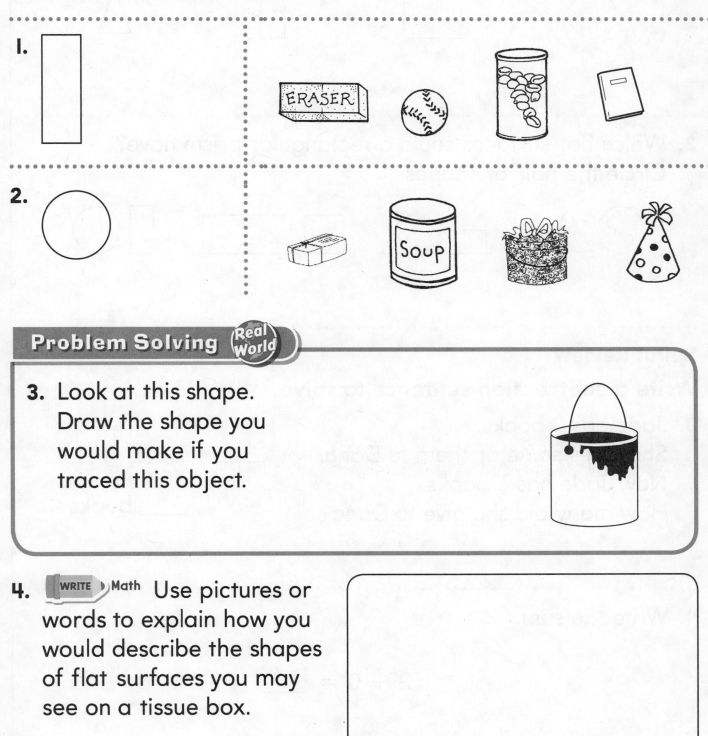

1.

2.

Problem Solving Real World

3. Look at this shape. Draw the shape you would make if you traced this object.

4. WRITE Math Use pictures or words to explain how you would describe the shapes of flat surfaces you may see on a tissue box.

Lesson Check

1. Which flat surface does a cone have?
Circle the shape.

2. Which flat surfaces could a rectangular prism have?
Circle the pair of shapes.

Spiral Review

Write a subtraction sentence to solve.

3. Jade has 8 books.
She gives some of them to Dana.
Now Jade has 6 books.
How many did she give to Dana?

_____ − _____ = _____

_____ books

4. Write the sum.

$$3 + 0 = \underline{}$$

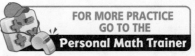

FOR MORE PRACTICE
GO TO THE
Personal Math Trainer

Name _____

Personal Math Trainer
Online Assessment and Intervention

1. Match each shape to the group where it belongs.

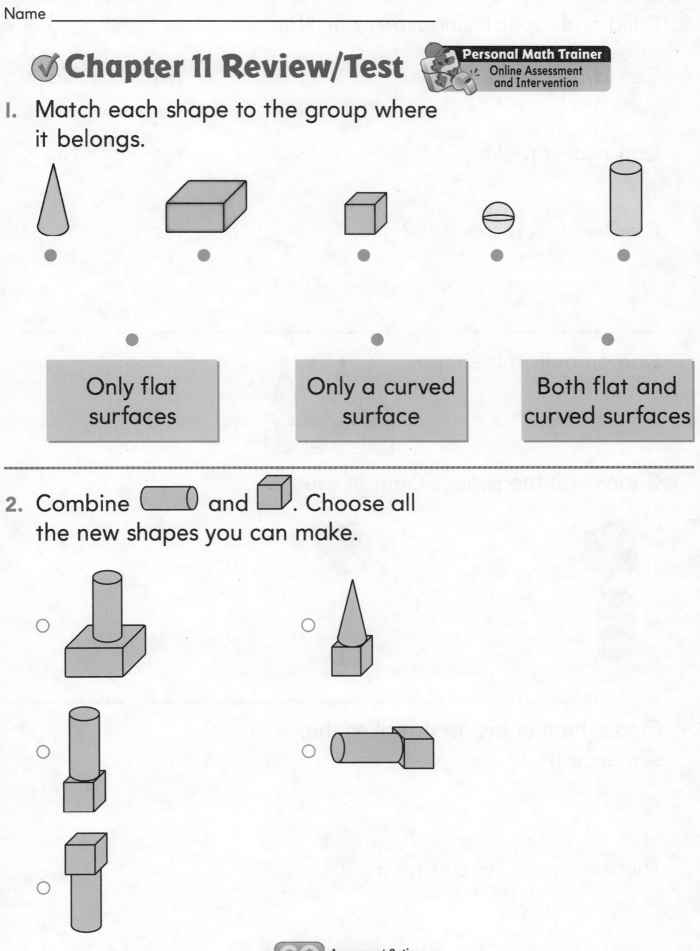

Only flat surfaces

Only a curved surface

Both flat and curved surfaces

2. Combine ⬭ and ⬛. Choose all the new shapes you can make.

© Houghton Mifflin Harcourt Publishing Company

3. Build and repeat. Choose Yes or No.

Can two make ?   ○ Yes   ○ No

Can two make ?   ○ Yes   ○ No

Can two make ?   ○ Yes   ○ No

---

4. Damon built this shape.

Choose all the shapes Damon used.

 ○

○

○

○

---

5. Circle the number that makes the sentence true.

There are | 0 |
         | 1 | circles on a 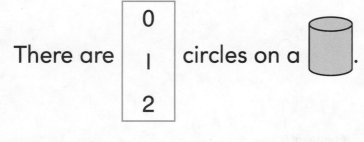 .
         | 2 |

Name _____

6. **GO DEEPER** Sara wants to trace a ◯. She finds these objects.

What would happen if she used the to trace a shape?

Draw the object Sara should trace.

7. Which shape has only 2 flat surfaces?

○

○

○

○

8. Look at the shape.

How many are used to make the shape?

9. Ellen built this shape.

Which shapes did Ellen use?
Circle them.

Draw another way to combine the objects.

10. THINK SMARTER + Hector built this shape.

Choose all the shapes Hector used.

© Houghton Mifflin Harcourt Publishing Company

Two-Dimensional Geometry

Curious About Math with
Curious George

Shapes can be found
in many places. What
shapes might you see
on a playground?

Name _____

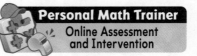
Sort by Shape

Circle the shape that belongs in each group.

1.

2.

Sort Shapes

Circle the shapes with 4 sides.

3.
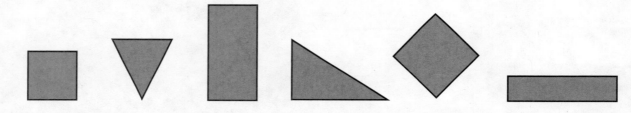

Identify Two-Dimensional Shapes

Color each square blue. Color each rectangle yellow.
Color each circle red.

4.

This page checks understanding of important skills needed
for success in Chapter 12.

Name _____

Review Words

circle
hexagon
rectangle
square
triangle

Vocabulary Builder

Visualize It

Complete the chart.
Mark each row with a ✔.

Word	I Know	Sounds Familiar	I Do Not Know
circle			
hexagon			
rectangle			
square			
triangle			

Understand Vocabulary

Write the number of each shape.

1. ____ circles

2. ____ squares

3. ____ triangles

Game Rocket Shapes

Materials

- ⊙ • 6 ■ • 8 ● • 14 ▲

Play with a partner.
Take turns.

1 Spin the ⊙.

2 Name the shape you spin.

3 Place that shape on the rocket if you can.

4 If you cannot place the shape, your turn is over.

5 The first player to cover a whole rocket wins.

Player 1

Player 2

circle círculo 5	**equal parts** partes iguales 18
fourth of cuarto de 21	**fourths** cuartos 22
half of mitad de 24	**halves** mitades 25
hexagon hexágono 26	**quarter of** cuarta parte de 43

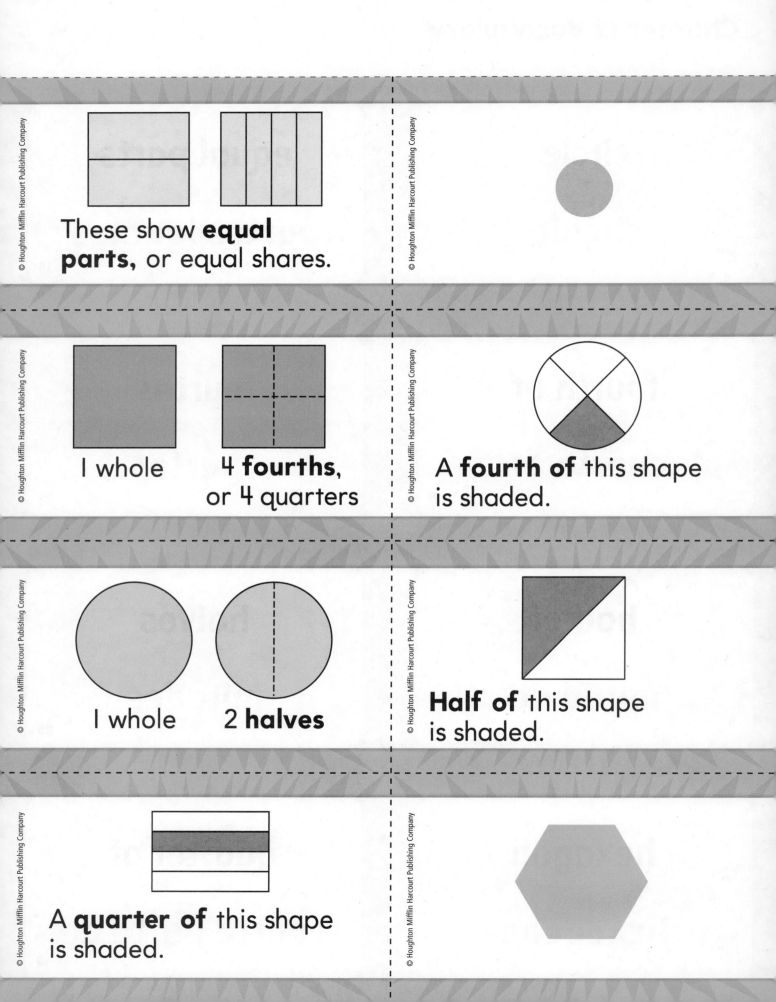

These show **equal parts,** or equal shares.

I whole

4 fourths, or 4 quarters

A **fourth of** this shape is shaded.

I whole

2 halves

Half of this shape is shaded.

A **quarter of** this shape is shaded.

quarters

cuartas partes

44

rectangle

rectángulo

45

side

lado

49

square

cuadrado

51

trapezoid

trapecio

58

triangle

triángulo

59

unequal parts

partes desiguales

60

vertex

vértice

61

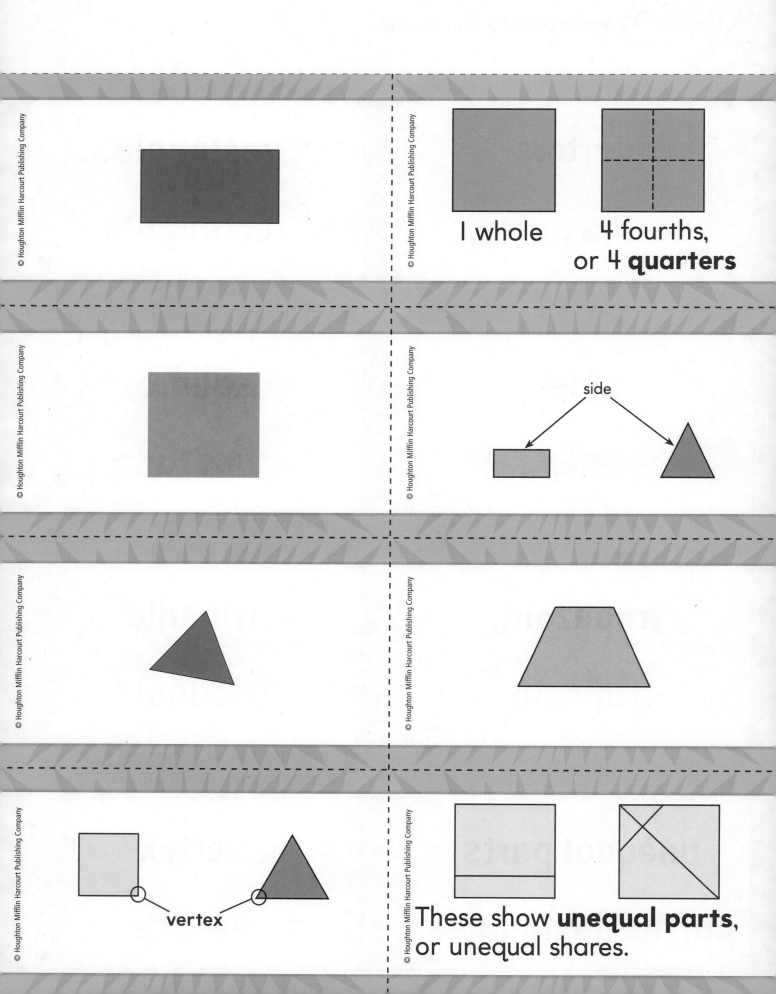

I whole

4 fourths, or 4 **quarters**

side

vertex

These show **unequal parts**, or unequal shares.

Guess the Word

Materials

timer

How to Play

Play with a partner.

1. Choose a math word from the Word Box.
   Do not tell your partner.
2. Set the timer.
3. Give a one-word clue.
4. Your partner tries to guess the secret word.
5. Repeat with a new one-word clue until your partner
   guesses correctly or time runs out.
6. Take turns.
7. The first player to correctly guess 5 words wins.

Word Box
circle
equal parts
fourth of
fourths
half of
halves
hexagon
quarter of
quarters
rectangle
side
square
trapezoid
triangle
unequal parts
vertex

The Write Way

Reflect

Choose one idea. Draw and write about it.

- Tell about two of your favorite shapes.

- Explain how you can combine shapes to make a new shape.

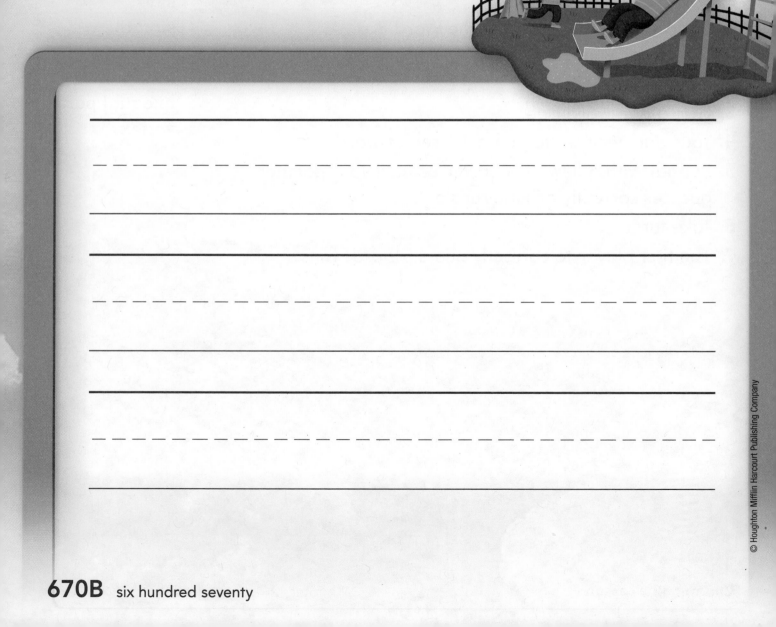

Name _____

Sort Two-Dimensional Shapes

Essential Question How can you use attributes to classify and sort two-dimensional shapes?

Learning Objective You will classify and sort two-dimensional shapes.

Listen and Draw Real World

Draw to sort the shapes.
Write the sorting rule.

_____   _____

- - - - - - - - - - - -   - - - - - - - - - - - -

_____   _____

FOR THE TEACHER • Read the following aloud. Devon wants to sort these shapes to show a group of triangles and a group of rectangles. Draw and write to show how Devon sorts the shapes.

Math Talk Math Processes and Practices 6

Explain Are there shapes that did not go in your groups?

Model and Draw

Here are some ways to sort two-dimensional shapes.

A **square** is a special kind of rectangle.

<u>curved</u> and closed shapes

circles

closed shapes with ____ **sides**

triangles

closed shapes with ____ **vertices**

rectangles

Share and Show MATH BOARD

Read the sorting rule. Circle the shapes that follow the rule.

THINK
Vertices (corners) are where the sides meet.

1. 4 vertices (corners)

2. **not** curved

☑3. only 3 sides

☑4. more than 3 sides

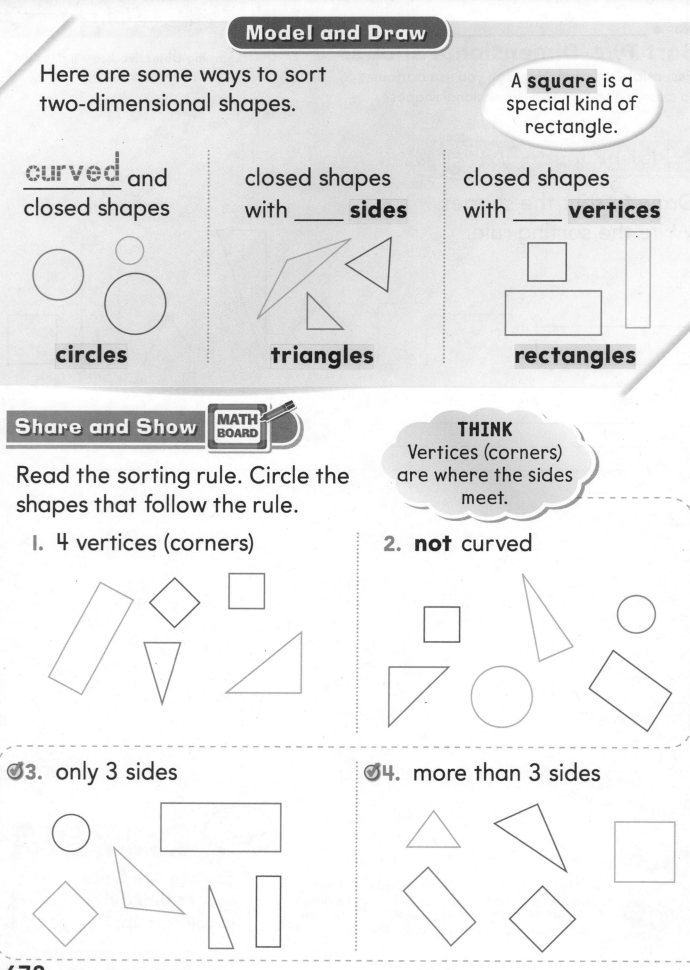

Name _____

Math Processes and Practices 6 **Use Math Vocabulary**

Circle the shapes that follow the rule.

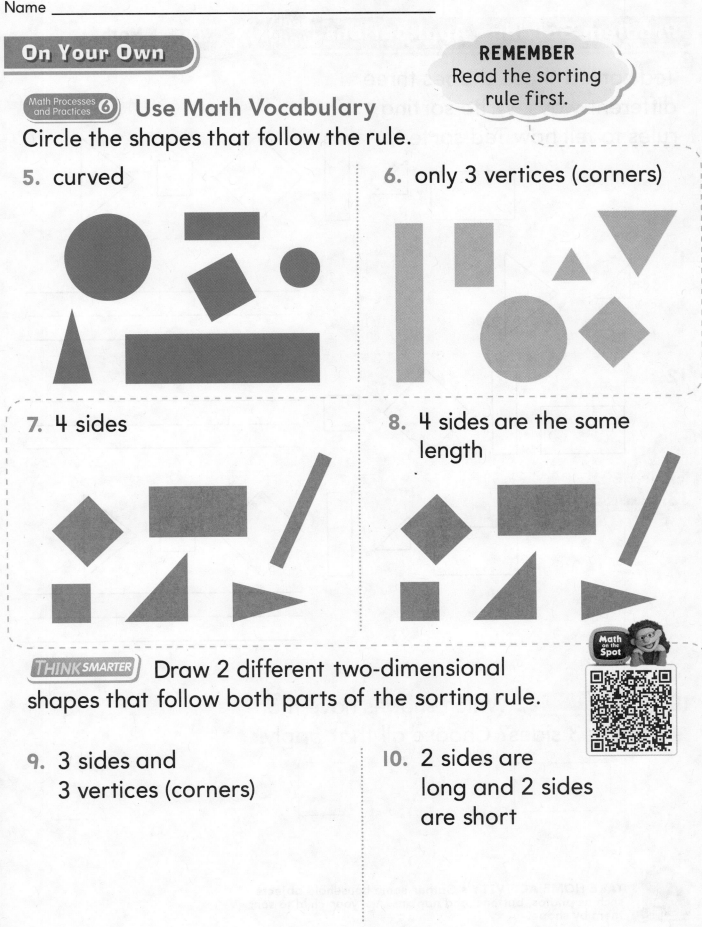

5. curved

6. only 3 vertices (corners)

7. 4 sides

8. 4 sides are the same length

THINK SMARTER Draw 2 different two-dimensional shapes that follow both parts of the sorting rule.

9. 3 sides and
3 vertices (corners)

10. 2 sides are
long and 2 sides
are short

Math on the Spot

© Houghton Mifflin Harcourt Publishing Company

Problem Solving • Applications (Real World)   WRITE ▶ Math

Ted sorted these shapes three different ways. Write sorting rules to tell how Ted sorted.

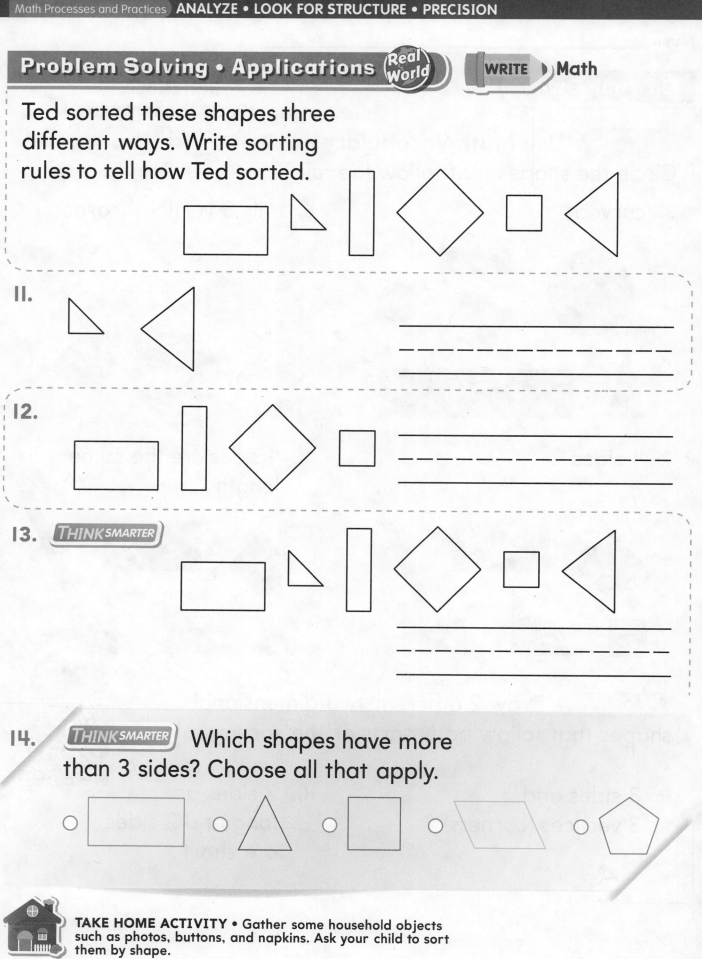

11. _____
    - - - - - - - - - - - - - - - - -
    _____

12. _____
    - - - - - - - - - - - - - - - - -
    _____

13. THINK SMARTER
    _____
    - - - - - - - - - - - - - - - - -
    _____

14. THINK SMARTER Which shapes have more than 3 sides? Choose all that apply.

TAKE HOME ACTIVITY • Gather some household objects such as photos, buttons, and napkins. Ask your child to sort them by shape.

Name _____

Sort Two-Dimensional Shapes

Learning Objective You will classify and sort two-dimensional shapes.

Read the sorting rule. Circle the shapes that follow the rule.

1. **not** curved

2. 4 vertices

Problem Solving Real World

3. Katie sorted these shapes. Write a sorting rule to tell how Katie sorted.

_____

_____

_____

4. WRITE Math Explain how you would name a sorting rule for I square, I rectangle, and I triangle.

_____

_____

_____

_____

Lesson Check

1. Circle the shape that would **not** be sorted into this group.

2. Circle the shape that has fewer than 4 sides.

Spiral Review

Solve. Draw or write to explain.

3. Clue 1: A black line is shorter than a white line.
   Clue 2: The white line is shorter than a gray line.
   Is the black line longer or shorter
   than the gray line? _____
   ____ ____ ____ ____ ____ ____
   _____

FOR MORE PRACTICE
GO TO THE
Personal Math Trainer

Name _____

Describe Two-Dimensional Shapes

Essential Question What attributes can you use to describe two-dimensional shapes?

Learning Objective You will describe two-dimensional shapes.

Listen and Draw

Use two-dimensional shapes. Sort them into two groups. Draw to show your work.

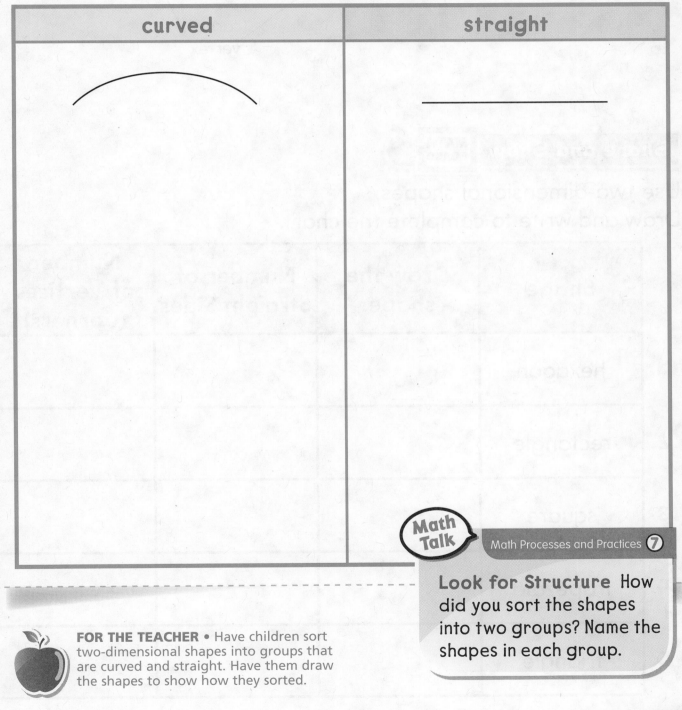

curved	straight

Math Talk

Math Processes and Practices ⑦

Look for Structure How did you sort the shapes into two groups? Name the shapes in each group.

FOR THE TEACHER • Have children sort two-dimensional shapes into groups that are curved and straight. Have them draw the shapes to show how they sorted.

Model and Draw

Some shapes have straight sides and vertices (corners).

side

trapezoid

hexagon

(corner)
vertex

Share and Show MATH BOARD

Use two-dimensional shapes.
Draw and write to complete the chart.

	Shape	Draw the shape.	Number of Straight Sides	Number of Vertices (Corners)
1.	hexagon			
2.	rectangle			
3.	square			
☑ 4.	trapezoid			
☑ 5.	triangle			

Name _____

Use to trace each straight side.
Use ✏️✏️ to circle each vertex (corner).
Write the number of sides and vertices (corners).

6. _____ sides

_____ vertices

7. _____ sides

_____ vertices

8. _____ sides

_____ vertices

9. _____ sides

_____ vertices

10. _____ sides

_____ vertices

11. _____ sides

_____ vertices

THINK SMARTER Draw a picture to solve.

12. I am a shape with 3 straight sides and 3 vertices.

13. I am a shape with 4 straight sides that are the same length and 4 vertices.

Problem Solving • Applications Real World   WRITE Math

Math Processes and Practices 6   **Use Math Vocabulary**

Draw shapes to match the clues.

14. Jake draws a shape that has fewer than 5 sides. It has 3 vertices.

15. Meg draws a shape with 4 sides. She labels it as a trapezoid.

16. **GO DEEPER** Ben draws two different shapes. They each have only 4 vertices.

17. **THINK SMARTER** Circle the number that makes the sentence true.

A △ has | 2 / 3 / 4 | vertices (corners).

🏠 **TAKE HOME ACTIVITY** • Have your child draw a square, a trapezoid, and a triangle. For each shape, have him or her show you the sides and vertices and tell how many of each.

Name _____

Describe Two-Dimensional Shapes

Learning Objective You will describe two-dimensional shapes.

Use (☐ BLUE ▷) to trace each straight side. Use (☐ RED ▷) to circle each vertex. Write the number of sides and vertices.

1.

_____ sides

_____ vertices

2.

_____ sides

_____ vertices

3.

_____ sides

_____ vertices

4.

_____ sides

_____ vertices

Problem Solving (Real World)

Draw a shape to match the clues.

5. Ying draws a shape with 4 sides. She labels it as a rectangle.

6. **WRITE** Math Use pictures and words to show the attributes of a hexagon.

Lesson Check

1. How many vertices does a triangle have?

   ____ vertices

2. How many vertices does a ☐ have?

   ____ vertices

Spiral Review

3. Circle the greater addend.
   Count on to find the sum.

   $$\begin{array}{r} 2 \\ + 9 \\ \hline \end{array}$$

4. Corey measures a crayon box
   with his paper clip ruler. About
   how long is the box?

   about ____ ⬭

FOR MORE PRACTICE
GO TO THE
Personal Math Trainer

Name _____

Combine Two-Dimensional Shapes

Essential Question How can you put two-dimensional shapes together to make new two-dimensional shapes?

Learning Objective You will write how many combined two-dimensional shapes are needed to make a new shape.

Listen and Draw

Use pattern blocks. Draw to show your work.

 FOR THE TEACHER • Have children use pattern blocks to act out the following problem. Karen has some pattern blocks. She puts two triangles together. Draw a new shape Karen could make.

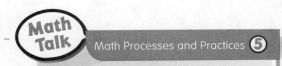

Math Talk Math Processes and Practices ⑤

Use Tools Describe the new shape Karen made.

© Houghton Mifflin Harcourt Publishing Company

Chapter 12

six hundred eighty-three **683**

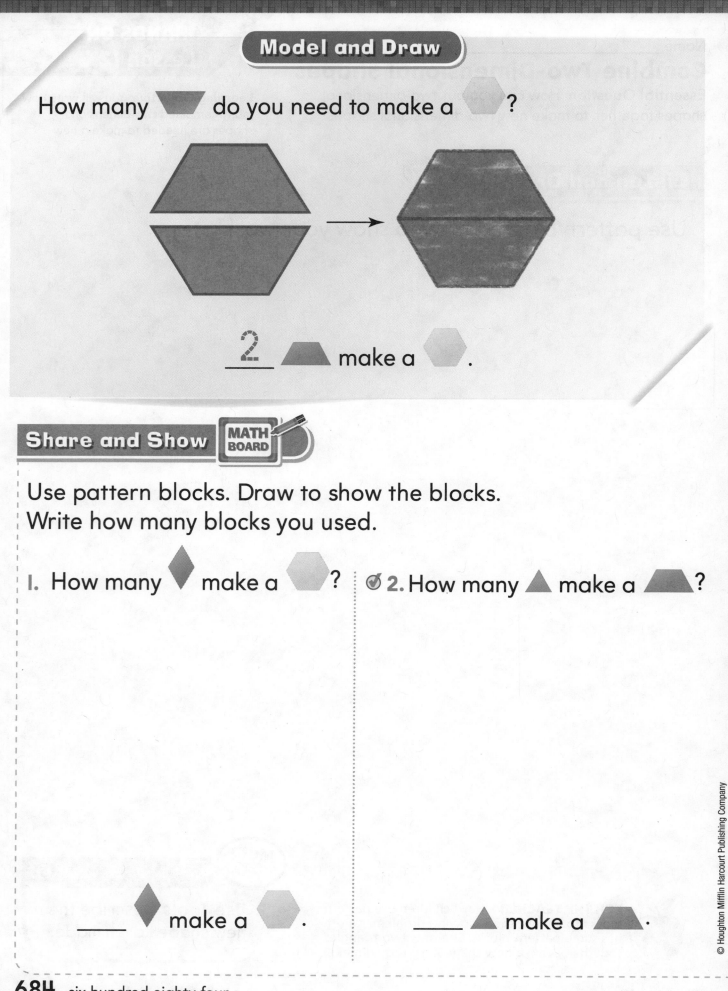

Model and Draw

How many ⬢ do you need to make a ⬡?

___2___ ⬢ make a ⬡.

Share and Show MATH BOARD

Use pattern blocks. Draw to show the blocks.
Write how many blocks you used.

1. How many ◆ make a ⬡?

2. How many ▲ make a ⬢?

____ ◆ make a ⬡.

____ ▲ make a ⬢.

Name _____

On Your Own

Math Processes and Practices 5 **Use a Concrete Model** Use pattern blocks. Draw to show the blocks. Write how many blocks you used.

3. How many ▲ make a ⬡ ?

____ ▲ make a ⬡.

4. How many ▲ make a ◆ ?

____ ▲ make a ◆.

5. **THINK SMARTER** Use me two times to make this shape. Which block am I? Circle a block to show your answer.

▲   ◆   ⬢

6. **GO DEEPER** Use these pattern blocks to make the shape. Write how many times you used each block.

▲   ◆   ⬢

____ ____ ____

Problem Solving • Applications (Real World)   WRITE Math

GO DEEPER Use pattern blocks.
Draw to show your answer.

7. 2 △ make a ◆.

How many △ make 3 ◆?

_____ △ make 3 ◆.

Personal Math Trainer

8. **THINK SMARTER +** How many △ make a ▱?
Use pattern blocks. Draw to show the
blocks you used.

TAKE HOME ACTIVITY • Have your child explain how
he or she solved Exercise 7.

Combine Two-Dimensional Shapes

Learning Objective You will write how many combined two-dimensional shapes are needed to make a new shape.

Use pattern blocks. Draw to show the blocks. Write how many blocks you used.

1. How many △ make a ⬠?

_____ △ make a ⬠.

2. How many △ make a ◇?

_____ △ make a ◇.

Problem Solving Real World

Use pattern blocks. Draw to show your answer.

3. 2 ⬠ make a ⬡.

How many ⬠ make 4 ⬡?

_____ ⬠ make 4 ⬡.

4. **WRITE** Math Draw the shapes you could put together to make a rectangle.

Lesson Check

1. How many △ do you use to make a ⬡?

_____ △ make a ⬡.

2. How many ◇ do you use to make a ⬡?

_____ ◇ make a ⬡.

Spiral Review

3. Use ▭. Which string is about 5 ▭ long? Circle the string that is about 5 ▭ long.

4. Look at the hour hand. Write the time.

_____

FOR MORE PRACTICE
GO TO THE
Personal Math Trainer

Name _____

Combine More Shapes

Essential Question How can you combine two-dimensional shapes to make new shapes?

Learning Objective You will combine two-dimensional shapes to make new shapes.

Listen and Draw

Use shapes to fill each outline.
Draw to show your work.

Represent Use the outline on the left to describe how two shapes can make another shape.

FOR THE TEACHER • Have children use two shapes to fill the outline on the left, and draw a line to show the two shapes. Then have children use three shapes to fill the outline on the right, again drawing lines to show the shapes.

Chapter 12

six hundred eighty-nine **689**

Combine shapes to
make a new shape.

or

How else could you
combine 2 ?

Share and Show MATH BOARD

Circle two shapes that can combine
to make the shape on the left.

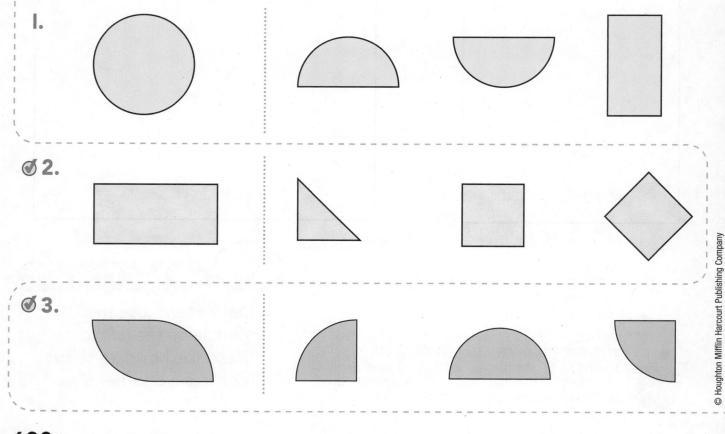

1.

✓ 2.

✓ 3.

Name _____

Math Processes and Practices 4 **Use Diagrams** Circle two shapes that can combine to make the shape on the left.

4.

5.

THINK SMARTER Draw lines to show two different ways to combine the shapes on the left to make new shapes on the right.

6.

7.

Problem Solving • Applications Real World   WRITE Math

THINK SMARTER Draw lines to show how the shapes on the left combine to make the new shape.

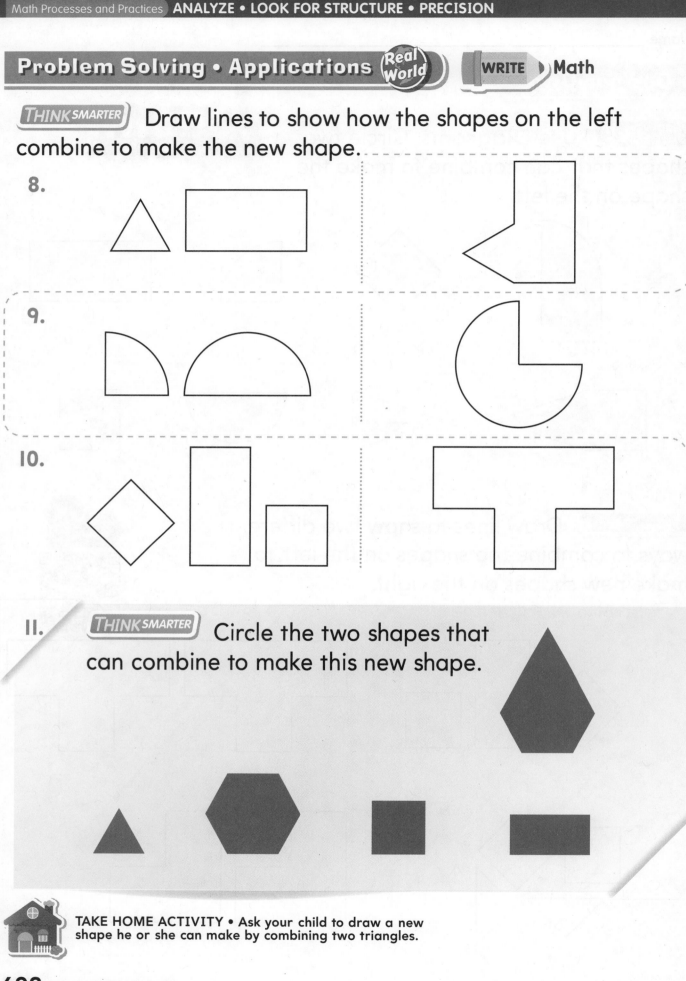

8.

9.

10.

11. **THINK SMARTER** Circle the two shapes that can combine to make this new shape.

🏠 **TAKE HOME ACTIVITY** • Ask your child to draw a new shape he or she can make by combining two triangles.

Combine More Shapes

Learning Objective You will combine two-dimensional shapes to make new shapes.

Circle two shapes that can combine to make the shape on the left.

1.

2.

Problem Solving Real World

3. Draw lines to show how the shapes on the left combine to make the new shape.

4. WRITE Math Draw two shapes. Then draw what they would look like if you put them together to make a new shape.

Lesson Check

1. Circle the shapes that can combine to make this new shape.

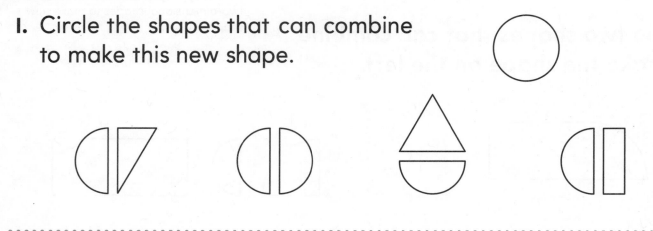

....

Spiral Review

Use the picture graph to answer each question.

Our Favorite Activity						
Swimming	☆	☆	☆			
Dancing	☆	☆	☆	☆		
Drawing	☆	☆	☆	☆	☆	☆

Each ☆ stands for 1 child.

2. How many more children chose ⬛ than 🏖 ?

_____ more children

....

3. How many children chose 🩰 and 🏖 ?

_____ children

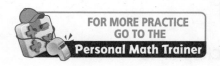
FOR MORE PRACTICE
GO TO THE
Personal Math Trainer

Name _____

Problem Solving • Make New Two-Dimensional Shapes

Essential Question How can acting it out help you make new shapes from combined shapes?

Learning Objective You will use the strategy *act it out* to solve real-world problems by combining shapes.

Cora wants to combine shapes to make a circle. She has ◺. How can Cora make a circle?

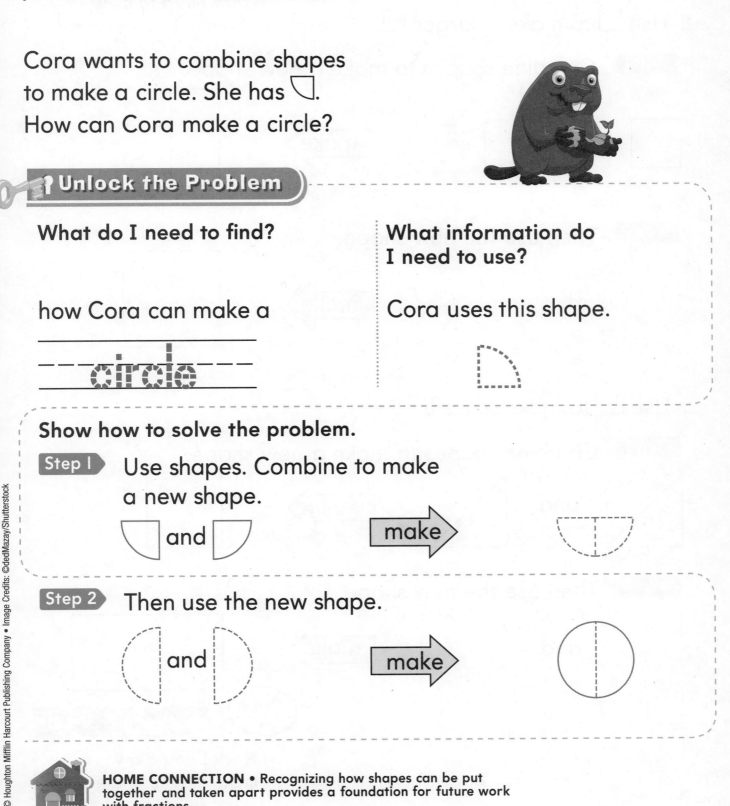

⚷ Unlock the Problem

What do I need to find?

how Cora can make a

_____
circle

What information do I need to use?

Cora uses this shape.

Show how to solve the problem.

Step 1 Use shapes. Combine to make a new shape.

◺ and ◿   **make**

Step 2 Then use the new shape.

◖ and ◗   **make**

HOME CONNECTION • Recognizing how shapes can be put together and taken apart provides a foundation for future work with fractions.

Try Another Problem

Use shapes to solve.
Draw to show your work.

- What do I need to find?
- What information do I need to use?

1. Use ▢ to make a larger ▢.

   Step 1 ▶ Combine shapes to make a new shape.

   ▢ and ▢ **make** ▶ ▯

   Step 2 ▶ Then use the new shape.

   and **make** ▶ ▢

2. Use ◺ to make a ▭.

   Step 1 ▶ Combine shapes to make a new shape.

   ◺ and ◺ **make** ▶ ▢

   Step 2 ▶ Then use the new shape.

   and **make** ▶ ▭

Math Talk

Math Processes and Practices ④

Model How did you make the rectangle in Exercise 2?

Name _____

Math Processes and Practices ① **Analyze Relationships** Use shapes to solve. Draw to show your work.

✓3. Use △ to make a ▭.

Step 1 Combine shapes to make a new shape.

and   **make** ▶

Step 2 Then use the new shape.

and   **make** ▶

4. **THINK SMARTER** Use ⬡ and △ to make a ▱.

Step 1 Combine shapes to make a new shape.

and   **make** ▶

Step 2 Then use the new shape.

and   **make** ▶

TAKE HOME ACTIVITY • Have your child explain how he or she solved Exercise 3.

Name _____

✓ Mid-Chapter Checkpoint

Concepts and Skills

Write the number of sides and
vertices (corners).

1. _____ sides

   _____ vertices

2. _____ sides

   _____ vertices

Circle the shapes that can combine
to make the new shape.

3.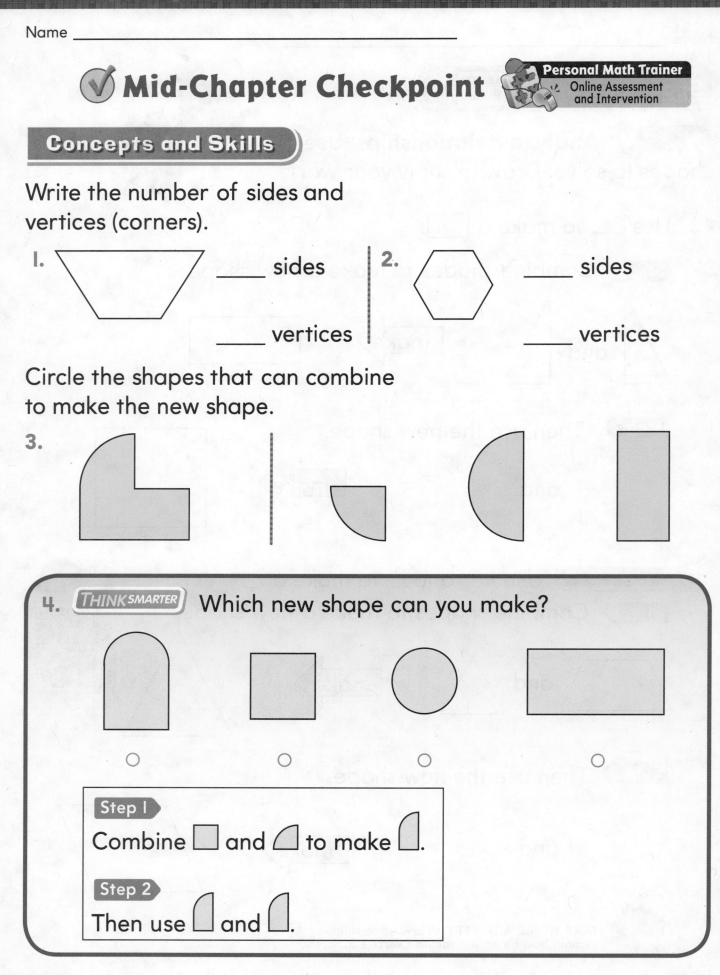

4. **THINK SMARTER** Which new shape can you make?

○   ○   ○   ○

Step 1
Combine ☐ and ◸ to make ◖.

Step 2
Then use ◖ and ◗.

Chapter 12

Problem Solving • Make New Two-Dimensional Shapes

Learning Objective You will use the strategy *act it out* to solve real-world problems by combining shapes.

Use shapes to solve.
Draw to show your work.

1. Use ☐ to make a ▭.

Step 1. Combine shapes to make a new shape.

☐ and ☐ →make→ ▭

Step 2. Then use the new shape.

▭ and ▭ →make→ ◇

2. WRITE Math Use pictures to show how you can make a new shape using a combined shape made from two trapezoids.

Lesson Check

Follow the steps.

1. Which new shape could you make?
   Circle your answer.

Step 1.
Combine and ⟋⟍ to make ☐.

Step 2.
Then use ☐ and ☐.

. . . .

Spiral Review

2. Circle the shape that has no flat surfaces.

. . . .

3. Which flat surface does a cylinder have?
   Circle your answer.

700 seven hundred

© Houghton Mifflin Harcourt Publishing Company

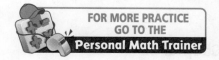

FOR MORE PRACTICE
GO TO THE
Personal Math Trainer

Name _____

Find Shapes in Shapes

Essential Question How can you find shapes in other shapes?

Learning Objective You will find shapes in other shapes.

Listen and Draw

Hands On

Use pattern blocks. What shape can you make with 1 and 2 ▲? Draw to show your shape.

Math Talk   Math Processes and Practices ⑤

Use Tools Can you use the same pattern blocks to make a different shape?

FOR THE TEACHER • Have children explore making new shapes with the given pattern blocks. Discuss different shapes that can be made using the same pattern blocks.

Chapter 12

Which two pattern blocks make this shape?

Use two pattern blocks to make the shape. Draw a line to show your model. Color the shapes. Circle the blocks you use.

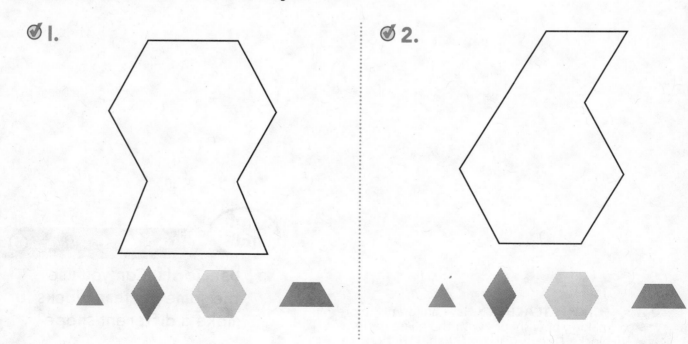

✔ I.

✔ 2.

Name _____

Math Processes and Practices **5**

Use a Concrete Model

Use two pattern blocks to make the shape.
Draw a line to show your model. Color the
shapes. Circle the blocks you use.

3.

4.

5.

6.

7. **THINK SMARTER** Use three pattern blocks to make
the shape. Draw lines to show your model.
Color the shapes. Circle the blocks you use.

Problem Solving • Applications Real World   WRITE Math

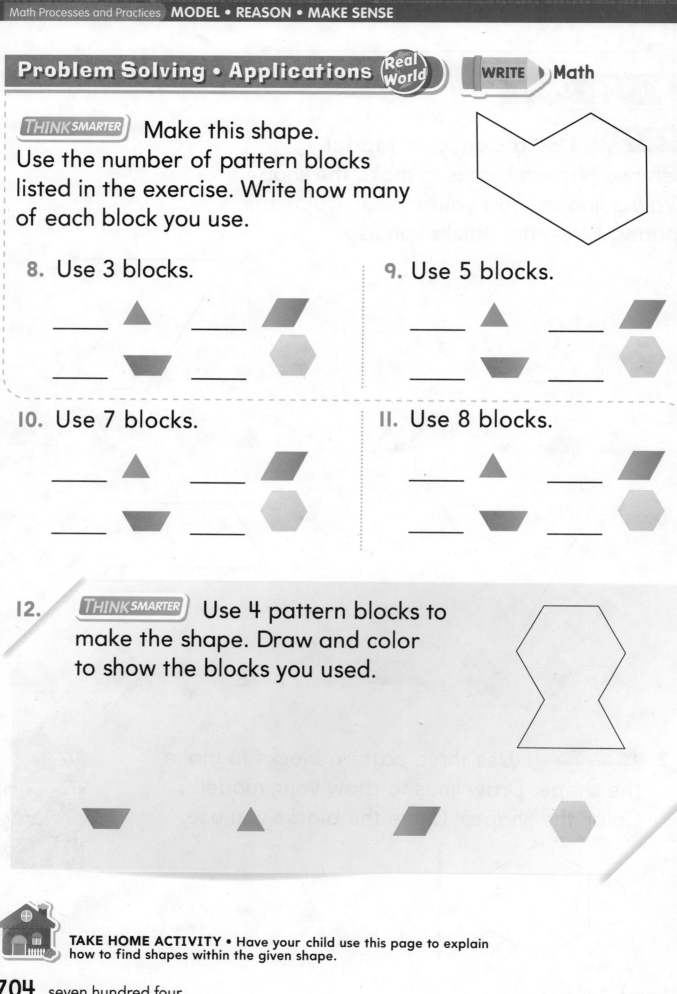

THINK SMARTER Make this shape.
Use the number of pattern blocks
listed in the exercise. Write how many
of each block you use.

8. Use 3 blocks.

_____ ▲   _____ ▰

_____ ▽   _____ ⬡

9. Use 5 blocks.

_____ ▲   _____ ▰

_____ ▽   _____ ⬡

10. Use 7 blocks.

_____ ▲   _____ ▰

_____ ▽   _____ ⬡

11. Use 8 blocks.

_____ ▲   _____ ▰

_____ ▽   _____ ⬡

12. **THINK SMARTER** Use 4 pattern blocks to
make the shape. Draw and color
to show the blocks you used.

▽   ▲   ▰   ⬡

© Houghton Mifflin Harcourt Publishing Company

🏠 **TAKE HOME ACTIVITY** • Have your child use this page to explain
how to find shapes within the given shape.

Name _____

Find Shapes in Shapes

Learning Objective You will find shapes in other shapes.

Use two pattern blocks to make the shape. Draw a line to show your model. Circle the blocks you use.

1.

2.

Problem Solving *Real World*

Make the shape to the right. Use the number of pattern blocks listed in the exercise. Write how many of each block you use.

3. Use 3 blocks.

____ △ ____ ▱ ____ ▱ ____ ⬡

4. **WRITE** *Math* Use pictures or words to explain what shapes can be put together to make a hexagon shape.

Lesson Check

1. Circle the pair of pattern blocks that can make this shape.

....

Spiral Review

2. Write the time.

_____

....

3. Write tally marks to show the number 8.

_____

....

4. How many vertices does a ☐ have?

____ vertices

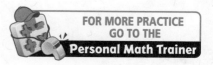

FOR MORE PRACTICE
GO TO THE
Personal Math Trainer

Name _____

Take Apart Two-Dimensional Shapes

Learning Objective You will take apart two-dimensional shapes into parts.

Essential Question How can you take apart two dimensional shapes?

Listen and Draw (Real World)

Color rectangles orange.
Color triangles purple.

FOR THE TEACHER • Read the following aloud. Angelina put some triangles and rectangles together. She drew pictures to show what she made. Color to show how Angelina put the shapes together.

(Math Talk)

Math Processes and Practices ⑦

Look for Structure
What shapes did Angelina make?

Chapter 12

seven hundred seven **707**

You can draw to show parts of a shape.

shows   and

Share and Show MATH BOARD

Draw a line to show the parts.

1. Show 2 ▭.

2. Show 2 △.

☑ 3. Show 2 ◻.

☑ 4. Show 2 △.

Name _____

Math Processes and Practices **7** Identify Relationships

Draw a line to show the parts.

5. Show 2 △.

6. Show 2 ▭.

7. Show 1 ▭ and 1 ◻.

8. Show 1 △ and 1 ⬯.

THINK SMARTER Draw two lines to show the parts.

Math on the Spot

9. Show 3 △.

10. Show 2 △ and 1 ⬯.

Problem Solving • Applications WRITE Math

11. **THINKSMARTER** How many squares are there?

_____ squares

12. **THINKSMARTER** Draw a line to show the parts. Show 2 ◡.

TAKE HOME ACTIVITY • Ask your child to explain how he or she solved Exercise 11.

Take Apart Two-Dimensional Shapes

Learning Objective You will take apart two-dimensional shapes into parts.

Draw a line to show the parts.

1. Show 2 ⬓.

2. Show 2 △.

Problem Solving Real World

3. How many triangles are there?

_____ triangles

4. WRITE Math Draw a shape. Then draw one or two lines to show parts of the shape.

Lesson Check

1. Look at the picture.
   Circle the pair that
   shows the parts.

Spiral Review

2. Use the graph.
   How many children chose ⚽ ?

Our Favorite Sport

⚽	soccer	�	�					
⚾	baseball	�	�	�	�	�	�	
🎾	tennis	�	�	�	�	�		

Each � stands for 1 child.

_____ children

3. Which new shape
   can you make?
   Circle your answer.

   Combine ▯ and ▯.

FOR MORE PRACTICE
GO TO THE
Personal Math Trainer

Name _____

Equal or Unequal Parts

Essential Question How can you identify equal and unequal parts in two-dimensional shapes?

Learning Objective You will identify equal and unequal parts or shares in two-dimensional shapes.

Listen and Draw

Draw to show the parts.

Show 2 .

Show 3 .

Math Talk

Math Processes and Practices **6**

Explain how the triangles shown in each square compare.

FOR THE TEACHER • Have children draw lines to show two triangles in one square and three triangles in the other square.

Chapter 12

seven hundred thirteen **713**

These show **equal parts**, or **equal shares**.

These show **unequal parts**, or **unequal shares**.

How can you describe equal shares?

Share and Show MATH BOARD

THINK
Are the parts the same size?

Circle the shape that shows equal parts.

1.

2.

☑ 3.

Circle the shape that shows unequal parts.

4.

5.

☑ 6.

© Houghton Mifflin Harcourt Publishing Company

Name _____

THINK
Equal shares means the same as equal parts.

Math Processes and Practices **6** **Use Math Vocabulary**

Color the shapes that show unequal shares.

7.

8.

Color the shapes that show equal shares.

9.

10.

THINK SMARTER Write the number of equal shares.

11.

_____ equal shares

12.

_____ equal shares

© Houghton Mifflin Harcourt Publishing Company

Problem Solving • Applications

WRITE Math

THINK SMARTER Draw lines to show the parts.

13. 2 equal parts

14. 2 unequal parts

15. 4 equal shares

16. 4 unequal shares

17. **THINK SMARTER** Does the shape show equal shares? Choose Yes or No.

○ Yes   ○ No

○ Yes   ○ No

○ Yes   ○ No

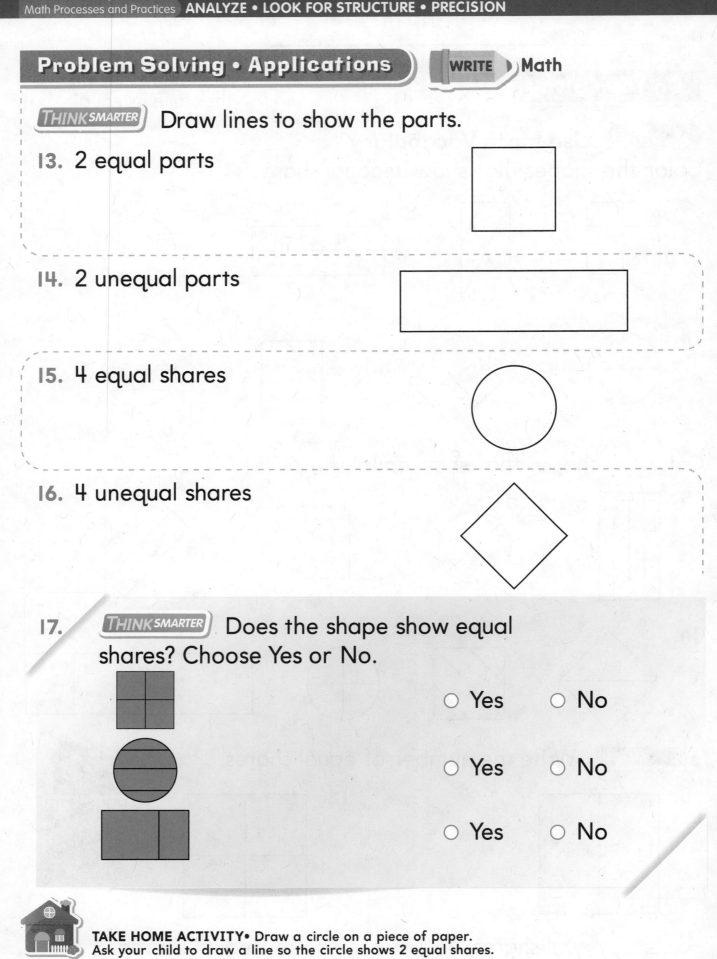

TAKE HOME ACTIVITY• Draw a circle on a piece of paper.
Ask your child to draw a line so the circle shows 2 equal shares.

Equal or Unequal Parts

Learning Objective You will identify equal and unequal parts or shares in two-dimensional shapes.

Color the shapes that show unequal shares.

1.

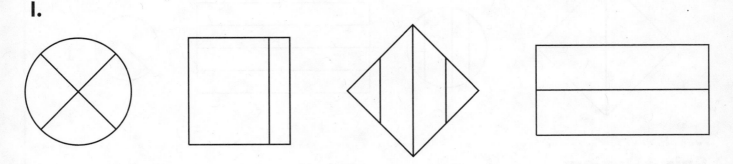

···

Color the shapes that show equal shares.

2.

Problem Solving Real World

Draw lines to show the parts.

3. 4 equal shares

4. WRITE Math Draw two rectangles. Draw lines on one rectangle to show equal parts. Draw lines on the other rectangle to show unequal parts.

Lesson Check

1. Color the shape that shows unequal shares.

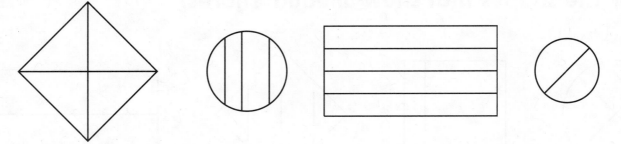

2. Which food did the most children choose?
Circle your answer.

Our Favorite Breakfast		Total
🍳 eggs	IIII	4
🧇 waffles	III	3
🥞 pancakes	ⵌⵌ I	6

3. Use the graph. How many children chose 🧸?

_____ children

FOR MORE PRACTICE
GO TO THE
Personal Math Trainer

Name _____

Halves

Essential Question How can a shape be separated into two equal shares?

Learning Objective You will separate shapes into two equal shares.

Listen and Draw

Draw to solve.

© Houghton Mifflin Harcourt Publishing Company

Math Talk

Math Processes and Practices ①

Analyze Will all four friends get the same amount of sandwich?

FOR THE TEACHER • Have children draw to solve this problem: Two friends share the sandwich on the left. How can they cut the sandwich so each gets an equal share? Then have children solve this problem: Two other friends share the sandwich on the right. How could this sandwich be cut a different way so each friend gets an equal share?

The 2 equal shares make 1 whole.

2 equal shares

Is **half of** the circle larger or smaller than the whole circle?

1 whole

2 **halves**

Share and Show MATH BOARD

Draw a line to show halves.

1.

☑ 2.

3.

☑ 4.

Name _____

On Your Own

Math Processes and Practices ❶ **Analyze Relationships**

Circle the shapes that show halves.

5.

6.

7.

8.

9.

10.

11.

12.

13.

14. **THINK SMARTER** Use the picture.
Write numbers to solve.

The picture shows ____ halves.

The ____ equal shares make ____ whole.

© Houghton Mifflin Harcourt Publishing Company

Problem Solving • Applications (Real World)   WRITE Math

Draw or write to solve.

15. Color half of each shape.

16. Linus cut a circle into equal shares. He traced one of the parts. Write **half of** or **halves** to name the part.

_____

_ _ _ _ _ _ _ _ _ _ _

_____ a circle

17. GO DEEPER Draw three different ways to show halves.

18. THINK SMARTER Circle the shapes that show halves.

TAKE HOME ACTIVITY • Draw a rectangle on a piece of paper. Ask your child to draw a line to show halves.

Halves

Learning Objective You will separate shapes into two equal shares.

Circle the shapes that show halves.

1.

2.

3.

4.

5.

6.

Problem Solving Real World

Draw or write to solve.

7. Kate cut a square into equal shares. She traced one of the parts. Write **half of** or **halves** to name the part.

_____

- - - - - - - - - - -

_____ a square

8. WRITE Math Draw a circle and separate it into halves. Color each half a different color.

Chapter 12

seven hundred twenty-three **723**

Lesson Check

1. Circle the shape that shows halves.

Spiral Review

2. Circle the new shape you can make.

Combine ◊ and ▱.

3. Circle the shape that has both flat and curved surfaces.

4. How many △ do you use to make a ◻? Draw to show your answer.

_____ △ make a ◻.

FOR MORE PRACTICE
GO TO THE
Personal Math Trainer

Name _____

Fourths

Essential Question How can a shape be separated into four equal shares?

Learning Objective You will separate shapes into four equal shares.

Listen and Draw Real World

Use what you know about halves. Draw to solve. Write how many.

There are ____ equal shares.

Math Talk

Math Processes and Practices ⑥

Explain How did you decide how to cut the pizza?

FOR THE TEACHER • Read the following problem. Two friends will share a pizza. Then two more friends come. Now four friends will share the pizza. How can the pizza be cut so each friend gets an equal share? How many equal shares are there?

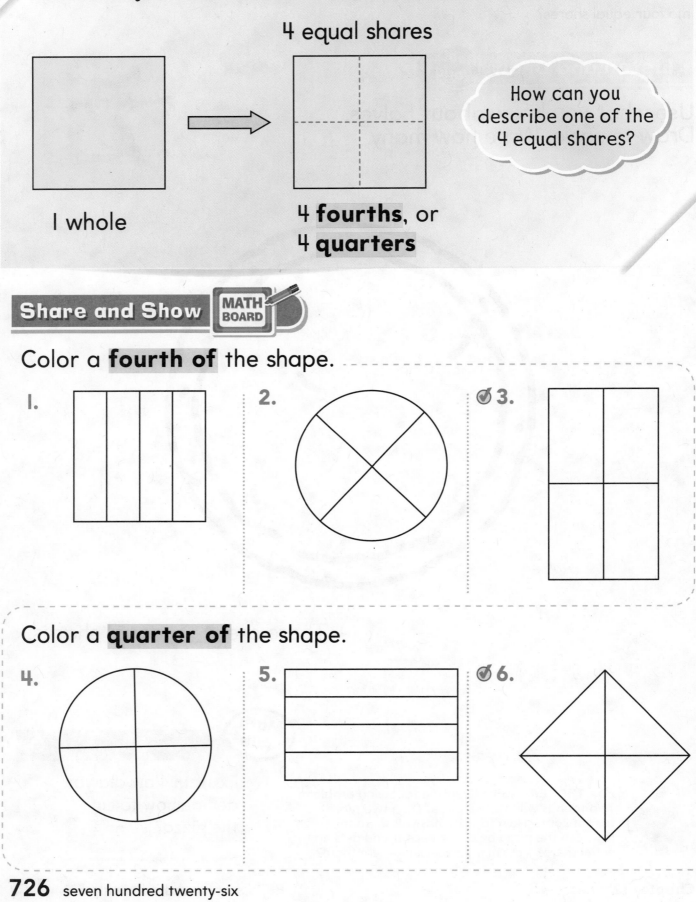

Model and Draw

The 4 equal shares make 1 whole.

4 equal shares

1 whole

4 **fourths**, or
4 **quarters**

How can you describe one of the 4 equal shares?

Share and Show MATH BOARD

Color a **fourth of** the shape.

1.

2.

✓3.

Color a **quarter of** the shape.

4.

5.

✓6.

© Houghton Mifflin Harcourt Publishing Company

Name _____

Math Processes and Practices 4 Use Diagrams Circle the shapes that show fourths.

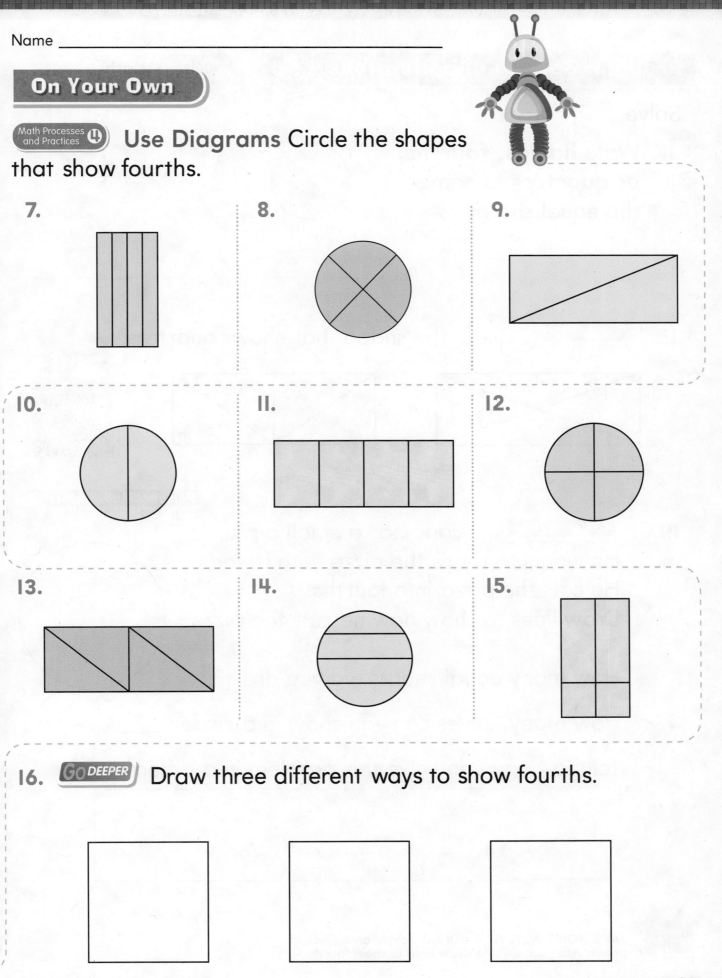

7.

8.

9.

10.

11.

12.

13.

14.

15.

16. **GO DEEPER** Draw three different ways to show fourths.

Chapter 12 • Lesson 10

seven hundred twenty-seven **727**

© Houghton Mifflin Harcourt Publishing Company • Image Credits: ©SketchMaster/Shutterstock

Problem Solving • Applications (Real World) WRITE Math

Solve.

17. Write **halves, fourths,** or **quarters** to name the equal shares.

_____   _____

18. **THINK SMARTER** Circle the shape that shows quarters.

19. **THINK SMARTER ⊕** Alano has a small pizza.
He wants to share the pizza with friends.
He cuts the pizza into fourths.
Draw lines to show how he cuts the pizza.

How many equal shares did you draw? _____

How many halves can you show in a circle? _____

Tell how you can solve this problem in a different way.

🏠 **TAKE HOME ACTIVITY** • Draw a circle on a piece of paper. Ask your child to draw lines to show fourths.

Fourths

Learning Objective You will separate shapes into four equal shares.

Circle the shapes that show fourths.

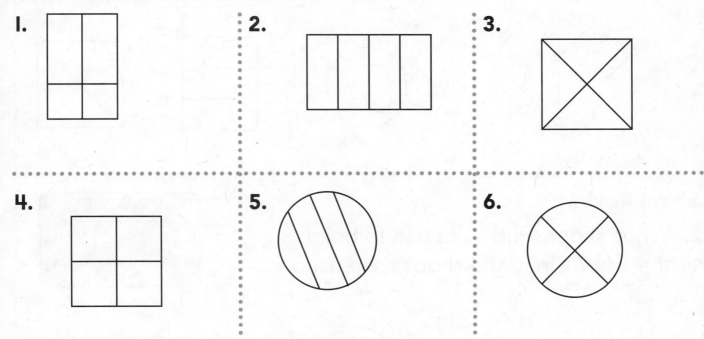

1.

2.

3.

4.

5.

6.

Problem Solving Real World

Solve.

7. Chad drew a picture to show a quarter of a circle. Which shape did Chad draw? Circle it.

8. **WRITE** Math Draw two squares. Draw lines to show fourths. Color a fourth of the first square. Color the second square to show a whole.

Lesson Check

1. Circle the shape that shows fourths.

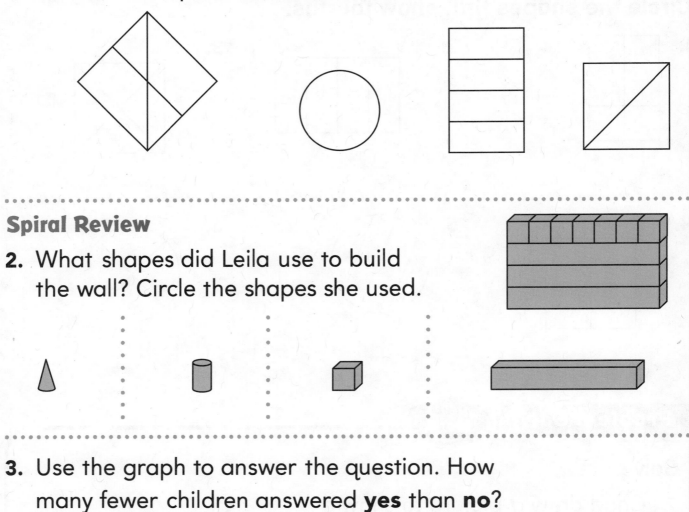

Spiral Review

2. What shapes did Leila use to build the wall? Circle the shapes she used.

3. Use the graph to answer the question. How many fewer children answered **yes** than **no**?

Answer	Do You Have a Pet?					
yes	○	○	○	○		
no	○	○	○	○	○	○

Number of Children

_____ fewer children

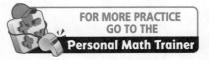

✓ Chapter 12 Review/Test

1. Which shapes have only 3 sides?
Choose all that apply.

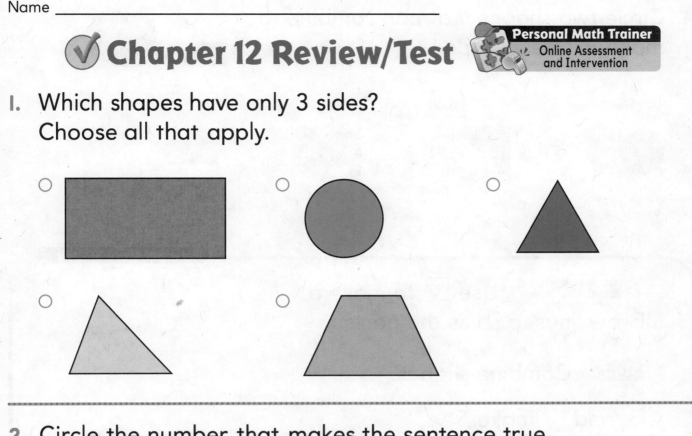

2. Circle the number that makes the sentence true.

A has

| 2 |
| 3 |
| 4 |

vertices (corners).

3. How many make a ?

Use pattern blocks. Draw to show
the blocks you used.

4. Circle two shapes that can combine to make this new shape.

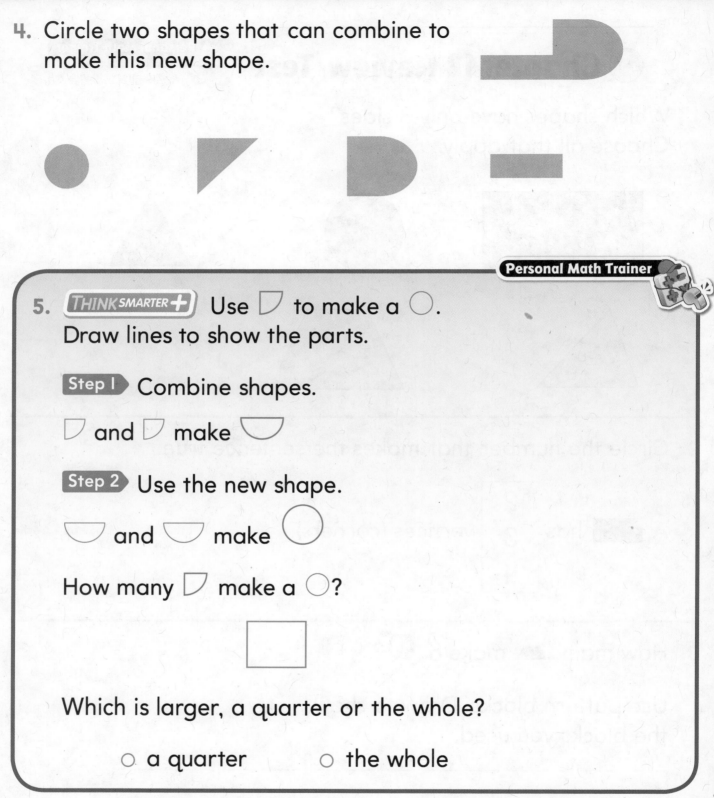

5. THINK SMARTER + Use ▱ to make a ◯. Draw lines to show the parts.

Step 1 Combine shapes.

▱ and ▱ make ⌒

Step 2 Use the new shape.

⌒ and ⌒ make ◯

How many ▱ make a ◯?

Which is larger, a quarter or the whole?

○ a quarter   ○ the whole

6. Use 4 pattern blocks to make the shape. Draw to show the blocks you used.

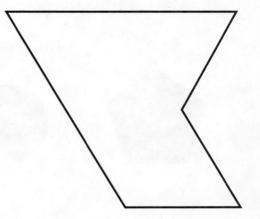

---

7. Draw a line to show the parts. Show 2 ▬ .

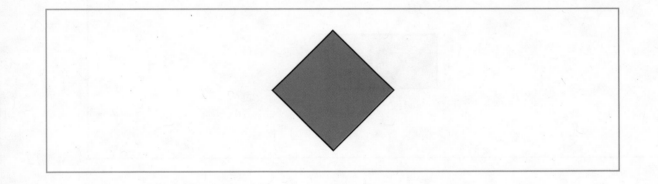

---

8. Does the shape show equal shares? Choose Yes or No.

    ○ Yes   ○ No

    ○ Yes   ○ No

    ○ Yes   ○ No

9. Circle the shapes that show halves.

---

10. **GO DEEPER** Draw lines to show fourths.

How many equal shares did you draw?

How many halves can you show in a rectangle?

Tell how you can solve this problem in a
different way.

Kinds of Energy
Develop Vocabulary

1. Write the definition using your own words.

energy:

_____

_____

_____

solar panel:

_____

_____

Develop Concepts

2. What are two kinds of energy you see on the pages? How is this energy collected?

_____

_____

_____

3. What are some advantages of making electricity in the ways shown? What are some of the problems?

_____

_____

_____

_____

Do the Math!

4. Eric saw 4 wind turbines turning and 3 wind turbines not turning. How many wind turbines did he see? Draw to show your work. Write the addition sentence.

5. Sarah has 6 solar panels on her house. Amy has 3 solar panels on her house. How many solar panels are on both houses? Draw to show your work. Write the sum.

_____ solar panels

Summarize

6. Look at the list of ideas we made about dams, wind farms, and solar panels. Have any of your ideas about them changed? Explain.

_____

_____

_____

Using Force
Develop Vocabulary

Use with *ScienceFusion*
pages 160–161.

1. Write the definition using your own words.

   force:

   _____

   _____

   _____

   speed:

   _____

   _____

   _____

Develop Concepts

2. How is kicking a ball different than catching a ball? What is going to happen to the ball in each of the two pictures?

   _____

   _____

   _____

   _____

3. How can you make a ball go faster or slower by kicking it?

   _____

   _____

   _____

Do the Math!

4. Write the number sentence and how many to solve.
   Jake and Alexa race their toy cars down a hill.
   Jake's car speeds down the hill in 10 seconds.
   Alexa's car speeds down the hill in 7 seconds.
   How much faster is Alexa's car?

_____ ◯ _____ ◯ _____   _____ seconds

....

5. Chen kicked 8 soccer balls. He kicked some soccer balls
   softly. He kicked 5 soccer balls hard. How many soccer balls
   did Chen kick softly? Draw to show your work.

....

Summarize

6. Describe what happens to the playground ball from the time
   it is placed in front of the kicker to when it is caught.

   _____

   _____

   _____

© Houghton Mifflin Harcourt Publishing Company

Name _____

Play Your Part

Develop Vocabulary

Use with *ScienceFusion*
pages 68–69.

1. Write the definition using your own words.

object:

_____

_____

_____

detail:

_____

_____

_____

Develop Concepts

2. Is part of an object bigger or is the whole object bigger? Explain.

_____

_____

_____

3. What has to happen before parts like a seat, handlebar, wheels, and frame can become a whole bicycle?

_____

_____

_____

Do the Math!

4. There are 18 bicycle parts in the box. Some are for a
   girl's bicycle and some are for a boy's bicycle.
   The number of parts for each bicycle is the same.
   Write a doubles fact to solve.

   ____ + ____ = ____

5. Lisa collected bicycle tires. She collected 3 on Tuesday,
   5 on Wednesday, and 7 on Thursday. How many tires did
   she collect? Draw a picture. Write the number sentence.

   ____ + ____ + ____ = ____ bicycle tires

Summarize

6. What details about bicycles can you find on these pages?
   What are some examples of details? How do the parts of
   the bicycle work together in the whole?

   _____

   _____

   _____

   _____

Name _____

Move It!
Develop Vocabulary

Use with *ScienceFusion*
pages 344–347.

1. Write the definition using your own words.

   adaptations:

   _____

   _____

   _____

   beak:

   _____

   _____

   _____

Develop Concepts

2. Look at the frog, the cheetah, the monkey, the fish, and the bird. How are these animals moving? What body parts are they using to move?

   _____

   _____

   _____

3. What different foods do a horse's teeth, a lion's teeth, and a bird's beak help each animal to eat?

   _____

   _____

   _____

© Houghton Mifflin Harcourt Publishing Company

Do the Math!

4. There were 16 seeds on the ground. The bird ate 9 of the seeds. How many seeds are still on the ground? Use the ten frames to make a ten to help you subtract.

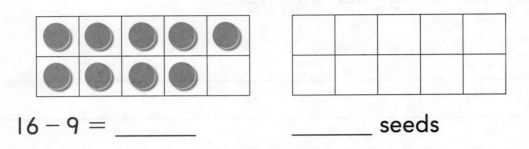

16 − 9 = _____   _____ seeds

5. Explain how you solved the problem.

_____

_____

_____

_____

Summarize

6. What adaptations help different animals to move in different ways and eat different kinds of foods? What are the body parts that help an animal in each type of activity?

_____

_____

_____

_____

_____

Name _____

Care for Earth!
Develop Vocabulary

Use with *ScienceFusion*
pages 222–225.

1. Write the definition using your own words.

reduce:

_____

_____

_____

reuse:

_____

_____

_____

recycle:

_____

_____

_____

Develop Concepts

2. How are *reduce* and *reuse* the same? How are they different?

_____

_____

_____

3. How are you caring for Earth when you decorate a plastic bottle to use as a vase?

_____

_____

_____

Do the Math!

4. The class collected 15 plastic bottles. Some of the bottles are green. 7 of the bottles are clear. Write two related number sentences about the plastic bottles.

___ + ___ = ___   ___ – ___ = ___

5. Draw a picture to show the related facts above.

6. The class needs to collect 14 shirts. How can you make the number 14 in different ways?

___ + ___ = ___

___ + ___ + ___ = ___

Summarize

7. Is making shirts from plastic bottles an example of *reducing*, *reusing*, or *recycling?* Explain your answer.

_____

_____

_____

Rocks and Soil
Develop Vocabulary

Use with *ScienceFusion*
pages 182–183.

1. Write the definition using your own words.

   rock:

   _____

   _____

   _____

   soil:

   _____

   _____

   _____

Develop Concepts

2. What useful products are made from rocks? Why do you think rocks make a good building material?

   _____

   _____

   _____

3. What is soil? What does it look and feel like? What useful products does soil help make?

   _____

   _____

   _____

Do the Math!

4. Marvin made a chart of the things he found. He found 23 things that come from plants, 15 things that come from animals, 54 things that come from rocks, and 38 things that come from something else.

Comes from plants	Comes from animals	Comes from rocks	Comes from something else
23	15	54	38

Marvin found 23 things that come from plants. Draw a quick picture to show the number. Write how many tens and ones there are.

_____ tens _____ ones

5. Marvin found 54 things that come from rocks. Draw quick pictures to show 54 two different ways.

Summarize

6. Why do we say that rocks and soil are natural resources?

_____

_____

_____

Name _____

What's It Like?

Use with *ScienceFusion* pages 92–95.

Develop Vocabulary

1. Write the definition using your own words.

    property:

    _____

    texture:

    _____

    weight:

    _____

    temperature:

    _____

Develop Concepts

2. What are some of the properties of matter? What are some words that describe an object's size? What are some ways to describe an object's shape?

    _____

    _____

3. Which would be heavier—a jar filled with pennies or a jar filled with one-dollar bills?

    _____

4. How do you know if a food is hot? Explain.

    _____

    _____

Do the Math!

5. There are 56 small cars and 85 large cars. Compare the numbers. Use quick pictures to show each number. Write <, >, or =.

_____ ◯ _____

6. The texture of the toys on the table is soft. 34 soft toys are on the table. There are 10 more soft toys in the toy box. How many toys are soft?

_____ soft toys

Summarize

7. List some properties we use to classify and describe matter. Think of an object and describe it using these properties.

_____

_____

_____

_____

Name _____

Plant Power
Develop Vocabulary

Use with *ScienceFusion* pages 384–385.

1. Write the definition using your own words.

plant:

_____

_____

_____

woody stem:

_____

_____

_____

Develop Concepts

2. What are some ways people use plants?

_____

_____

_____

3. How have plants been used to build or make things in our classroom?

_____

_____

_____

Do the Math!

4. Draw a quick picture. Use tens and ones to add. The farmer's market has 35 green apples and 26 red apples. How many apples are at the farmer's market?

_____ apples

5. There are 58 tomatoes in the field. He picks 20 to sell at the farmer's market. How many tomatoes are still in the field?

_____ tomatoes

6. Explain how you solved exercise 4.

_____

_____

_____

Summarize

7. Explain why plants are important to people.

_____

_____

_____

Name _____

Measuring Up
Develop Vocabulary

Use with *ScienceFusion*
pages 30–31.

1. Write the definition using your own words.

   measurements:

   _____

   _____

   _____

   _____

   _____

Develop Concepts

2. If you measure your desk with the crayon and then the marker, would you find the same measurements? Explain.

   _____

   _____

   _____

   _____

   _____

3. Which science tools could you use to get an accurate measurement of the length of your desk?

   _____

   _____

   _____

   _____

   _____

Do the Math!

4. Use square tiles to measure each object. Write the measurement in the table.

desk	book	crayon	folder

....

5. Draw 3 objects in order from longest to shortest.

....

Summarize

6. Why do science tools "measure up"? Why do tools like shoes not "measure up"?

_____

_____

_____

_____

Set Things in Motion
Develop Vocabulary

Use with *ScienceFusion* pages 146–147.

1. Write the definition using your own words.

motion:

_____

_____

_____

speed:

_____

_____

_____

Develop Concepts

2. Why do you think the log ride climbs slowly? Why do you think it zooms down fast?

_____

_____

_____

3. Do you think the rabbit can move both slowly and fast? Explain.

_____

_____

_____

Do the Math!

4. Based on the graph, write the waiting time for each ride in the table.

Ride	Waiting Time (Minutes)
Carousel	
Teacups	
Swings	

5. Which ride had the shortest waiting time? Why is it easy to tell this from the graph?

_____

_____

_____

6. What was the difference between the longest and the shortest waiting times? Explain.

_____

_____

_____

Summarize

7. Give some examples from pages 146–147 of motion that is fast and motion that is slow.

_____

_____

_____

Name _____

Good Night, Sky
Develop Vocabulary

Use with *ScienceFusion*
pages 276–277.

1. Write the definition using your own words.

moon:

_____

_____

_____

sphere:

_____

_____

_____

Develop Concepts

2. Think about what the moon is made of. Why can't the moon make its own light?

_____

_____

_____

3. What are two ways the moon and the sun are alike? How are they different?

_____

_____

_____

Do the Math!

4. Color the spheres.

5. Which shapes above are the same shape as the sun and the moon?

_____

_____

_____

6. Give examples that show the difference between a sphere and a circle.

_____

_____

_____

Summarize

7. Explain what you know about the nighttime sky.

_____

_____

_____

Name _____

So Salty
Develop Vocabulary

Use with *ScienceFusion* pages 206–207.

1. Write the definition using your own words.

   ocean:

   _____

   _____

   _____

   _____

   _____

Develop Concepts

2. Identify and describe the body of water on pages 206–207.

   _____

   _____

   _____

   _____

3. Should we drink ocean water? Why do you think animals that live in the ocean cannot live in lakes?

   _____

   _____

   _____

   _____

   _____

Do the Math!

4. Color the part of the circle that shows how much of Earth is covered with land.

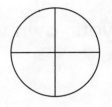

. . . .

5. Does the circle show equal shares? Explain.

_____

_____

_____

. . . .

6. Draw two more ways to make fourths.

. . . .

Summarize

6. What is the main idea on pages 206–207?

_____

_____

_____

Picture Glossary

add sumar

$$3 + 2 = 5$$

addend sumando

$$1 + 3 = 4$$

addend

addition sentence enunciado de suma

$2 + 1 = 3$ is an **addition sentence**.

bar graph gráfica de barras

Flowers in the Garden

Kinds of Flowers

daisies

sunflowers

Number of Flowers

0 1 2 3 4 5 6 7

circle círculo

compare comparar

Subtract to **compare** groups.

$$5 - 1 = 4$$

There are more .

cone cono

count back contar hacia atrás

$8 - 1 = 7$

Start at 8.

Count back 1.

You are on 7.

count on contar hacia adelante

$4 + 2 = 6$

Say 4.

Count on 2.

5, 6

cube cubo

curved surface superficie curva

Some three-dimensional shapes have a **curved surface**.

cylinder cilindro

difference diferencia

$$4 - 3 = 1$$

The **difference** is 1.

---

digit dígito

13 is a two-digit number.

The 1 in 13 means 1 ten.
The 3 in 13 means 3 ones.

---

doubles dobles

$$5 + 5 = 10$$

doubles minus one dobles menos uno

$5 + 5 = 10$, so $5 + 4 = 9$

---

doubles plus one dobles más uno

$5 + 5 = 10$, so $5 + 6 = 11$

---

equal parts partes iguales

These show **equal parts**,
or equal shares.

equal shares porciones iguales

These show equal parts, or **equal shares**.

fewer menos

3 **fewer** 🐦

flat surface superficie plana

Some three-dimensional shapes have only **flat surfaces**.

fourth of cuarto de

A **fourth of** this shape is shaded.

fourths cuartos

I whole   4 **fourths**, or 4 quarters

half hour media hora

A **half hour** has 30 minutes.

half of mitad de

Half of this shape is shaded.

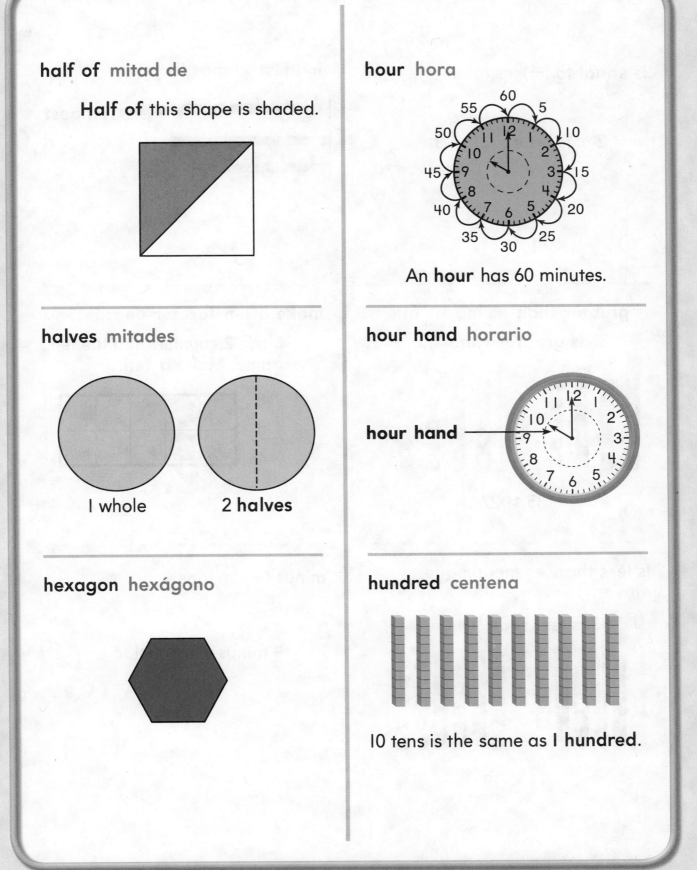

hour hora

An **hour** has 60 minutes.

halves mitades

I whole   2 **halves**

hour hand horario

hour hand

hexagon hexágono

hundred centena

10 tens is the same as **I hundred**.

is equal to (=) es igual a

2 plus 1 **is equal to** 3.

$$2 + 1 = 3$$

longest el más largo

longest

---

is greater than es mayor que

35 **is greater than** 27.

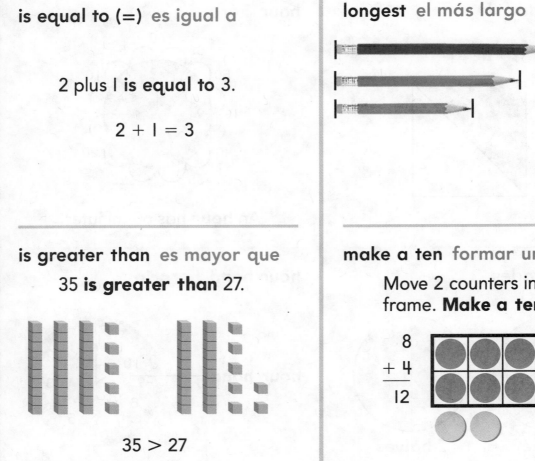

$$35 > 27$$

make a ten formar una decena

Move 2 counters into the ten frame. **Make a ten**.

$$\begin{array}{r} 8 \\ + 4 \\ \hline 12 \end{array}$$

---

is less than es menor que

43 **is less than** 49.

$$43 < 49$$

minus (−) menos

4 **minus** 3 is equal to 1.

$$4 - 3 = 1$$

minute hand minutero

minute hand

minutes minutos

An hour has 60 **minutes.**

more más

$5 - 1 = 4$

There are **more** .

ones unidades

10 **ones** = 1 ten

order orden

You can change the **order** of the addends.

$1 + 3 = 4$ $3 + 1 = 4$

picture graph gráfica con dibujos

Our Favorite Activity at the Fair							
🦌 animals	👤	👤	👤	👤	👤		
🎡 rides	👤	👤	👤	👤	👤	👤	👤

Each 👤 stands for 1 child.

plus (+) más

2 **plus** 1 is equal to 3.
2 + 1 = 3

quarter of cuarta parte de

A **quarter of** this shape is shaded.

quarters cuartas partes

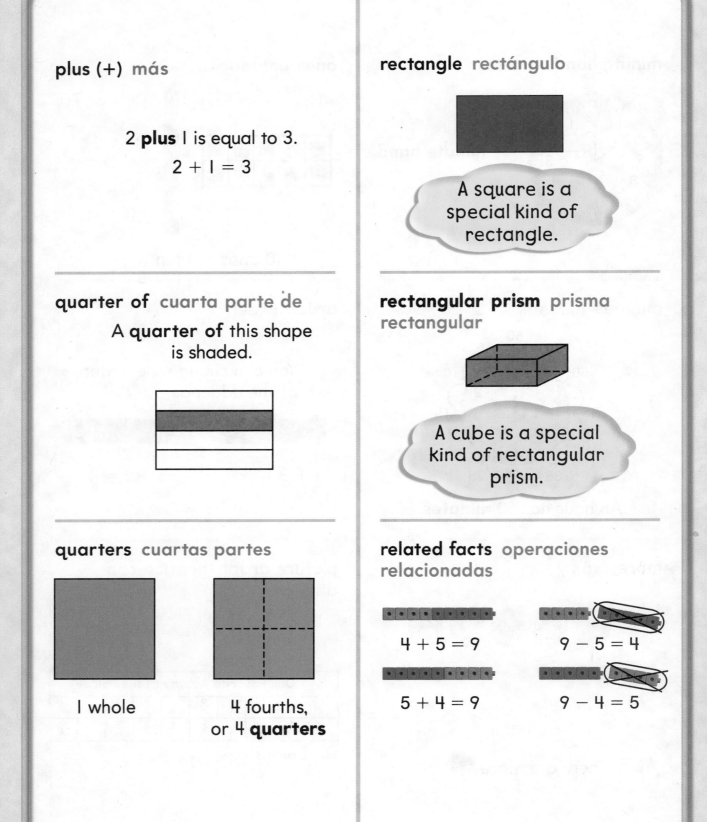

1 whole   4 fourths,
                 or 4 **quarters**

rectangle rectángulo

A square is a special kind of rectangle.

rectangular prism prisma rectangular

A cube is a special kind of rectangular prism.

related facts operaciones relacionadas

4 + 5 = 9   9 − 5 = 4

5 + 4 = 9   9 − 4 = 5

shortest el más corto

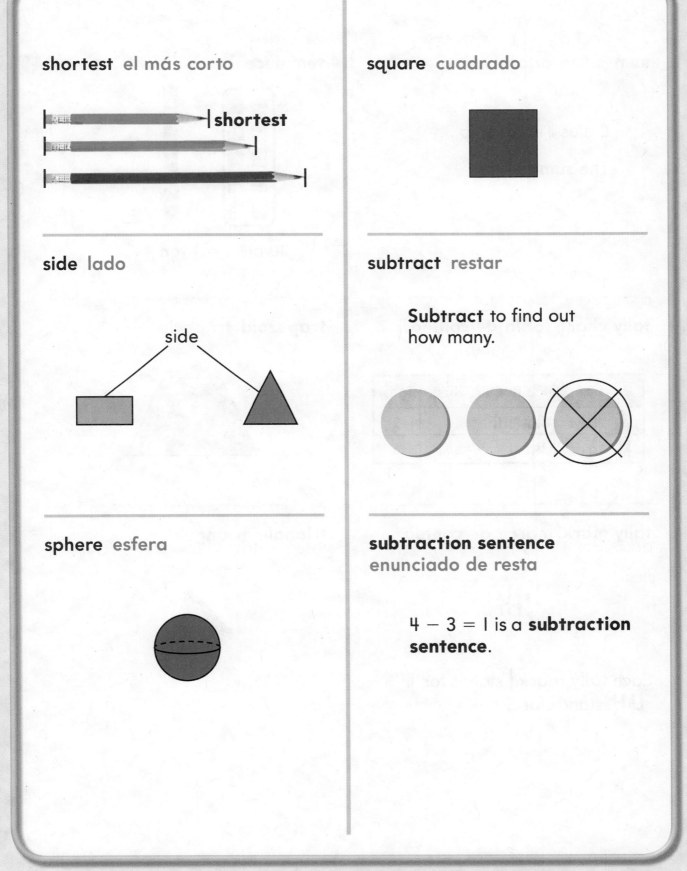

shortest

side lado

side

sphere esfera

square cuadrado

subtract restar

Subtract to find out how many.

subtraction sentence
enunciado de resta

$4 - 3 = 1$ is a **subtraction sentence**.

sum suma o total

2 plus 1 is equal to 3.

The **sum** is 3.

---

tally chart tabla de conteo

Boys and Girls in Our Class		Total
boys	‖‖‖ ‖‖‖	9
girls	‖‖‖ ‖	6

---

tally mark marca de conteo

Each **tally mark** ‖ stands for 1.
‖‖‖ stands for 5.

ten decena

10 ones = 1 **ten**

---

trapezoid trapecio

---

triangle triángulo

H10

unequal parts partes desiguales

These show **unequal parts**, or unequal shares.

---

unequal shares porciones desiguales

These show unequal parts, or **unequal shares**.

---

vertex vértice

vertex

zero 0 cero

When you add **zero** to any number, the sum is that number.

$5 + \mathbf{0} = 5$

Index

Doubles plus one, 155–158, 161–163
Draw a Picture, 197–200, 479–482

E

*e***Glossary,** *See* Multimedia eGlossary
Equal and not equal, 303–306
Equal parts, 713–716
Equal shares, 713–716
Equal to
   number sentences, 303–306
   symbol, 20, 411–413, 417–420
Essential Question, In every lesson.
   Some examples are: 13, 37, 361, 411,
   639, 725
*e***Student Edition,** *See* Technology and
   Digital Resources

F

Family Involvement
   Home Connection, 31, 87, 197, 211,
      241, 255, 267, 285, 297, 373, 417,
      479, 537, 543, 555, 611, 651, 695
   Take Home Activity, 16, 22, 28, 33, 40,
      46, 52, 58, 72, 78, 84, 90, 96, 101,
      108, 114, 120, 134, 140, 146, 152,
      158, 163, 170, 176, 182, 188, 194,
      200, 214, 220, 225, 232, 238, 244,
      258, 264, 270, 275, 282, 288, 294,
      300, 306, 312, 334, 340, 346, 352,
      357, 364, 370, 376, 382, 388, 402,
      408, 413, 420, 426, 440, 446, 451,
      458, 464, 470, 476, 482, 488, 516,
      522, 528, 534, 539, 546, 552, 558,
      564, 578, 584, 590, 595, 602, 608,
      614, 636, 642, 647, 654, 660, 674,
      680, 686, 692, 697, 704, 710, 716,
      722, 728
Fewer, 93–96, 576–577, 584, 596, 612
Fewest, 588, 605
Figures, *See* Three-dimensional shapes;
   See Two-dimensional shapes
Flat surface, 634–636, 657–660

For the Teacher, In most lessons. Some
   examples are: 13, 37, 361, 405,
   645, 725
Fourth of, 725–728
Fourths, 725–728

G

Games
   Addition Bingo, 12
   Add to Subtract Bingo, 254
   Ducky Sums, 130
   Graph Game, 574
   Measure UP!, 512
   Neighborhood Sums, 436
   Rainy Day Bingo, 398
   Rocket Shapes, 670
   Shape Match Bingo, 632
   Show the Numbers, 330
   Subtraction Slide, 68
   Under the Sea, 210
Geometry, *See* Three-dimensional
   shapes; *See* Two-dimensional shapes
Go Deeper, In some Student Edition
   lessons. Some examples are 77, 90,
   200, 376, 642
Graphs
   bar graphs, 587–590, 593–595, 596,
      611–614, 617, 619
   picture graphs, 575–578, 581–584,
      596, 617, 618
Greater than, 400
   compare two numbers, 399–402,
      411–413, 417–420
   symbol, 399–402, 411–413, 417–420

H

Half hour, 549–552, 555–558, 561–564,
   567, 569
Half of, 719–722
Halves, 719–722, 731
Hands On, 19, 25, 43, 49, 75, 81, 99, 111,
   143, 149, 155, 167, 173, 185, 217, 229,
   261, 279, 297, 349, 355, 361, 367, 379,

2. Abstract and Quantitative Reasoning. In many lessons. Some examples are 69, 75, 81, 87, 93, 99, 167, 169, 173, 179, 197, 229, 241, 255, 285, 309, 337, 349, 367, 385, 417, 443, 445, 467, 473, 481, 485, 525, 531, 549, 555, 599, 639, 645

3. Use and Evaluate Logical Reasoning. In many lessons. Some examples are 163, 187, 191, 217, 241, 291, 343, 349, 423, 437, 449, 485, 491, 513, 519, 531, 537, 575, 581, 587, 593, 599, 605, 611, 639, 645, 713

4. Mathematical Modeling. In many lessons. Some examples are 15, 20, 27, 33, 43, 50, 72, 83, 87, 99, 146, 170, 181, 194, 219, 255, 282, 299, 312, 399, 405, 411, 440, 464, 479, 561, 575, 581, 587, 593, 599, 605, 633, 657, 689, 701, 719

5. Use Mathematical Tools. In many lessons. Some examples are 21, 49, 87, 99, 137, 151, 175, 255, 339, 373, 379, 385, 485, 587, 593, 596, 611, 617, 619

6. Use Precise Mathematical Language. In many lessons. Some examples are 57, 119, 139, 157, 291, 305, 311, 343, 351, 363, 449, 473, 513, 525, 543, 611, 639, 657, 671, 683, 713

7. See Structure. In many lessons. Some examples are 45, 113, 145, 217, 261, 269, 273, 281, 309, 333, 355, 379, 399, 405, 443, 543, 651, 671, 707

8. Generalize. In many lessons. Some examples are 7, 37, 49, 137, 191, 229, 261, 267, 273, 279, 331, 337, 357, 411, 449, 479, 491, 525, 549, 593, 633, 651, 671, 677

Math on the Spot Videos, In every Student Edition lesson. Some examples are: 90, 108, 339, 375, 642

Math Story, *See* Vocabulary Reader

Math Talk, In every lesson. Some examples are: 13, 25, 367, 385, 707, 725

Measurement
  length, 513–516, 519–522, 525–528, 531–534
  compare and order, 513–516, 519–522
  indirect measurement, 519–522
  nonstandard units, 525–528, 531–534
  time, 543–546, 549–552, 555–558

Mid-Chapter Checkpoint, 34, 102, 164, 226, 276, 358, 414, 452, 540, 596, 648, 698

Minus sign, 76, 81–84, 100–101

Minute, 555–558

Minute hand, 555–558, 562–563

Missing addends, *See* Unknown numbers

Model
  addition
    adding to, 19–22, 461–464
    addition sentences, 20–22, 25–28, 31–33, 43–46, 50–51
    make a model, 31–33, 255–257
    make a ten to add, 173–176, 179–182
    math triangles, 285–288
    putting together, 25–28
    tens, 173–176, 179–182
    ways to make numbers to ten, 49–52
    word problems, 31–33, 146, 170, 194, 255–257, 282, 294, 312, 440, 464, 479–482
  bar graphs, 587–590, 593–595, 596, 611–614, 617, 619
  bar models, 31–33, 87–90, 99–101, 255–258
  compare, subtraction, 99–101
  numbers in different ways, 373–376, 379–382, 385–388, 485–488
  subtraction
    bar models, 87–90, 99–101, 255–258
    to compare, 99–101
    make a model, 87–90, 99–101, 255–257
    make a ten to subtract, 229–232
    math triangles, 285–288

take apart numbers from ten or less, 117–120

taking apart, 81–84

taking from, 75–78

tens, 229–232, 449–451

word problems, 78, 84, 87–90, 220, 241–244, 255–257

tens, 355–357

Model and Draw, In every lesson. Some examples are: 14, 38, 362, 386, 702, 726

Model, Reason, Make Sense, In most lessons. Some examples are: 28, 78, 270, 370, 654, 710

More, 93–96, 576–578, 581–582, 588–590, 594, 600, 606, 612, 614, 617

Most, 583, 588, 589, 595, 601, 605, 607, 608

 N

Number(s)

compare, 399–402, 405–408, 411–413, 417–420, 423–426

expand, 349–352

identify place value, 343–346, 349–352, 355–357, 361–364, 367–370, 373–376, 399–402, 405–408, 411–414, 417–420, 473–476

show in different ways, 373–376, 379–382, 385–388, 485–488

as tens and ones, 343–346, 349–352, 361–364, 367–370, 373–376, 379–382, 385–388, 399–402, 405–408, 467–470, 473–476

two-digit numbers, *See* Two-digit numbers

Number sentences

addition, 20

model, 20–22, 25–28, 31–33, 43–46, 50–51

word problems, 40, 131, 140, 170, 134, 194, 258, 312

subtraction, 76

model, 75–78

word problems, 78, 96, 106–108, 214, 219

O

Ones, 344

count on with a hundred chart, 331–334, 455–458

group to make tens, 349–352, 355–357, 361–364

On Your Own, In every lesson. Some examples are: 15, 39, 363, 387, 703, 727

Order, 44

of addends, 43–46, 131–134

length, 513–516, 519–522

P

Part-whole relationships

addition, 31–33, 256–257

subtraction, 87–90,

Personal Math Trainer, In some Student Edition lessons. Some examples are 78, 152, 200, 364, 482, 584

Picture Glossary, H1–H11

Picture graphs, 575–578, 581–584, 596, 617, 618

Place value, *See* Two-digit numbers

Plane figures, Plane shapes, *See* Two-dimensional shapes

Plus sign, 20

Practice and Homework

Practice and Homework. In every Student Edition lesson. Some examples are: 215, 265, 335, 415, 517, 643

Problem Situations

Addition Problem Situations

Add to/Change Unknown, 9, 16, 32, 62, 217, 248, 256–257, 294, 334, 439–440

Add to/Result Unknown, 13, 19, 31–37, 40, 55, 62, 127, 134, 137, 140, 143, 146, 170, 197, 199–200, 204, 223, 251, 258, 261, 273, 282, 292, 293–294, 343, 443, 455, 461, 464, 467, 470, 479–481, 485, 498, 590

Rectangle, 657–660, 671–674

Rectangular prism, 633–636

Related facts, 261–264, 267–270, 279–288

Shapes, *See* Three-dimensional shapes; *See* Two-dimensional shapes

Share and Show, In every lesson. Some examples are: 14, 38, 362, 380, 708, 726

Shortest, 509, 513–516

Show What You Know, 10, 66, 128, 208, 252, 328, 396, 434, 510, 572, 630, 668

Side(s), 672
number of, 671–674, 677–680

Solid figures, Solid shapes, *See* Three-dimensional shapes

Sort
to represent data, 593, 599, 605, 611–614
three-dimensional shapes, 633–636
two-dimensional shapes, 671–674

Sphere, 633–636

Square, 657–660, 671–674

Story problems, *See* Word problems

Strategies, *See* Addition Problem Solving Application; *See* Subtraction

Subtraction
all or zero, 105–108
checking with addition, 273–275
to compare, 93–96, 99–101
missing numbers, *See* Unknown numbers, using related facts to find
model
bar models, 87–90
make a ten to subtract, 229–232
math triangles, 285–288
part-whole relationships, 87–90
subtract to compare, 99–101
take apart numbers from ten or less, 117–120
taking apart, 81–84

taking from, 75–78
word problems, 78, 84, 87–90, 220, 241–244, 255–257
part-whole relationships, 87–90
related facts, 267–270, 279–282, 285–288
strategies
break apart to subtract, 235–238
count back, 211–214
make a ten to subtract, 229–232
think addition to subtract, 217–220, 223–225
Subtraction Problem Situations
Take Apart/Addend Unknown, 81, 84, 88–90, 102, 108, 124, 220, 229, 232, 243, 258, 279, 282, 291, 293–294, 312, 316, 376, 449, 612
Take Apart/Both Addends Unknown, 111, 182, 244, 420
Take Apart/Total Unknown, 223
Take from/Change Unknown, 88–90, 108, 214, 225, 242, 243, 249, 255–256, 292, 294, 310, 451
Take from/Result Unknown, 69, 72, 75, 78, 84, 87, 105, 117, 120, 182, 200, 207, 214, 217, 223, 235, 238, 241, 244, 257, 261, 273, 282, 292, 310, 312, 317, 327, 440, 470
Take from/Start Unknown, 107, 220, 232, 243, 249, 488
take apart numbers from ten or less, 117–120
taking from
model, 75–78
use pictures, 69–72
tens
break apart to subtract, 235–238
make a ten to subtract, 229–232
subtract, 229–232, 449–451
twenty
basic facts to, 309–312
ways to make numbers to, 297–300
two-digit numbers, 449–451
unknown numbers, using related facts to find, 279–282, 285–288
word problems
Act It Out, 241–244
Choose an Operation, 291–294
model, 78, 84, 87–90, 255–257